Praise for previous editions of

# Massachusetts
# Off the Beaten Path™

*"Massachusetts: Off the Beaten Path* is a must read for anyone who wants to discover the very best of Massachusetts."
—Massachusetts Office of Travel and Tourism

"Report(s) on unusual places that are worth making a detour for."
—*The Boston Sunday Globe*

"For your ... getaways, there are dozens of enticing possibilities."
—*The Patriot Ledger*

"Recommended for destination-bound visitors ... blends history with specifics on local fare and little-known tourist choices."
—*The Bookwatch/Midwest Book Review*

"The ultimate non-tourist travel book."
—*The Boston Parents' Paper*

## Help Us Keep This Guide Up to Date

Every effort has been made by the authors and editors to make this guide as accurate and useful as possible. However, many things can change after a guide is published—establishments close, phone numbers change, and facilities come under new management.

We would love to hear from you concerning your experiences with this guide and how you feel it could be improved and be kept up to date. While we may not be able to respond to all comments and suggestions, we'll take them to heart and we'll also make certain to share them with the authors. Please send your comments and suggestions to the following address:

The Globe Pequot Press
Reader Response/Editorial Department
P.O. Box 833
Old Saybrook, CT 06475

Or you may e-mail us at:
editorial@globe-pequot.com

Thanks for your input, and happy travels!

OFF THE BEATEN PATH™ SERIES

# Massachusetts

THIRD EDITION

Off the Beaten Path™

Barbara Radcliffe Rogers
and Stillman Rogers

with Pat Mandell

The Globe Pequot Press

Old Saybrook, Connecticut

Illustrations by Carole Drong
Cover and text design by Laura Augustine
Maps created by Equator Graphics © The Globe Pequot Press
Cover photo by Kindra Clineff/Index Stock

**Library of Congress Cataloging-in-Publication Data is available.**

ISBN 0-7627-0398-9

Manufactured in the United States of America
Third Edition/First Printing

*To Eliot, Allie, and Erik*

# EXPERIENCE THE WONDER OF FOXWOODS.

Nestled in the beautiful New England countryside, you'll find the world's favorite casino. Foxwoods Resort Casino, now even more breathtaking than ever. Inside our magnificent new Grand Pequot Tower, you'll find a world class hotel, with 800 luxurious rooms and suites. With gourmet restaurants, and more table games, slot machines and chances to win.

Our new hotel is the perfect complement to our 312-room AAA rated four diamond Great Cedar Hotel, and our quaint Two Trees Inn, with 280 charming rooms.

Foxwoods is fine dining with 24 fabulous restaurants. And room service is available 24 hours a day, for your convenience. Foxwoods is five different gaming environments, with over 5,750 Slot Machines, Blackjack, Craps, Roulette and Baccarat,including a Smoke-Free casino.

Foxwoods is High Stakes Bingo, Keno, a Poker Room and the Ultimate Race Book.

Foxwoods is entertainment. With stars like Aretha Franklin, Engelbert Humperdinck, Paul Anka and Bill Cosby. It's two challenging golf courses. It's Championship Boxing. It's Cinetropolis, with the 1,500-seat Fox Theater. It's a Turbo Ride, Cinedrome, and our Dance Club. With its Hotels, Restaurants, Gaming and Entertainment, it's no wonder that Foxwoods has become the hottest entertainment destination in the country.

## EXPERIENCE THE WONDER OF THE CONNECTICUT WOODS.
Conveniently located in Mashantucket. Exit 92 off I-95 in southeastern CT.
### Call 1-800-PLAY-BIG
Visit our website at www.foxwoods.com
Mashantucket Pequot Tribal Nation

# Contents

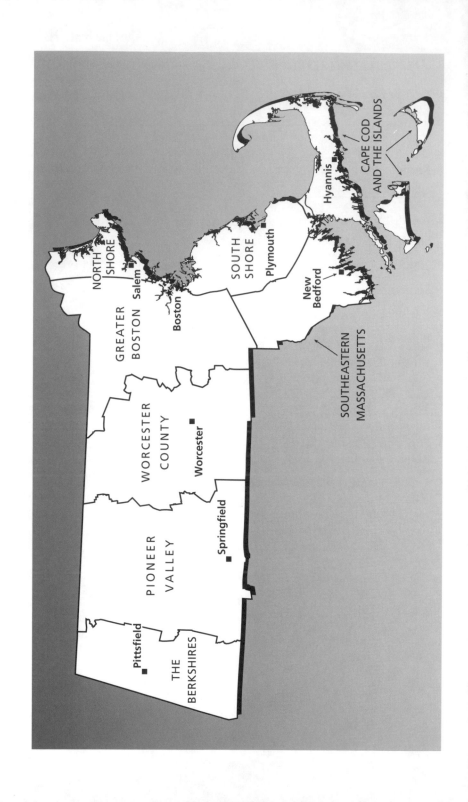

# Introduction

Almost the entire state of Massachusetts is off the beaten path, quietly waiting to be discovered. It's true that Massachusetts is New England's most populous state and its most densely settled one. And yes, Boston, Cape Cod, and the Berkshires must batten their hatches against the invasion of summer visitors.

But outside these tourist centers, the whole state is off the beaten path. If you've never visited the southern Berkshires, you'll discover a world of turn-of-the-century farmland and forests little touched by time. A wide swath of Massachusetts—Worcester County and the Pioneer Valley—is virtually unknown except to locals.

Even in downtown Boston, New England's largest city, there are little-known places where the tourists don't go. Hear change bell ringing at the Church of the Advent, one of only fifteen places in America where you can hear change-ringing bells. Find out why you should visit Boston's tiny Chinatown. Walk along the nation's first Women's Heritage Trail, or visit Castle Island, where Edgar Allan Poe conceived *The Cask of Amontillado*.

And Boston is just the beginning of the journey. This book covers eight regions, from the Cape to the Berkshires, highlighting almost 200 attractions in detail. The choices were often arbitrary, because there are actually hundreds more. But making those choices was a lot of fun; you never can tell when straying from the well-beaten path will lead you to a collection of endangered farm animals whose breeds date back centuries or the country's only museum devoted to plastic. In truth, this book barely scratches the surface of the off-the-beaten-path possibilities in this state. Think of it as a taste of the best.

Massachusetts's best includes unique scenic wonders, from glacial potholes big enough to swim in to a "natural" bridge that nature made out of marble. You can spend the night in a lighthouse on a windswept island off Cape Cod or visit a reservation where sixty-five varieties of holly grow.

This book will help you discover man-made wonders like the Bridge of Flowers, a millionaires' row rivaling Newport's, and the longest

---

## Just the Facts, Ma'am

**Population:** 6,041,185, in the 1994 census

**Nickname:** The Bay State

**Capital:** Boston, which is also New England's largest city

**Area:** 8,257 square miles

**Highest elevation:** Mt. Greylock (3,491 feet)

**Miles of Atlantic coast:** 192

**Miles of shoreline:** 1,519

**Major Airport:** Logan International Airport (3 miles from downtown Boston)

wooden bridge on the East Coast. American history has its deepest roots in Massachusetts. You'll visit the homes of John Adams, Daniel Webster, and John Alden. You'll also meet some distinctly lesser-known historic personages, such as "the witch of Wall Street" and "the Copper King."

You will tour museums devoted to everything from the legendary Tom Thumb to dolls, shipbuilding, and Shakers. At farms and orchards, you'll sample Massachusetts's largesse: chèvre cheese, maple syrup, cider, and cranberry wine, to name just a few.

Revel in the quirky place and the oddball attraction, too: a house made entirely of newsprint and the country's only vintage plumbing museum.

Massachusetts is where you'll find the country's oldest continuously operating museum and its oldest continually operating church, the oldest art festival, and the longest-running carillon-concert series in North America.

## To Learn More

Call (800) 447–MASS to receive a free "Massachusetts Getaway Guide," and for seasonal updates, including events, fall foliage reports, and ski conditions, call (800) 227–MASS or visit the state's Web site at www.mass-vacation.com. If you need answers to specific questions, call the Massachusetts Office of Travel and Tourism at (617) 727–3201.

"Massachusetts Down on the Farm Directory" contains information on farm stays, farm tours, hay rides, and other farm-related activities and is available from the Massachusetts Department of Food and Agriculture, 100 Cambridge Street, Boston 02202; (617) 727–3000, ext. 187, or at its Web site, www.massgrown.org.

This state's beaches and parks are some of its most special places. Take the hidden barrier beach on Nantucket, reachable only by four-wheel drive, or the North Shore park that was once a wealthy estate and still has its carriage trails and rhododendron and laurel.

Some of Massachusetts's best-kept secrets are off-season delights, such as wintertime cruises to see harbor seals. Even the shops are an adventure: One sells shining, antique potbellied stoves; another is an eighteenth-century wooden boat shop.

When you're hungry, stop in at a nineteenth-century ice-cream parlor that still makes egg creams, a tearoom serving scones and cream, or a romantic alfresco dessert-only spot overlooking a salt marsh on the Cape.

Bed-and-breakfast inns along the way offer a comfortable and friendly place to lay your head at night during your travels.

For their generous help in researching this book, we would like to thank the Massachusetts Office of Travel and Tourism, the Plymouth County Development Council, the Bristol County

# INTRODUCTION

Development Council, the Martha's Vineyard Chamber of Commerce, the Nantucket Island Chamber of Commerce, the Worcester Convention and Visitors Bureau, the Franklin County Chamber of Commerce, and the Berkshires Visitors Bureau.

We also wish to add our note of gratitude to Glen Faria and Bill DeSousa, Julie and Lura Rogers, Gail Gavert, Sue and Gordon Follansbee, Chris Lyons, Miriam Curran, Arsene Davignon, Kim Adams, Tom Bross, Pat Mandell (the original author of this book), and Eliot, Allie, and Erik Lee.

## What's Up?

*Most newspapers run weekly entertainment guides or at least a weekly calendar of events. Many also print special summer activity supplements, which tell about local activities and attractions. In Boston, look for the* Phoenix *for alternative and arts events, and to the daily newspapers, the* Boston Globe *and the* Boston Herald. The Martha's Vineyard Times, *the* Springfield Republican, Cape Cod Times, *and the* Worcester Telegram and Gazette *cover their respective areas.*

## There's No Such Thing as Typical Weather

*N*ew England is renowned for its fast-changing, unpredictable climate. Summer temperatures can be in the low 70s or mid-90s, with humidity higher and breezes stronger near the coast. In the winter, expect coastal humidity and wind to make the low 30s temperatures seem much colder. Winter snow cover is more likely as you move west, especially when you reach the Berkshires.

But it is the changeability that makes the weather "interesting." The warmest summer day may suddenly turn chilly, and the day that began in a downpour may be bathed in brilliant sunshine by noon. As a rule of thumb, be prepared for anything, and bring clothes for cool evenings even in mid-summer. Weather changes so abruptly here that radio announcers joke that they need to go out and look at the sky before reading the weather report.

*The prices and rates listed in this guidebook were confirmed at press time. We recommend, however, that you call establishments before traveling to obtain current information.*
*Maps provided are for reference only and should be used in conjunction with a road map. Distances suggested are approximate.*

On any given day in downtown Boston, you'll see tourists rooted to a painted red line on the sidewalk, staring transfixedly at their maps. The ribbon of red marks the Freedom Trail, and they are happy to follow it to the Old North Church, Faneuil Hall, and Paul Revere's House—in and out of town in one day. But they miss 95 percent of what's here.

Step off the Freedom Trail and you'll discover a world of neighborhoods so distinct that exploring them is like traveling from village to village—which these neighborhoods once were. You would never mistake the brownstones and wide Parisian boulevards of the Back Bay for the brick Federal-style houses and narrow nineteenth-century lanes of Beacon Hill. The old waterfront wharf buildings have been remade into condos and shops, surrounded by office towers and luxury hotels. Rather than clipper ships, today cruise boats and commuter ferries depart the quays.

The industrial landscape of South Boston also houses some unique museums and the city's fish piers and shipping terminals. Though almost no tourist knows where the South End is, it's the city's largest neighborhood. It was built on filled-in land—like the Back Bay, but long before it. The South End's Victorian brick townhouses bear a striking similarity to those of Back Bay. Despite the scruffy character of parts of the Fenway section, which winds around the Back Bay fens, it too holds hidden treasure. The midtown area wears a 1960s urban-renewal look but holds such nineteenth-century architectural master-pieces as Trinity Church and the Boston Public Library. The size of Boston's Chinatown doesn't rival New York's or San Francisco's, but its heart does. More far-flung areas such as Cambridge and towns to the west and north are not to be overlooked either.

Boston is a compact and walkable city—just don't try to drive here.

## *Downtown and Waterfront*

The best way to get to know Boston's neighborhoods is by taking a tour with the *Historic Neighborhoods Foundation.* HNF focuses

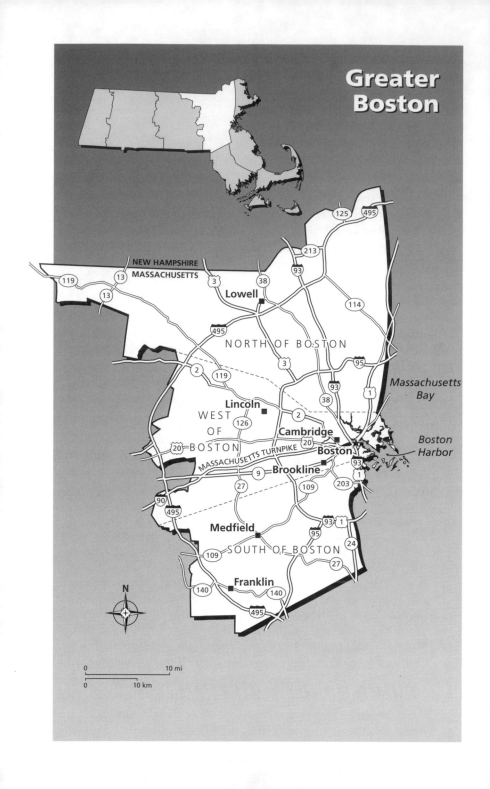

on one neighborhood at a time. In summer, weekly tours visit the waterfront and Chinatown. Tours of Beacon Hill and the Italian North End go off the Freedom Trail to find hidden courtyards and gardens and discover social history. "Make Way for Ducklings" tours for children follow the route of author Robert McCloskey's famous mallards through the Public Garden, where young tourists will find larger-than-life-size sculptures of the storybook ducks. HNF headquarters are at 99 Bedford Street (617–426–1885).

While they stroll the waterfront, many people don't look beyond the shops and offices. But a plaque here and there will tell you how much history is at hand. Look at the facades and you'll see that some of the old warehouses were designed to emulate Renaissance palazzi and Greek temples. John Hancock had his countinghouse on cobblestoned **Long Wharf.** Built in 1760, the countinghouse is now the **Chart House restaurant** and still has Hancock's black iron safe embedded in the wall. Nathaniel Hawthorne served as a customs inspector at Long Wharf. Built in 1710, it is the granddaddy of all the wharves. The British marched ashore on Long Wharf when they occupied the city in 1768— and beat a hasty retreat back down it when the colonists routed them in 1776. In later years, Long Wharf bid adieu to missionaries, California-bound gold rushers, and clipper traders. One little jewel you should look for is **Waterfront Park** (immediately north of Long Wharf on Atlantic Avenue), a nicely landscaped pocket park with brick walkways and benches that offers a lovely harbor view along with respite.

With such a magnificent harbor—getting cleaner by the month—you would expect to find outdoor restaurants springing up all around the shoreline to take advantage of the almost five months of good weather that Boston has. But for outdoor dining along the waterfront, you have only one reliable choice: **Rowes Wharf Café.** Luckily, it is terrific, with good food, pleasant service, and cafe tables set out overlooking the harbor boats. Located at the Boston Harbor Hotel (617–439–7000), the cafe serves breakfast, lunch, and dinner from Memorial Day into October. You'll probably have to wait for a table at lunch, but you won't mind because the harbor is lovely and the mix of people getting on and off water taxis and excursion boats makes for an interesting diversion.

**Post Office Square Park,** adjacent to the Hotel Meridien, along Franklin and Milk streets, is the new centerpiece of Boston's downtown.

The city leveled an eyesore garage to build a wonderful green space with white latticework, brick walkways, fountains, beautiful flowers and plants, and trees from Harvard's Arnold Arboretum, all edged with low-lying granite walls. At all hours of every nice day, the park is full of people having coffee or lunch, chatting, and enjoying the sun and flowers. Children often play in the fountain at one end of the park, and a cafe at the other end serves snacks and drinks.

Four centuries of notable Boston women have been recalled along the **Women's Heritage Trail,** believed to be the country's first. Four walking routes cover downtown, the North End, Beacon Hill, and the Chinatown/South Cove area, linking the stories of some fifty women. Among them are Phillis Wheatley, a slave who became the first publicly recognized African-American woman poet, and Abigail Adams, wife of President John Adams. Louisa May Alcott lived on Beacon Hill, and Fannie Merritt Farmer published her world-famous cookbook from Tremont Street. The National Park Service Visitor Information office at 15 State Street (617–242–5642) sells a guide booklet with a map. Boston by Foot (617–367–2345) leads similarly themed tours called "Great Women of Boston."

Steps away from Government Center, the **Harrison Gray Otis House** conceals behind its Federal exterior one of the most opulent interiors in Boston. This three-story brick house, built in 1796, was the first of three that Charles Bulfinch designed for his friend Otis, a prominent lawyer and member of Congress. Everywhere you look are imported wallpapers and carpets, heavy swag curtains, and gilt-framed mirrors. High-relief dancing figures of maidens grace an Adam-style mantel in the drawing room. Neoclassical motifs frame every doorway and window; a dado depicts scenes of Pompeii. The Otis house, at 141 Cambridge Street, is headquarters for the Society for the Preservation of New England Antiquities (617–227–3956). It's open from noon to 5:00 P.M. Tuesday through Friday and from 10:00 A.M. to 5:00 P.M. Saturday. Admission is $4.00.

At 131 Cambridge Street, right next to the Harrison Gray Otis House, is the **Old West Church,** designed by an architect as famous in his day as Charles Bulfinch: Asher Benjamin. Benjamin wrote handbooks for builders and carpenters to guide them in working with his neoclassical style, thus influencing American architecture from the East Coast to the Midwest. Designed in 1805, Old West is a signature model of simplicity and symmetry. Three brick stories narrow to an Ionic cupola and a Doric third-story porch, with the gables of each story topped by graceful urns. The cupola has twelve columns flanking a clock garlanded in the Adam style.

# GREATER BOSTON

A few blocks from Cambridge Street is a restaurant that will delight beer fans: the *Commonwealth Brewing Company,* at 138 Portland Street (617–523–8383), which makes all its own beer in the basement. There are more than a dozen varieties on tap, plus several seasonal brews, such as an India pale ale. Copper and brass shine everywhere in the vast dining room, where enormous beer kegs stand about. Dinners range from grilled fresh fish to meat pie and three-alarm chili. Downstairs in the taproom, you can watch the English-trained brewers at work behind glass walls while you sit in a Hofbrau-style bar.

Although few sightseers think to enter the *Nynex Building,* at 185 Franklin Street (formerly known as the New England Telephone Building), inside it is one of the most splendid murals in town. Called *Telephone Men and Women at Work,* the depiction circles the rotunda in a 197-foot oval, 12 feet high. The mural traces telephone history, starting with a muttonchopped Alexander Graham Bell giving a telephone demonstration in Salem in 1877. Scenes of the 1880s are rich in period detail of top-hatted gents and long-skirted women. Also in the building is Bell's Garret, a dark little corner full of memorabilia where Bell worked to develop the telephone in 1875.

Except for its restaurants, most guidebooks don't bother to list Boston's tiny *Chinatown.* Chinatown may be small, but it's intensely and authentically Chinese. Green-pagoda-topped gates guarded by Chinese Foo dogs mark the main entrance, at Beach Street and Surface Road. Even the phone booths are roofed with red-and-green Chinese pagodas. Stores and restaurants advertise in Chinese characters. Among the shops you might poke into are *Eastern Live Poultry,* at 48 Beach Street, which sells squawking live chickens; *Hing Shing Pastry,* at 67 Beach Street (617–451–1162), for its mouthwatering array of traditional Chinese pastries; and *Chin Enterprises,* at 33 Harrison Avenue (617–423–1725), where you can buy a professional-quality wok. Restaurants fill every block, but one of the more intriguing ones is the *Chinatown Eatery,* at 44 Beach Street, which resembles a Hong Kong

**April 19**
*Battle Reenactment,* Lexington Green, Lexington, at dawn each Patriot's Day (a legal holiday in Massachusetts).

**Mid-May**
*Lilac Sunday,* Arnold Arboretum, Jamaica Plain, features tours of North America's second-largest collection of lilacs—more than 400 varieties; (617) 524-1718.

**Mid-May**
*Annual Kite Festival,* Franklin Park, Boston, colors the sky with thousands of kites; (617) 635-4505.

**Late September**
*Gallop's Island Applefest,* Harbor Islands State Park, with island tours, apple ice cream, candy apples, and cider-making; (617) 223-8666.

**Late September**
*Banjo and Fiddle Contest,* Boardinghouse Park, Lowell, where performers from all over the East Coast compete; (978) 970-5000.

food market in its bedlam. Five take-out stands surround cafeteria-style tables, and menus on the wall are handwritten in Chinese as well as English.

At the corner of Harrison Avenue and Oak Street, you'll see a building-size mural that depicts the history of the Chinese in Boston—the *Unity/Community Chinatown Mural.* Among its pigtailed Chinese figures are construction workers, a launderer, and women at sewing machines.

For a window on Chinese culture, stop in at the *Chinese Culture Institute* at 272 Tremont Street (617–542–4599), which exhibits the work of Chinese artists. Other offerings include concerts, plays, and workshops in traditional crafts. The annual *Chinese Lantern Festival* celebrating the Chinese New Year sets the streets to glowing with lanterns and features a splendid costumed parade.

From Chinatown, it's just a few steps to *South Station,* whose curved, 1898 beaux arts facade fronts on Summer Street and Atlantic Avenue. Once terribly dilapidated, South Station has been gorgeously restored, its interior designed to resemble a European market square. The light-filled concourse sparkles with polished marble floors, brass railings, gleaming oak benches, and restaurants and shops within elegant dark green kiosks. Travelers and nontravelers alike enjoy being here. On sale are flowers, gourmet chocolates, foreign magazines, freshly baked croissants, frozen yogurt, and perfume.

If you're looking for an off-the-beaten-path place to stay in Boston, try one of the bed-and-breakfast services. They might place you in a brick Federal home on Beacon Hill with fireplaces, four-posters, and a lovely hidden garden; a classic 1890 Back Bay brownstone with mahogany floors; or perhaps a South End Victorian townhouse. Contact Bed and Breakfast Associates Bay Colony, P.O. Box 57–166 Babson Park, Boston 02157–0166 (800–347–5088 or 617–449–5302; doubles $75–$125) or Bed and Breakfast Agency of Boston, 47 Commercial Wharf, Boston 02110 (617–720–3540 or 800–248–9262; doubles $70–$120), which specializes in the downtown area.

# Beacon Hill and Back Bay

One of the most photographed streets on Beacon Hill is tiny *Acorn Street,* a nineteenth-century byway only one lane wide and one block long. The antique charm of this street is undiminished. Acorn Street is so remarkably unchanged that it's easy to picture a horse and carriage rumbling down it. It's one of the few old cobblestoned streets left on Beacon Hill and one of the oldest-looking places in Boston. Coachmen and servants of the wealthy once lived on Acorn Street. Their Federal brick townhouses resemble their owners' mansions, graced with black shutters and windowboxes, as well as black iron gaslights. Acorn Street is 1 block north of Chestnut Street, between West Cedar and Willow streets.

Behind Beacon Hill houses are lovely, walled gardens. Some are opened to the public during the *Hidden Gardens of Beacon Hill* tour the third Thursday in May. The tour reveals how artfully these tiny backyard spaces have been landscaped, with everything from flowering shrubs to herbs and some very old trees. Unusual accents might be a Japanese wind sculpture, stone cupids, antique French urns, or painted faux trellises. For tickets, which include refreshments, contact the Beacon Hill Garden Club, P.O. Box 302, Charles Street Station, Boston 02114 (617–227–4392).

Charles Bulfinch won his greatest fame for designing the Massachusetts *New State House.* Its regal facade crowns the summit of Beacon Hill. Freedom Trail tourists dutifully regard the outside but often don't bother with the inside. Inside, however, you'll see a patterned floor made of twenty-four kinds of marble, murals of the American Revolution, and hundreds of historic flags returned after duty in American wars. A stained-glass skylight depicts the seals of the original thirteen colonies. The black iron railings leading up the elegantly wide main staircase are a unique pattern of ironwork called "black lace." (The molds were broken after the railings were cast.) Don't miss the Sacred Cod in the House of Representatives chamber—a wooden fish hung there in 1784 to symbolize the importance of the fishing industry to Massachusetts. Free tours of the State House are given from 10:00 A.M. to 4:00 P.M. weekdays; call (617) 727–3676.

Just across Beacon Street from the State House is the beginning of the *Black Heritage Trail,* fourteen stops that follow the history of African-American life on Beacon Hill in the nineteenth century. The first stop is the *Robert Gould Shaw and 54th Regiment Memorial,* a bas-relief sculpture by Augustus Saint-Gaudens that pays tribute to the first black regiment recruited for the Civil War. The *African Meeting House* is the oldest standing black church in America, built in 1806. It was known in the abolitionist era as the Black Faneuil Hall, and Frederick Douglass and William Lloyd Garrison spoke here. The trail also takes you to one of the first schools for black children and to a house that served as an Underground Railway station and was visited by Harriet Beecher Stowe. Walking-tour maps are available at the Boston Common Visitor

Information kiosk and at the *Museum of Afro-American History,* 46 Joy Street (617–742–1854), a stop on the trail.

*The Boston Athenaeum,* at $10^1/_2$ Beacon Street (617– 227–0270), has occupied this building, with its dogwoods flanking the front door, since 1849. There is no better place to go to find true New England personalities and sensibilities. Although it is a private library, the first two floors are open to the public after a stop at the door to sign in. The interior features high vaulted ceilings, pillared archways, and scores of marble busts. In addition to an extensive collection of books, the Athenaeum also has a collection of fine art, including works by Gilbert Stuart, John Singer Sargent, and Chester Harding. Fresh and lively flower arrangements are scattered throughout the reading rooms, which are furnished with solid wooden reading tables and red leather, brass-studded armchairs. On Wednesday afternoons, the library hosts one of the finest teas in Boston, indulged in by New England types who could have been ordered up through central casting. Visit especially the second-floor exhibit area, where quirky but always delightful thematic art exhibits are on display.

When people say *Charles Street,* they almost always mean the Beacon Hill part, stretching from the corner of the Boston Common and Public Garden to the Charles River. Lining it are excellent restaurants, neighborhood shops, and forty or so antiques stores offering everything from old New England lithographs to elegant English, French, and Chinese furnishings. Some shops, such as those selling linens and garden accessories, specialize in the new decorative arts, thereby adding to the feeling that you could supply an entire house from the goods offered here. The side streets also hold a few shops, so you may want to pick up an antiques map at any of the stores or ask passersby to point out good side-street shops. The prices can be reasonable compared with regions of the country where antiques are less available.

Every Sunday morning, the bell ringers at the *Church of the Advent,* at the corner of Mount Vernon and Brimmer Streets, play concerts for the churchgoers from about 10:30 A.M. until 11:00 A.M. services. Advent, built during the 1880s and 1890s, has a set of eight change-ringing bells. There are only fifteen sets of change-ringing bells in America, with more than half of them in Massachusetts. *Change bell ringing* is an English tradition in which hanging bells are worked by ropes according to mathematical patterns. The bell ringers, many associated with Massachusetts Institute of Technology, personify the popular wisdom that mathematicians are musical. They ring the bells in different patterns so that no tune is ever repeated on a Sunday morning. As church services begin at Advent, they head over to Old North Church in the North End to give a concert for that neighborhood.

One of the most enduring symbols of Boston is the famous *Swan Boats* that ply the lagoon in the Public Garden. The Swan Boats were launched in 1877 by Robert Paget, who was inspired by the swan boat scene in Wagner's opera *Lohengrin.* They have been operated by the Paget family ever since. Many Bostonians never ride these boats; I did not for ten years. The big surprise is that riding the Swan Boats is fun. These unique pedal-powered boats make a leisurely circuit of the lagoon, trailed by quacking ducks certain of a handout. The Swan Boats operate 10:00 A.M. to 5:00 P.M. daily from mid-April to mid-September; tickets cost $1.75 for adults and 95 cents for children. Call (617) 522–1966.

With all the homage paid to Colonial and Federal architecture in Boston, the Victorian age gets short shrift. But at the *Gibson House,* a Victorian house museum, you can see the lifestyle of the Back Bay Victorians in all its full-blown opulence. This Italian Renaissance Revival home maintains its original 1859 interior of gold-embossed faux leather wallpaper and black walnut paneling. Family pieces include plush Turkish ottomans, eighteenth-century heirloom furniture, china, and porcelain, and paintings and photographs. The Gibson House, at 137 Beacon Street, is open from Wednesday through Sunday May through October and on weekends in winter. Tours are given at 1:00, 2:00, and 3:00 P.M. Admission is $4.00. Call (617) 267–6338.

If you're a Francophile, check out the *French Library,* a unique bastion of French culture in an 1867 Back Bay townhouse at 53 Marlborough Street (617–266–4351). It was founded after World War II by a group of

Swan Boats, Boston Public Garden

Free French enthusiasts. French films and concerts are presented in the exquisite Louis XV theater, with its carved paneling accented in gold leaf. Films range from old Marcel Carné and Jean Luc Godard classics to contemporary cinema. A series of candlelight concerts presents French music, plus wine and cheese; art shows, cooking demonstrations, and lectures are also offered. The highlight of the year is Bastille Day (July 14), celebrated with a bang-up dinner and block dance.

***Commonwealth Avenue,*** a grand boulevard with a tree-filled park in its center, runs the length of Back Bay, an area that was literally a bay. The shore line was at the foot of the Public Garden, where Commonwealth Avenue begins. The street is lined with stately brick and brownstone townhouses almost all the way to Kenmore Square.

On the way, it crosses busy Massachusetts Avenue (which you will meet later in Cambridge), and on the corner is Boston's venerable Eliot Hotel and the stylish restaurant ***Clio.*** We choose Clio especially for Sunday brunch. Boston takes on an entirely different persona on Sundays, and we like to begin ours in a leisurely way over a pot of real brewed tea and a plateful of caramelized exotic fruits and a mound of sugary beignets, or with poached eggs and sweet potato hash with ham. Service is silk-smooth, the formality of the white-paneled room is lightened with contemporary wooden lamps and a somewhat-improbable leopard-print carpet, and the music is Parisian. The dinner menu changes each day as the chef creates anew with the freshest and the best: Begin with a salad of potatoes and wild mushrooms with a balsamic glaze or one of our favorites, a panroast of mussels with chanterelles and fennel. On the entree menu, you might find swordfish au poivre with braised shallots or garlic-rubbed chicken with a cassoulet of fresh vegetables, bacon, and potato gnocchi, beginning at $21. A daily vegetarian dish is $18–$23. Chef Ken Oringer's summer desserts make up for the fact that brunch is not served in July and August (although breakfast is offered until noon). Finish off dinner with a tart of fresh apricots with crème fraîche ice cream or a warm ricotta tart with thyme honey and strawberries. If you simply can't decide, or want to sample several dishes, choose the nightly tasting menu; (617) 536–7200.

# *The North End*

Although Boston's Little Italy is no secret, and tourists head to Hanover Street to find color and good food, few go farther than the line of trendy new cafes with glass-paneled fronts that open onto the street in fair weather. These recent additions are designed to look like what people think Italy looks like. But farther down Hanover, and in the streets adjacent to it, you'll find yourself in a neighborhood with rich traditions. Even though many Italian families have been replaced by young professionals, this is still the cultural heartland of Boston's Italian community. Those who have moved to the suburbs return often, on celebratory occasions and to renew their cultural and family ties. For many, this is their return to the "old country" and to their roots.

On Salem Street people still shop for their daily groceries, and you won't find a supermarket in the entire area. Individual shops sell fish, vegetables, bread, meats cut to order, or cheese and pastas. Food is a way of life here, and the aromas emanating from the many restaurants are tantalizing. We can't possibly name them all—not even all the really great ones. But we can tell you that the hands-down choice for canoli, which should *always* be filled fresh while you watch, is **Maria's Bakery,** at 46 Cross Street, where you can also find an array of breads, cookies, and sweets.

The best way to learn about the North End and its food-rich heritage is on a **North End Market Tour,** with food expert Michele Topor. She knows everyone, so if a chef slips out of the kitchen for a minute, she'll stop and introduce you to him as he passes on the street. She wanders in and out of food shops and bakeries, tossing out cooking and buying hints—even recipes—in her wake and plucking up samples for you to try. You'll learn why real balsamic vinegar is so expensive (it's aged twelve years) and how to tell good dry pasta from mediocre. You'll taste seasonal fruits, sample grappa, nibble on cheeses and proscuitto, and learn about foods you never knew existed. And you'll leave with a list of food markets and shops. Three-hour tours begin at 10:00 A.M. and 2:00 P.M. each Saturday and Wednesday and cost $35; (617) 523–6032; fax (617) 367–2185.

Michele also points out some of the best restaurants as you walk around the North End, giving you the latest inside information on who's serving what and how. You can't go wrong with her advice. Our own favorites in the North End? We could write a book. Almost across the street from each other on Salem Street, **Antico Forno** and **Terramia** share a jovial chef, Mario Nocera, recently arrived from Italy. Dishes emerge from the giant wood oven (*forno*), for which one restaurant is named, redolent in warmly mingled flavors and earthy, smoky fragrances. And the bill, with tip and a glass of wine, will barely top $20 at Forno (617–523–3112), maybe $10 higher at the more upscale Terramia (617–723–6733). In the same price range as Antico Forno—even a bit less expensive—is **Artu,** at 6 Prince Street, which serves plain, unadorned, and wonderfully flavorful dishes from the Italian countryside. The food gets more attention than the atmosphere; (617) 227–9023.

At the upscale end, a place you'd choose for a very special occasion or very special person is **Mama Maria's** on North Square. Don't expect the checkered tablecloths the name suggests; several intimate dining rooms are impeccably turned out in white linens and are newly and stylishly renovated. You'll hardly notice the pleasant views from large windows once the food arrives. Although the menu changes often to reflect the seasons, you are likely to find the baked goat cheese and smoked tomato tart leading the appetizers, since loyal patrons demand it, and for good reason. Other choices for starters might be a delicate ravioli of smoked sturgeon or a salad of an infinite variety of baby greens with preserved pears and walnut-encrusted gorgonzola. From the entree menu, we've had pan-seared scallops skewered on rosemary branches and served over pearl-sized couscous with cured tomatoes and lemon, or a perfectly-cooked loin of tuna over squid-ink pasta with olives and capers. All the pasta is handcut, made right in the restaurant. Most entrees are $19 to $24 and the extensive wine list begins at $22. The maître d'hôtel is knowledgeable, and you can rely on him to choose the best wine in a price range; diners often ask his advice. The restaurant is handicapped-accessible (rare in the North End) and has valet parking, a blessing for out-of-town travelers. You will need reservations, since, although it's tucked into a corner far from Hanover Street, it's not a secret anymore; (617) 523–0077.

# South Boston

South Boston is home to two unique museums. When you cross the Congress Street Bridge, you'll see a giant white milk bottle—the **Hood Milk Bottle.** A landmark lunchstand from the 1930s, it sells snacks today and signals the beginning of **Museum Wharf.** Especially if you have children, you won't want to miss the **Children's Museum,** one of the best in the country. It's also the country's second-oldest, founded in 1913. There are four floors of hands-on exhibits here, many creative and witty. A skeleton wearing a top hat and bow tie illustrates anatomy. Children can try out the giant-bubble maker or clamber up a two-story climbing sculpture of chicken wire and wood. As they explore and role-play in a mock garage and neighborhood market, kids learn about jobs. An exhibit on cultural diversity, racism, and ethnicity, to prepare children for a multicultural nation, is the first of its kind in the country. The museum is at 300 Congress Street (617–426–6500). Admission is $7.00 for adults, $6.00 for children and teens ages two to fifteen, and $2.00 for one-year-olds. From September to June, the museum is open from 10:00 A.M. to 5:00 P.M. Tuesday through Sunday and until 9:00 P.M. on Friday; Friday evenings, admission is only $1.00 per person. From July through Labor Day, the museum is open 10:00 A.M. to 7:00 P.M. Monday through Thursday, 10:00 A.M. to 9:00 P.M. Friday, and 10:00 A.M. to 5:00 P.M. Saturday and Sunday.

Upstairs in the same brick building is the world's only museum devoted solely to computers—the **Computer Museum.** Just how fast technology changes is dramatically illustrated in the exhibits, which cover more than forty years of computing. Whereas an early Air Force vacuum-tube computer took up the space of a four-story building, the same computing power is now available in a desktop microcomputer. After you check out the CAD/CAM program used to design the sole of a Nike Air shoe, you can see "smart" robots, computer-animated films, and a computer made of 10,000 Tinker Toys that actually works. You might design a car on-screen or have Aaron the computer draw your picture. For an up-close look at how computers work, take a stroll through the giant walk-through computer, with its 25-foot keyboard and bumper-car-size mouse. The Computer Museum keeps the same hours as the Children's Museum. Admission—$7.00 for adults and $5.00 for students—is half-price on Sunday from 3:00 to 5:00 P.M. Children four and under are admitted free. Call (617) 426–2800.

# Copley Square, Fenway, South End

When you're traveling, you might not think to stop at the library. But the **Boston Public Library** in Copley Square is worth a visit even if you never check out a book. Built in 1895 after the manner of an Italian Renaissance palace, the library has been recently restored so that its McKim, Mead, and White architecture, its Saint-Gaudens sculpture, and its Puvis de Chavannes murals glow as they did when

## Halifax's Annual Thank-You

*T*he tall, perfectly shaped Christmas tree that stands each year at the Prudential Center is not just any tree. Each December since 1918, the city of Halifax, Nova Scotia, has sent the finest tree available as a gift to the people of Boston in appreciation for their outpouring of generosity after the explosion in Halifax Harbor during World War I that left 2,000 dead and most of the city in ruins. Help from Boston came quickly and continued until Halifax was rebuilt and the homeless were housed, fed, and clothed. Haligonians have never forgotten this bond that ties them to Bostonians.

Henry James walked through here one hundred years ago. Daniel Chester French did the elegant relief work on the massive bronze doors on Dartmouth Street. The grand entrance hall sweeps up an imposing marble staircase past twin stone lions. Siena marble arches and Corinthian columns frame frescoes of the muses. The landing overlooks a lovely central courtyard with a fountain and benches. A second-floor room is based on the library of the Doge's Palace in Venice. The library's main entrance is at 666 Boylston Street; call (617) 536–5400, extension 212.

Behind the Public Library, at 116 Huntington Avenue, is a well-named restaurant, *Ambrosia,* with one of Boston's most sophisticated menus. While chef/owner Anthony Ambrose's culinary style is clearly rooted in the traditions of southern France, he plays this off brilliantly with flavors and ingredients as diverse as Asian and native New England. We have begun dinner there with a sashimi of tuna served with squid-ink capellini and roasted garlic butter, flavors few chefs dare offer together. We especially applaud the creative respect Ambrose shows for vegetables, again often in a fusion of styles, pairing julienned potatoes in a terrine with nori and serving neglected vegetables, such as celariac, with venison. Desserts are creative and often based on fruits (frozen peach parfait on a shortbread cookie) or sorbets in combinations of herb flavors (camomile and lavender with peach). Pastas and risottos begin at $15, evening entrees are $22 to $30. Lunch is served on weekdays; (617) 247–2400.

The world's only stained-glass globe big enough to walk through is located at the First Church of Christ, Scientist. Thirty feet in diameter, the *Mapparium* represented the "global village" long before that concept was popular. Six hundred and eight glass panels make up the countries of 1931 and send visitors' voices echoing hollowly. A glass bridge spans the middle, where you can get a bird's-eye view of any country in the world—precisely the architect's intention. Although visitors once could see through the bridge underneath their feet to Antarctica, it so bothered people to be standing in the middle of nowhere that the church put a carpet down. The Mapparium, at 175 Huntington Avenue, is open Monday through Saturday from 9:30 A.M. to 4:00 P.M. Call (617) 450–2000.

The *Museum of Fine Arts* is not only easy to find on Huntington Avenue, it's also among the best-known art collections in the country. But in addition to its knock-out French Impressionists, its mummies, and its major traveling exhibitions, it has some corners visitors rarely reach. One is the series of period rooms featuring furnishings and decorative arts from a variety of times and places. Another is the small but well-chosen collection of Medieval art, which includes an exceptionally fine stone-carved doorway. A Buddhist temple hides within the stunning Asian galleries, and outside is a Japanese garden, which you can enter without paying museum admission, although you cannot take your lunch there. The entire museum is free on Wednesday evenings. The MFA has guidebooks for families and free drop-in workshops for ages 6-12; (617) 267–9300.

During the growing season, one of the gems of Boston is the Fenway *Victory Gardens.* The gardens, under cultivation since World War II, have been expanded many times. The small plots hold mature fruit trees, vines and canes, perennial vegetables such as rhubarb and Jerusalem artichoke, and radishes, peas, and zinnias for cutting. Many of the gardeners are talented landscapers as well as vegetable growers. Their paths, retaining walls, and small shelters are labors of love and peacefulness. The vegetation and the nearby Muddy River draw songbirds by the dozens.

Although a 1990 multimillion-dollar art heist focused international attention on the *Isabella Stewart Gardner Museum,* it still gets bypassed in favor of the Museum of Fine Arts. Hidden away behind a deceptively unprepossessing exterior is a fifteenth-century-style Venetian palazzo. Enter through a four-story courtyard with stone porticoes, arches, and columns; beautiful flowering plants; and Moorish-style windows. It's a suitably fabulous showcase for the personal art collection of Isabella Stewart [Mrs. Jack] Gardner, a wealthy Victorian matron whose independent spirit provoked Bostonians to label her an eccentric. "Mrs. Jack" liked to wear her two largest diamonds on gold wire springs over her head, among other unusual habits. Her collection, amassed over a lifetime of travel to Europe and opened to the public in 1903, spans an extraordinary range: Roman sarcophagi, Chinese porcelain, Flemish tapestries, Italian Renaissance paintings, American and British paintings, sculpture, furniture, and many prints and drawings. The museum also has a little lunchtime cafe and offers weekly chamber music concerts and Thursday afternoon tours. It's located at 280 The Fenway; call (617) 566–1401. Tickets cost $10.00 for adults, $7.00 for seniors, and $5.00 for students; children under twelve are admitted free. Admission is $3.00 for those showing a college ID card on Wednesdays. The museum is open from 11:00 A.M. to 5:00 P.M. Tuesday through Sunday.

Boston's largest neighborhood, the South End, is listed on the National Register of Historic Places as the largest concentration of Victorian brick row houses in the country. Once the height of fashionable living, it was eclipsed by Back Bay and lapsed into decline. But in the 1960s, an influx of professionals renovated the dilapidated buildings and in their wake drew the chic boutiques, restaurants, and nightclubs that now line the main thoroughfares of Columbus Avenue and Tremont Street. The neighborhood has a Bohemian edge to it, lent by the many artists and gays living here. South End artists exhibit regularly at the **Mills Gallery** at 549 Tremont Street. (A call to 617–426–7700 will give you a schedule of this and other Boston events.) In late October, **house tours** are given by the South End Historical Society, located at 532 Massachusetts Avenue (617–536–4445). The jewel of the South End is **Bay Village,** the few blocks just southeast of Arlington and Stuart streets. This warren of narrow little streets looks more like Beacon Hill than Back Bay. Black shutters and iron grillwork doorways and windowboxes accent its brick row houses—and wrought-iron gaslights line the sidewalks, just as they do on Beacon Hill.

# Cambridge

Although it has its own rich share of the Hub's claim on history, Cambridge's ethnic neighborhoods and its colleges—Harvard, MIT, and others—give it a vibrant life in the here-and-now. Each weekend some saint's day, some holiday, some festival, or just good weather brings people to the streets. Kids in costumes wave banners, men in suits carry heavy statues, and everybody eats street food, which we often suspect to be the real purpose of it all.

Some of these events stop traffic in busy Harvard Square itself, but many others are tucked away in neighborhoods, such as the **Feast of Cosmo and Damian** in the Italian enclave above Inman Square, which spreads over into Somerville. Each September a parade of local bands, costumed kids, and women who wish they were wearing more-comfortable shoes follows the lines of men who carry the two saints, winding their way along a route lined by festively decorated houses whose porches and windows seem to be overflowing with people eating.

The parade doesn't move very fast—the statues are heavy—and it stops often, in front of houses where gifts of money are pinned to the robes of the little saints, until you can hardly see the statues for the bills. The grand finale is at Flowers by Sal, on Cambridge Street, where long rolls of ribbon with dollar bills pinned to their entire length are rolled from upper story windows and wrapped around the by now nearly smothered statues.

**Inman Square** is the Portuguese heart of the Boston area. Although not as intensely so as New Bedford, and mixed with Italian and other influences, it's still a recognizable piece of Portugal. Several restaurants are as genuine as the broa in the bakeries: At *Casa Portugal,* you can order *caldo verde*—a soup of kale and potatoes punctuated with slices of spicy sausage—then dive into a melange of fresh shellfish or pork Allentejo, a delectable combination of pork and clams. Casa Portugal is at 1200 Cambridge Street; (617) 491–8880.

Irish pubs seem to thrive in the *auld sod* of Cambridge. These, unlike Boston's Irish bars, are the hangouts of those newly arrived from the land of green, and they ring with the poetic cadences of Dublin's Grafton Street. In Inman Square, look for *The Druid* at 1357 Cambridge Street, a Dublin-style pub where you'll hear poets, music, and an occasional Irish theatrical performance; (617) 497–0965.

Behind Porter Square, just over the line into Somerville, is Davis Square, where *The Burren* serves up Irish brew on tap and good rugged pub food, including traditional bangers and mash or the Guinness stew. The Burren is at 247 Elm Street; (617) 776–6896. *Grafton Street Grill* is more centrally located, on Massachusetts Avenue—MassAve to locals—opposite Harvard Yard, a couple of doors down from the Harvard Bookstore.

Harvard, which can rarely be accused of modesty, hides several fine museums within its historic walls, all within a short walk of Harvard Square. From ancient Chinese jades to dinosaur bones, these museums have it all. The *University Museum* is four museums in one, housing exhibits on botany, gems and minerals, zoology, and archaeology and ethnology. The spirit of nineteenth-century collectors who chased through

## Booklovers' Stop

*F*ew bibliophiles can resist the lure of the family-owned **Harvard Book Store,** the very persona of Harvard Square. I worked there when I was in college, and my daughter was drawn to a job there by the same muse. Its young clerks know and love books, and several are writers themselves; all are readers. So engrossed was I late one evening, just before closing, in "shelving books" (a euphemism that thinly disguised reading in a secluded corner) that I didn't notice the time until the lights went off and I heard the big door at the top of the stairs close. Fortunately, it was winter, and another employee saw that my coat was still on the rack, so he came looking for me. To this day, although the store is larger and a door no longer separates the used book section in the basement, I won't browse down there at night.

—*Barbara*

jungles and mountains with butterfly nets and specimen boxes lingers here in the antique, glass-topped wooden display cases. The most celebrated exhibit in the *Botanical Museum* is the Glass Flowers, handmade glass replicas of 847 species of plants for teaching botany. The first time I saw them, I walked by them, thinking, "Oh, those are real," and looking elsewhere for the glass flowers. Strawberry and peach blossoms and palm leaves made of colored glass and wire rest gently in their cases. Larger-than-life glass bees pollinate some specimens. In the *Peabody Museum of Archaeology and Ethnology,* prehistoric and other early cultures, from pre-Columbian Central American peoples to South American and North American Indians, highlight the collections. Whale skeletons hang from the ceiling of the *Museum of Comparative Zoology,* where rooms full of collected critters and stuffed beasties range from iridescent butterflies, giant beetles, and fish to a Mongolian tiger and six hundred species of hummingbirds. The collection in the *Mineralogical and Geological Museum* dates back to 1784 and ranges from precious gems to meteorites. The University Museum, at 24 Oxford Street, is open from 9:00 A.M. to 4:15 P.M. Monday through Saturday and from 1:00 to 5:00 P.M. on Sunday. Admission is $5.00 for adults, $4.00 for seniors, $3.00 for students and children (for all four museums). Call (617) 495–3045.

Harvard has three art museums, all close together. The *Busch-Reisinger Museum,* at 24 Kirkland Street, with its noted collections of Central and Northern European art, is the only such museum in the country. The *Fogg Art Museum,* at 32 Quincy Street, holds master paintings by Fra Angelico, Rubens, van Gogh, Renoir, Homer, and Pollock. In a strikingly contemporary building opened in 1985, the *Sackler Museum,* at 485 Broadway, displays ancient, Near Eastern, and Oriental art, including an unparalleled collection of Chinese jade and cave reliefs. The art museums are open daily from 10:00 A.M. to 5:00 P.M. Admission is $5.00 for adults, $4.00 for seniors, and $3.00 for students. Visitors under eighteen are always free, and no admission fee is charged from 10:00 A.M. to noon on Saturdays. Call (617) 495–9400.

Especially in the spring, there's no more beautiful place in Cambridge than *Mount Auburn Cemetery.* Acres of flowering plants and trees surround the graves in America's first garden cemetery, founded in 1831. Everywhere you look, trees towering over your head hang their soft petals in pink, white, lavender, and yellow over the ornate Victorian statuary and grave markers, gently obscuring the rough stone. A weeping willow leans soulfully into a pond. Many of the 2,500 trees in 380 species are rare—such as cedar of Lebanon, weeping flowering dogwood, and White Russian mulberry—but no less beautiful are the more common varieties: star magnolia, Corinthian dogwood, several types of cherry tree, and purple crabapple. The trees attract so many birds that birders come here regularly to spot them, and the cemetery is one of the best places to see the spring warbler migration. Other birds bring the number of species sighted in Mount Auburn to over 235. And most of those famous Bostonians whose names you recognize are buried here—Henry Wadsworth Longfellow, Winslow Homer, Oliver Wendell Holmes, Charles Bulfinch, Amy Lowell, Julia Ward Howe, Henry Cabot Lodge, R. Buckminster Fuller, and Isabella Stewart Gardner, to name just a few. A map of the graves and an audiotape tour are available at the gatehouse. Burials take place regularly, and you cannot picnic, jog, play Frisbee, or otherwise disport yourself in a disrespectful manner. The main cemetery gates are at 580 Mount Auburn Street (Route 16). Members of the Friends of Mount Auburn Cemetery (617–864–9646) lead seasonal walks and give lectures on the cemetery year-round.

As you might expect, the Harvard Square area bursts at the seams with places to eat, many of them no more than that. For some years, the highlight of the area was Harvest, where many of Boston's brightest chefs got their start. Then it fell on difficult times and finally closed. In 1998, it did what restaurants never do: It reopened under the same name, with the same high standards of its prime years, and has made a rousing success of it. Hidden in a passageway behind Crate and Barrel, at 44 Brattle Street, *Harvest* opens into a garden courtyard filled with tables shaded by full-grown trees. Lunch entrees include several standouts borrowed from the starters menu at dinner: a tartlet of Nunsuch goat cheese, a potpie of cepes, or a salad of Maine crab in creamy cucumber dressing layered with crisp-coated fried green tomatoes. Each day's menu features a risotto special, which might include shelled mussels and basil with tart flavor bursts of whole tiny cherry tomatoes. The main courses, which range from $13, might include filet mignon topped with marrow and herb butter, and dessert could be a spiced plum and blackberry shortcake or a banana split made with caramelized banana and a warm brownie. Service is adroit and highly informed. Sunday brunch is a three-course, all-inclusive menu; (617) 868–2255.

Between Harvard and Porter Squares, MassAve is dotted with restaurants. On the corner of Shepard Street, *Chez Henri* blends the flavors of France and Cuba in a pleasant fusion that treasures the nuances of individual ingredients. Look for the likes of grilled pork chops with an ancho chili glaze, saffron-infused conch chowder served with sweet potato biscuits, crabcakes with a jalepeño mango glaze, or curried coconut shrimp with black beans. The dessert chef is excellent, too. The upscale dining room is not undiscovered, so make a reservation; (617) 354–8980.

Porter Square, two subway stops up MassAve from Harvard Square, is the center of the Japanese community, which congregates in the food courts in the *Porter Exchange.* This art deco building, which was once the main Sears store, has a Japanese grocery and a row of eateries that serve big bowls of fat udon noodles, cooling plates of chilled soba in the summer, and steaming nabe pots in the winter. The faces, the voices, the aromas, and the tastes could make you believe you're in Kyoto.

One of the few bed-and-breakfasts that you can book independently in Cambridge is called *A Cambridge House,* an 1892 home listed on the National Register of Historic Places. It's nicely restored and richly furnished with floral print fabrics, patterned wallpapers, period antiques, and Oriental rugs. A number of rooms are available in an adjacent carriage house and another nearby property. Write A Cambridge House at 2218 Massachusetts Avenue, Cambridge 02140, or call (617) 491–6300 or 800–232–9989. Room rates (doubles $119–$225) include wine and cheese in the evening and an elaborate breakfast, which might feature chocolate waffles with fresh strawberries.

If you want to stay right in the Square, and in style, the *Charles Hotel* is convenient to all the action in Harvard Square, with upscale rooms and the *Regattabar,* headquarters for haute-jazz in the Boston area. The likes of Wynton Marsalis and Dizzy Gillespie have played here. To reserve a room at the Charles, call (800) 882–1818. Like most city hotels, it has special summer weekend rates.

# South of Boston

I f you're driving to Boston from the south, there's an unusual sight on Route 3. Heading north, look to your right at exit 13 and you'll see a white *Boston Gas Company tank* painted with huge swashes of bright colors in a spectrum of red, yellow, orange, blue, green, and purple. The rainbow-colored artwork gives a lift to a dreary urban landscape. It's signed simply "Corita." The artist was the late Corita Kent, a former Los Angeles nun who left her order and moved to Boston. She designed the popular love postage stamp and countless pop art silkscreen prints. Her gas tank design has been a Boston landmark ever since 1971 and is the world's largest copyrighted work of art. During the Vietnam War, many criticized the design, saying the blue stripe resembled the profile of North Vietnamese leader Ho Chi Minh. Corita denied it.

Incongruously neighbored by huge cranes and warehouses, **Castle Island** is a windswept green park with a long promenade perfect for strolling. It's also the oldest continuously fortified site in North America. The fort, rebuilt several times, has stood here since 1634. The hilly lawns surrounding the high granite ramparts are a fine place to picnic. Edgar Allan Poe, who enlisted at Castle Island, based his story *The Cask of Amontillado* on an incident that took place here involving a young lieutenant who was killed in a duel and whose friends sealed up his killer in one of the fort's lowest dungeons. Weekend tours of the fort are offered in the summer. The park is at the end of William J. Day Boulevard in South Boston; call (617) 727–5290.

One of Boston's best-kept secrets is the **Boston Harbor Islands.** This group of some thirty islands scattered from Boston Harbor down the coast to Quincy and Hingham is accessible only by private boat or commercial ferry. Eight of them form a state park, with each island permeated by a unique flavor and character. The hub is Georges Island, where the ferry stops first and you can catch a free interisland water taxi during the summer. Exploring Civil War–era Fort Warren is the highlight of a trip to Georges Island, the most developed of the group. Peddocks Island, the largest, has a diverse terrain of woodlands, salt marsh, rocky beaches, and open fields. Tales of buried pirate treasure continue to surround Lovells Island, which also has a nice swimming beach. Berry pickers love Grape Island, where they can gather raspberries, blackberries, and wild rose hips, meanwhile watching the wide variety of birds the berries attract. Bumpkin Island is known for its beautiful wildflowers, Great Brewster for its profusion of wild roses. For information on Peddocks and Lovells islands, call the Boston Metropolitan District Commission's Harbor Region Office at (617) 727–5290. For Georges and the other islands, call the Boston Harbor Islands State Park in Hingham at (617) 740–1605.

To get to the islands, you can depart from Boston, Hingham, or Hull. The Boston-based Bay State Cruise Company, on Long Wharf (617–723–7800), sails daily in summer and on weekends through the spring and fall. The Friends of the Boston Harbor Islands sponsors special boat trips and tours, such as sunset cruises and trips to Boston Light, the nation's first lighthouse, on Little Brewster Island; call (617) 523–8386.

To explore the harbor and its islands by kayak, sign on for a trip with **Zoar Outdoors**. Camping trips visit several islands, including the deserted POW camp on **Peddocks Island**, staying overnight on Grape

Island. B&B trips are also available, with day paddles. Contact Zoar through its Web site at www.zoarout@aol.com or call (800) 532–7483.

# West of Boston

The famed architect of Boston's Emerald Necklace lived and worked on a quiet, tree-lined street in a Brookline neighborhood. His former home and office are now the *Frederick Law Olmsted National Historic Site,* which holds photographs of Olmsted's work and a vault full of thousands of his landscape plans. The rustically paneled second floor served as offices, but Olmsted, ever a lover of the outdoors, often took his desk out to a shady hollow in the yard to work. The house, located at 99 Warren Street, is open from 10:00 A.M. to 4:30 P.M. Friday through Sunday. Call (617) 566–1689.

As you drive on busy Route 16 in Waltham, you'd never know that just off it is a nineteenth-century country estate set in an oasis of green lawns, cornfields, and sheep pastures. One of the finest examples of Federal architecture in America, *Gore Place* was built in 1805 as the country seat for Christopher Gore, a wealthy lawyer who served as Massachusetts's first U.S. attorney, in 1789, as well as state representative, U.S. senator, and governor. The symmetrical brick facade has a bowfront center flanked by two long wings, accented with lunette windows and black shutters. The Great Hall sets the tone, with its King of Prussia marble floor, 17-foot ceiling, and a three-story staircase that curves as gracefully as a swan's neck. Some of the furnishings are Gore family possessions, among them silver, crystal, and china, along with family portraits. One of the mansion's most unusual features is the Oval Drawing Room, an entirely oval room echoed in an oval sitting room upstairs. To accommodate this unusual room, windows and sliding doors had to be curved as well, and a unique set of servants' stairs are incorporated into the wall depth separating the oval from the adjacent dining room. To replace the wallpaper, Gore Place recently had to engage the same paperers who do the Oval Office in the White House. During a tour here, you will learn a great deal of fascinating historical information, including the story of the Gores' major-domo, Robert Roberts, author of first book in America to be written by a black person. His *House Servants Directory* was published in 1827 and quickly became the standard for the managing of a well-ordered household.

On the extensive grounds are formal gardens, one completely walled by a tall hedge. In summer these are a riot of bright phlox, hollyhocks, thistle, bee balm, and day lilies. A rare knot garden is close by.

Programs at Gore Place include summer concerts, a Christmas open house with period decorations, and an annual sheepshearing festival in April, complete with spinning and weaving demonstrations, crafts, folk music, and food. Two rotating exhibits emphasizing the Federal period are displayed throughout the house, which is open to the public from April 15 to November 15. Gore Place is at 52 Gore Street, (617– 894–2798). Hours are 10:00 A.M. to 5:00 P.M. Tuesday through Saturday and 2:00 to 5:00 P.M. Sunday. (Last tours are at 4:00 P.M.) Admission is $4.00 for adults and teens and $3.00 for children ages five to twelve.

Another fine estate in Waltham is on Lyman Street, off Route 20. *The Vale* was begun in 1793, and although the Federal house itself is not open for individual visitors, its remarkable greenhouses are. These were built in 1804, are among the oldest in America, and are filled with a succession of blooms from bougainvillea in May to an entire greenhouse filled with camellias in late January and early February. During the summer you can buy plants here, including hard-to-find herbs such as lemon grass and patchouli. Other sales are scheduled throughout the year and include orchid plants in November. Admission to the greenhouses is $1.50, Monday through Saturday from 9:00 A.M. to 4:00 P.M., and you can tour the grounds and gardens as well; (781) 891–4882, ext. 244.

Waltham made its name with watches and clocks. When we had railways connecting towns across the nation—and when they ran on time—they ran on Waltham watches. Some of America's best-known clock towers have Waltham works.

## And It All Ran Like Clockwork

*T*he Waltham factories did more than make the world's best timepieces and first fiber-to-finished-fabric; they were the first to see the importance of taking care of workers. Many of these were young women who came from farms and rural communities and were not used to city life, so their company built them boarding houses and made sure they had good food, safe and affordable lodgings, transportation to work, and even recreational facilities. Waltham Watch maintained a gymnasium and a fleet of canoes that its employees could paddle in the Charles River. The company sponsored concerts for them on an island where everyone arrived by canoe. In the winter it provided ice skates and kept the ice cleared so employees could skate on their lunch hour.

The Waltham Watch factory building is still there—and still handsome, with fine brickwork and good architectural lines—overlooking the Charles River, its original source of power. You can get a good view of it from the mile-long *Riverwalk,* which borders the opposite bank from the Moody Street Bridge to the Prospect Street Bridge, or you can float past it by boat, on the *M. V.* **Totem Pole.** Leaving Cronin's Landing, at the Moody Street Bridge, four times a day on weekends (and for lunch cruises on Wednesday and Friday), this pleasant open boat with a shade canopy tours the quiet, tree-lined stretch of the Charles between Waltham and Newton. Along with the mills, it passes the sites of two of the Boston area's most famous ballrooms, Nuttings on the Charles and The Totem Pole, where all the greats performed—Frank Sinatra, Bing Crosby, and the "big bands"—and the island where John Philip Sousa and his band played to an audience of 5,000 people listening from canoes in the river. The cruise stops in Newton, where you can walk around in the riverbank park. You can board the boat from this end at the Newton Marriott's landing. The cost is $8.00 for adults, $7.00 for seniors, and $5.00 for children; (781) 894–8604.

Along with ducks, geese, and swans, you'll see a lot of canoes in the river, and you can join them by renting a canoe or kayak at the half-timbered Newton Boathouse, opposite the Mariott in Newton, from *Charles River Canoe and Kayak;* (617) 965–5510. This section of the river is known as the Lakes District because the river is so placid and the islands and coves seem more like lakes than a river. You can paddle alone or join a tour. The company also offers kayaking trips to Gloucester and other harbors and moonlight canoe trips on the Charles. Rentals start at $9.00 an hour or $36 a day.

Back in Waltham, in another set of old mill buildings, themselves a National Historic Landmark, is the *Charles River Museum of Industry.* The Waltham mills are considered the fourth most important in America's Industrial Revolution, and this museum focuses not only on the whats and hows of manufacturing but also on the experience of the workers and how mills changed American life forever. Here you will see an early paper bag machine spitting out 600 bags per minute (and learn that the flat-bottomed bag was invented by Margaret Knight, who patented it in 1871). You'll also learn how the Industrial Revolution created the need for clocks, shoes, and lunchboxes. Admission is $4.00, $2.00 for children and seniors, and the museum is open Monday through Saturday from 10:00 A.M. to 5:00 P.M.; 154 Moody Street; (781) 893–5410, www.crmi.org/~crmi.

Aficionados of art deco architecture should look at the two facing buildings on Moody Street just south of the river. One is the Cronin Building and the other is the Watch City Brewing Company, each a classic of its type. Moody Street also offers restaurants, running the gamut of nationalities from Indian to Ecuadorian, with ample free public parking just a block or so away, near the river. As you stroll along, it will seem that every other entrance leads to food. *Tuscan Grill,* at number 361, is consistently rated among the best Italian restaurants in the Boston area, serving hearty dishes in an informal (and somewhat-cramped) setting; (781) 891–5486. A couple of doors up the street, we like *Lizzy's Homemade Ice Cream,* but not just for the ice cream. It's a cafe with sandwiches, soups, and light lunch dishes, and no table service; (781) 893–6677. At number 313, *Iguana Cantina* serves Mexican food; (781) 891–3039.

The rural setting of the *DeCordova Museum* in Lincoln is a big attraction. Set in a wooded, green, thirty-acre park that overlooks a lake, this is a peaceful and uncrowded art museum. Its holdings in twentieth-century American art include paintings, sculpture, graphics, and photography. The outdoor jazz concerts in the summer are especially intimate gatherings. The museum also sponsors chamber music, ballet, modern dance, and rock music performances. The DeCordova is located on Sandy Pond Road; call (781) 259–8355. It's open from 11:00 A.M. to 5:00 P.M. Tuesday through Sunday. Tickets to the museum cost $6.00 for adults, $4.00 for seniors, students, and children.

## They Saw It Here First

*T*he Boston Manufacturing Company, which opened here in 1814, in the building that now houses the Museum of Industry, had a long list of "firsts," including:

- *The first time in the world that spinning and weaving were combined in a single operation in the same building*

- *The first power loom used in the United States*

- *The first time silk was woven by machine*

- *The first time young women were an important part of the paid workforce*

- *The first brick textile mill*

- *The first large successful manufacturing company in the United States (and the prototype for the modern corporation)*

- *The first industrial labor strike in the United States—in 1821*

Walter Gropius, founder of the Bauhaus school of art and architecture in Germany, designed and built his family home in the rolling green hills of Lincoln. *Gropius House* so perfectly embodied the Bauhaus principle of economy in design over ornamentation that it became much-visited by architects. Industrial-style materials typical of Bauhaus are seen in the glass-block wall dividing the study and dining room and in the welded tubular steel staircase railing. Much of the furniture was designed by Gropius's friend Marcel Breuer. And Gropius's artist friends, among them Henry Moore, contributed works of art. From June 1 to October 15, the Gropius House, at 68 Baker Bridge Road, is open for hourly tours beginning at 11:00 A.M., with the last tour beginning at 4:00 P.M., Wednesday through Sunday. From November 1 to May 30, the house is open the first full weekend of the month. Call (781) 259–8098. Admission is $5.00 adult, $4.50 senior, and $2.50 student.

At the *Drumlin Farm Education Center and Wildlife Sanctuary,* in Lincoln, you can visit injured animals and birds in their native habitat as you walk along the trails. Inside, in the Burrowing Animals Building, you see an underground exhibit with a cutaway of small animals in their tunnels. Special one-way glass lets you watch their activities without disturbing them.

Most likely, the *Willow Pond Kitchen* will stay the way it is until kingdom come—it's done so since at least about 1927. The ma-and-pa, down-home atmosphere walks on the wild side with its decor of moth-eaten stuffed bobcat, coyote, and even skunk. You sit at Formica tables in ancient wooden booths where you are served great homemade food on paper plates. You can always count on lobster roll and lobster pie, steamed clams, and lots of fish dishes—also burgers, sandwiches, and soups made from scratch. The restaurant, at 745 Lexington Road in Concord, is open for lunch and dinner. Call (508) 369–6529.

Portugese wines are sadly neglected on most restaurant wine lists, but not at the beguiling *Guida's* in Concord's historic railway depot. Wine plays a serious role in the cuisine of this talented young chef, and you'll find meltingly tender squid simmered in Dão. The fishcakes, made with hearty *baccalau* (salt cod), are served with a delicate creamy cilantro sauce on the side. Few places in Portugal have Guida's way with a steaming *caldeira* of mixed seafoods, and the grilled sardines are manna from heaven. Speaking of manna, ask if she's baked the dense cornmeal *broa,* a flat bread from northern Portugal, exuding a rich, earthy aroma. The menu has many New American selections, but we go there for expert modern interpretations of traditional Portuguese dishes. Take the commuter rail train from Porter Square right to Guida's door; 84 Thoreau Street; (978) 371-1333.

# North of Boston

**M**ore *snowy owls* congregate at Boston's Logan Airport than any- where else in New England. From November to May, snowy owls migrate from their tundra habitats in Greenland, northern Canada, and Alaska to sit out the Arctic winter. To the owls, the vast landing fields of the airport look just like the tundra of home. As many as forty-seven snowy owls have been banded here in one winter by Norman Smith, director of the Trailside Museum in Milton and a lifelong raptor fan. You can rarely see the snowy owls out your airplane window, but you can see them at Plum Island on the North Shore. (See the next chapter.)

There are just six professional quilt museums in the United States, and one is in Lowell—the **New England Quilt Museum,** the only one in New England. The seventy or so quilts in its permanent collection date back more than a hundred years. Rotating exhibits also showcase antique, traditional, and contemporary quilts, and the Christmas quilt show is especially colorful. The museum is located at 18 Shattuck Street; call (978) 452–4207. Admission is $2.00. Hours are from 10:00 A.M. to 5:00 P.M. Tuesday through Saturday and from noon to 5:00 P.M. on Sunday, with reduced winter hours.

New England's only butterfly park, **Butterfly Place** at Papillon Park, delights with hundreds of butterflies on view. Enclosed in a glass atrium, the mostly North American species feed on flowering plants set along brick pathways, where you can easily see them. The climate is kept warm and humid for the butterflies, and classical music playing in the back- ground makes this a real escape for humans. You might see a kite- shaped butterfly with sky blue and black striped wings, a luna moth, and plenty of monarchs. An observation area shows a video about butterflies and displays larvae and caterpillars, and a naturalist answers questions in the atrium. Butterfly Place is open from 10:00 A.M. to 5:00 P.M. daily from April 15 through Columbus Day. Admission is $6.00 for adults and teens and $5.00 for seniors and for children ages three to twelve; chil- dren under three are free. At exit 34 from Route 3, take Westford Road for half a mile and bear left onto Swan Road, which becomes Tyngsboro Road; the park is a mile down on the right. Call (978) 392–0955.

Bucolic Route 113 meanders westward through farmlands, never far from New Hampshire and passing through the attractive town of

Pepperill before joining Route 119 in Townsend. Here, in the tiny settlement called Townsend Harbor, the Historical Society maintains the **Reed Homestead,** an 1809 home with a nice garden and a small museum shop; (978) 597–2106. Next to it, at South and Main Streets, **The Cooperage** stands above the falls that once powered its wood-shaping equipment. Now the mill houses a shop selling herbs, dried flowers, wool, and antiques, and the owner invites you to picnic in the herb garden overlooking the old mill pond and dam, and even provides a table. An early gristmill faces The Cooperage from across South Street, completing a nice ensemble of historic buildings.

Beyond, Route 119 goes through **Willard Brook State Forest,** a deep, bosky terrain of stone walls and bridges cut by hiking and bicycle trails and bridle paths. In the winter it is popular with cross-country skiers and snowmobilers. The park headquarters, at the Ashby town line, has trail maps. A wooded campground with twenty-one campsites is 1 mile west of the headquarters; (978) 597–8802.

MORE PLACES TO STAY
IN GREATER BOSTON

**Hotel Buckminster,**
645 Beacon Street,
at Kenmore Square,
Boston 02215;
(617) 236–7050 or
(800) 727–2825.
Plain and comfortable, this hotel often has rooms available when chain hotels are full and offers bargain rates and vouchers for breakfast in neighborhood bakeries.

**Midtown Hotel,**
220 Huntington Avenue,
Boston 02115;
(617) 262–1000 or
(800) 343–1177.
Near Copley Square, with attractive rooms at attractive prices; free parking and a pool.

**Mary Prentiss Inn,**
6 Prentiss Street,
Cambridge 02138;
(617) 661–2929.
A modest but comfortable lodging a block off Massachusetts Avenue between Porter and Harvard squares; inexpensive for the city.

**Irving House,**
24 Irving Street,
Cambridge 02138;
(617) 547–4600.
A plain-Jane walk-up motel near Harvard Square with rooms under $100.

MORE PLACES TO EAT
IN GREATER BOSTON

**Aurora,**
30 Congress Street,
Boston;
(617) 350–6001.
In a ship anchored in the harbor, offering a smashing view of the city, Russian dishes, and seafood.

**Pomodoro,**
319 Hanover Street
(North End), Boston;
(617) 367–4348.
Although chefs change often here, the quality doesn't, nor does the familiar air, where everyone seems to know the owner. Entrees are under $20.

**Marcuccio's,**
125 Salem Street
(North End) Boston;
(617) 723–1807.
A contemporary take on
the Italian theme, with
an outstanding fusion
menu and most entrees
under $20.

**Sandrine's Bistro,**
8 Holyoke Street,
Cambridge;
(617) 497–5300.
Just off Harvard Square,
serving Alsatian dishes,
which combine French and
German influences; the
choucroute Alsacienne, a
blend of sausages, meats,
and sauerkraut, would feed
an army on the march;
prices are below the norm
in the Square.

**Portugalia,**
723 Cambridge Street,
Cambridge;
(617) 491–5373.
Near Inman Square,
serves reasonably priced
Portuguese favorites in a
traditional old-country
atmosphere.

**Jae's Cafe,**
1281 Cambridge Street,
Cambridge
(617) 497–8380.
Not fancy, but good food
from all around the Pacific
Rim; some of the best
Korean food in the city.

**Guida's,**
84 Thoreau Street,
Concord;
(978) 371–1703.
Stylish restaurant serving
creative dishes in an historic building; the wine list
is particularly rich in
hard-to-find Portuguese
selections.

---

WORTH SEEING IN
GREATER BOSTON

**John F. Kennedy Library
and Museum,**
Columbia Point,
Boston;
(617) 929–4523,
admission $8.00 adults.

**Museum of Science,**
Science Park,
Boston;
(617) 723–2500.
One of the finest, with an
OMNI theater and state-of-
the-art displays.

**New England Aquarium,**
Central Wharf,
Boston;
(617) 973–5200.
Sea creatures of all types in
realistic environments.

**Paul Revere House,**
North Square
(North End), Boston;
(617) 523–2338.
The only building left in
Boston from the 1600s.

**USS** *Constitution*,
"Old Ironsides,"
Charlestown Navy Yard,
Boston;
(617) 426–1812.
One of the major
experiences of a trip to
New England.

---

TO LEARN MORE ABOUT
GREATER BOSTON

For complete travel infor-
mation, contact the Greater
Boston Convention and
Visitors Bureau, Prudential
Plaza West, P.O. Box 490,
Boston 02199
(617) 536–4100.

For the best current information on what's happen-
ing in the Boston area,
check the web page of
Frank Avruch, "Boston's
Man About Town" and well-
known authority on classic
movies and the arts in general: www.bostonman.com.

# North Shore

I t's ironic that most people's introduction to the North Shore of Boston comes by way of whizzing Route 1, arcadelike in its density of fast-food shops and gas stations and the famous fiberglass cows outside Saugus's Hilltop Steakhouse, for just beyond this urban surrealism lies some of the territory most prized by blue bloods, exclusive and expensive residential areas for Boston commuters. Three-hundred-year-old colonial towns with quaint seventeenth-century houses. Farmland and horse country, including a polo club in Hamilton where spectators throw champagne tailgate picnics and Princess Anne has been known to show her face.

Lining the coast all the way up to the Merrimac River and New Hampshire are seaports and fishing and boatbuilding capitals that became famous all over the world in the nineteenth century: Salem, Essex, Gloucester, and Newburyport. Serious yachters around the globe know of chichi Marblehead, which has a long tradition of maritime prowess—it was Marblehead men who ferried George Washington across the Delaware. And America's Cup contender Ted Hood makes sails here.

Magnificent white sand beaches stretch along miles of open ocean in Ipswich, Newbury, and Nahant. Cape Ann is known not only for fishing and boatbuilding but also for its artists' colonies, one of which is the oldest in the country.

But back to Route 1. Despite the fact that this is not the most attractive stretch you'll see in Massachusetts, it brings you to some interesting towns with industrial histories, among them Saugus, site of a Puritan ironworks, and Lynn, once known as "Shoe City." And you won't stand in line in these towns.

## Industrial Towns

T ucked away in Saugus is an unusual piece of history: the *Saugus Iron Works National Historic Site.* Here the Puritans built an ironworks in 1650 to supply the growing colony with nails and wrought

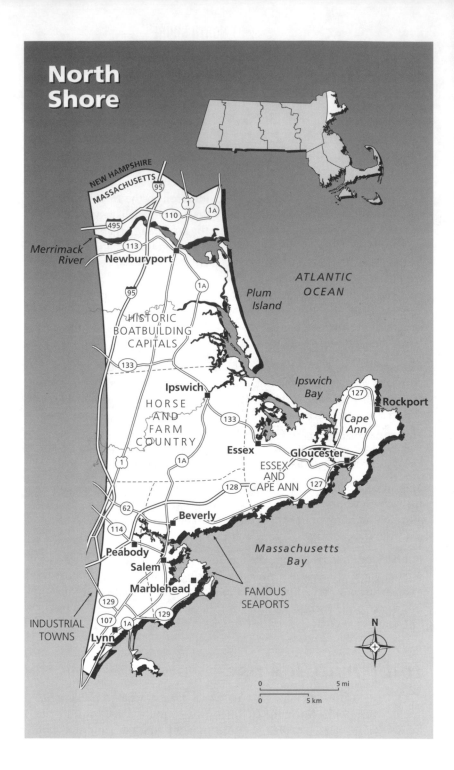

# North Shore

NEW HAMPSHIRE
MASSACHUSETTS

95
1
110
1A

495

113
Merrimack
River

Newburyport

95

1A

Plum
Island

ATLANTIC
OCEAN

HISTORIC
BOATBUILDING
CAPITALS

133

Ipswich
Bay

127
Rockport

Ipswich

HORSE
AND
FARM
COUNTRY

133

Cape
Ann

1

1A

Essex

Gloucester

ESSEX
AND
CAPE ANN

128

127

62

Beverly

114

Massachusetts
Bay

Peabody

Salem

Marblehead

FAMOUS
SEAPORTS

INDUSTRIAL
TOWNS

129

107
1A
129

N

Lynn

0          5 mi

0          5 km

# NORTH SHORE

**AUTHORS' FAVORITES ON THE NORTH SHORE**

*Saugus Iron Works*

*Peabody Essex Museum*

*Hammond Castle Museum*

*Beauport*

*Essex River Cruise*

iron previously shipped at great cost from England. The buildings have been faithfully reconstructed. Guided tours lead you from the two-story blast furnace, with its 18-foot bellows, to the forge, with its giant hammer and anvil, and to the rolling-and-slitting mill, where iron was flattened and cut for various products. The guide sets the waterwheel to turning, powering the blast furnace bellows. In the casting shed down below, it smells all dank and iron-y.

The site is so peaceful today that it's hard to imagine the hellish noise and heat the men worked in back then. Now it looks like a green park. You might even see a snapping turtle laying its eggs on the slag heap, or a field of yellow coreopsis in bloom. A nature trail winds along the Saugus River, once mighty enough to power seven waterwheels, now a tidal marsh. A museum holds artifacts found on the site and exhibits on the ironworks' history. There's also a tour of the seventeenth-century ironworks house. To get to the Central Street site, follow signs from either exit 43 off Interstate 95 or the Main Street exit off Route 1. It's open from 9:00 A.M. to 5:00 P.M. daily, 9:00 A.M. to 4:00 P.M. in winter. Admission is free. Call (781) 233–0050.

The city of Lynn became a shoemaking center in the eighteenth century and was nationally known by the end of the 1800s. Shoemaking exhibits are displayed at the **Lynn Historical Society** in a small yellow house on a quiet side street. Hanging on the wall is a large medallion under glass, almost 5 feet in diameter and made entirely of tiny shoe soles in concentric rings. The 234 soles, each unique to the maker, represented all the Lynn shoe manufacturers and dealers of the day at the 1893 Chicago Exposition. Ladies' turned shoes were Lynn's specialty; they were turned inside out to make the stitching fashionably invisible. Other exhibits are shoemakers' tools, antique clothes, postcards, and an 1896 switchboard. Lynn's 1860 shoemakers' strike made national news. A walking-tour brochure of some of the old shoe factories is available at the museum, at 125 Green Street. It's open from 1:00 to 4:00 P.M. Monday through Saturday. Admission is $3.00 for adults and $1.00 for children.

I've been to a lot of ice-cream places that offer toppings doled out by a teaspoon-wielding staffer. But at the **Putnam Pantry,** an old-fashioned place with worn wooden floors, you can custom-make your own sundae, ladling out endless quantities of sliced strawberries, hot fudge, real whipped cream, cherry caramel, and more, set out in generous bins. You sit at marble-topped tables in ice-cream-parlor chairs with heart-shaped backs. Take heed: To get to the dining room, you pass through a vintage candy store, its shelves loaded with chocolates, hard candies, gumdrops, fudge, stick candy, and lollipops. Open daily from 11:00 A.M. to 10:00 P.M., the Putnam Pantry is located on Route 1 north, just north of Route 62; call (978) 774–2383.

You've never seen a magic show like **Le Grand David and His Own Spectacular Magic Company** in Beverly. The show is held in the Cabot Street Cinema Theatre, a beautifully restored art deco movie palace built in 1920, all frescoed and gold-leafed. In the red plush lobby, a top-hatted accordion player, a juggling jester, a puppet show, and popcorn and candy for sale amuse children before the two-hour show and during intermission. "Spectacular" doesn't do justice to the grand, turn-of-the-century-style, elaborately painted silk backdrops, lavish costumes out of the *Arabian Nights,* and music of *Scheherazade.* The stars of the show, Le Grand David and Marco the Magi, perform classic feats of prestidigitation, Houdini-like escapes, and levitation, as well as sawing people in boxes and making doves and ducks disappear. The large, three-generation cast has performed together for almost twenty years, and includes David's two young nieces, veteran performers at the ages of seven and nine. Performances are given at 3:00 P.M. Sundays from mid-September through July. Tickets cost $12.00 for adults and $8.00 for children under twelve; call (978) 927–3677. The Cabot Street Cinema Theatre is located at 286 Cabot Street, off Route 1A south, in Beverly.

# Famous Seaports

Marblehead Harbor is one of the most beautiful harbors in New England. The fine shops and restaurants here, as well as three centuries of architecture that wind up and down the climbing narrow streets of its Old Town, draw big summer resort crowds. Still, there's no disputing the beauty of a drive out **Marblehead Neck** (take Pleasant Street to Ocean Avenue to reach the connecting causeway). The winding road passes a pretty beach and fantastic mansions, and then a stone castle. A sign on the right marks **Castle Rock,** where a short path leads to the rock, which you can climb for a gorgeous view of the coast. The road ends at **Chandler Hovey Park,** a pocket park high up that's a vantage point for stirring ocean views, and the Marblehead Light.

At a quiet remove from downtown is a splendid old English Tudor mansion cresting a seaside cliff, **Spray Cliff on the Ocean Bed and Breakfast.** Guests can enjoy the ocean views from three terraces, one reached via a cliffside stairway, and from a private beach. The living room is light-filled, airy, and spacious. Seven guest rooms, each with private bath, are decorated in a casual California country style, with whimsically painted furniture. Breakfast offers bounteous choices of quiches and muffins. Spray Cliff is located at 25 Spray Avenue, Marblehead (doubles $149–$189). For reservations, call (781) 631–6789 or (800) 626–1530.

Salem is so filled with maritime wonders that you could easily spend a week here. Boosted by its maritime trade, Salem was once the nation's sixth-largest city. By 1800, so many Salem ships filled Asian ports that some traders thought Salem was a country. You can see a great wealth of this history at the **Peabody Essex Museum,** a complex of several buildings in downtown Salem on the Essex Street Mall. The first is the former **East India Marine Society,** founded in 1799 by sea captains who knew they were bringing home rare oddities. Their "museum of natural and artificial curiosities" is housed in the original 1824 granite building with a black anchor in front and is the oldest continuously operating museum in America.

It also must be the most treasure-filled maritime museum in all of New England. Thirty brightly designed galleries hold maritime artifacts, Asian export art, and exhibits in ethnology, natural history, and archaeology. Among the "natural curiosities" you'll encounter are a ship's model made entirely of cloves, a 6-inch tall hair comb elaborately carved from a single scale of a Pacific tortoise, and a stuffed scarlet ibis from Brazil. Ships' figureheads and paintings of Salem ships and Chinese ports feature prominently, as do exotic treasures from Bombay to Zanzibar. Asian export art made just for trade with the West includes engraved silver teapots, a secretary made entirely of carved ivory, and a Chinese "moon bed" whose oval-shaped, dark wood canopy is inlaid with ivory and cut out with hundreds of infinitesimally small designs of people, pagodas, and boats.

Diagonally across the Essex Street Mall are a gallery and three historic houses that span three centuries of architecture: the 1684 **John Ward House,** the 1727 Georgian **Crowninshield–Bentley House,** and the 1804 **Gardner–Pingree House,** considered the Federal masterpiece of

**Late May**
*Annual Seaport Festival,*
Salem, includes historic tours, a craft show and demonstrations;
(508) 740–1650.

**Late June**
*St. Peter's Fiesta,*
Gloucester, with parades, Italian food, and the highlight, a greased pole contest at sea;
(800) 649–6839

**Mid–September**
*Essex Clamfest,* Memorial Park, Essex, the town where fried clams were invented;
(978) 283–1601.

**Mid–late October**
*Haunted Happenings,*
Salem, brings creepy doings throughout town;
(800) 298–2929

**December**
*Christmas Boat Cavalcade,*
Gloucester, when thirty pleasure boats decorated for the holidays go up Plum River and around the harbor;
(800) 649–6839.

**December**
*Christmas Celebrations,*
Newburyport (see page 46);
(978) 462–6680.

famed Salem architect Samuel McIntire. The Gardner-Pingree House has many elaborate details: door and window corners with carved sheaves of wheat (symbols of prosperity), painted floor cloths, and Adam-style marble mantelpieces. Museum holdings, in a beautiful gallery with white Corinthian columns and a vaulted ceiling, feature oil portraits of such leading figures as Nathaniel Hawthorne and Daniel Webster, as well as period silver pieces. Also among the collections are hundreds of pieces of eighteenth- and nineteenth-century European porcelain and glassware.

The museum complex is open from 10:00 A.M. to 5 P.M. Monday through Saturday, and from noon to 5:00 P.M. Sundays. The three historic houses and gallery are also open until 8:00 P.M. Thursdays. Tickets cost $7.00 for adults, $6.00 for students, $4.00 for children, and $18 for families.

Magnificent sea captains' houses line the entire length of quiet, tree-shaded *Chestnut Street,* just west of the Essex Street Mall. Federal-style temples to wealth stand in neat rows, painted in pastels of creamy yellow, white, or taupe. Wonderful period details stand out: a gold eagle medallion over a door, urn-topped fence posts, fanlight windows, white pillared porticoes, and tidy black shutters.

Down near the waterfront, *The Grapevine,* at 26 Congress Street (978–745–9335), offers an Italian-inspired seafood and pasta menu, rounded out with *pizzettas* and meats. An enchanting alfresco patio evokes Florence. The restaurant is open for lunch and dinner, with dinner entrees from $14 to $23.

# Horse and Farm Country

A genteel atmosphere of yesteryear still lingers at the *Wenham Tea House,* which opened in 1910 as a fund-raising arm of the Wenham Village Improvement Society. Ladies brought their daughters for birthdays and bridal showers to the tearoom, with its painted yellow chairs and flowered curtains. Dainty and traditional lunches include creamed chicken on toast, lobster roll, and cottage cheese with fruit. Lunch is served by reservation only at 11:30 A.M., 12:30 P.M., and 1:30 P.M. Tea, served from 3:15 to 4:30 P.M., is a delicious affair of scones with whipped cream and raspberry jam, cinnamon sticks, and tea bread. A really nice gift shop sells jams, teas, cookies, and candies; a profusion of books on gardening, cooking, birds, and travel; and such handcrafts and housewares as Waterford crystal, silver, handbags, and painted ceramics. The teahouse, on Route 1A in the center of Wenham, is closed on Sundays; (978) 468–1398.

Right across the street is the **Wenham Museum,** at 132 Main Street (978–468–2377), offering a fantastic collection of dolls—unique, unusual, and antique ones. Besides nineteenth-century German bisque-head dolls and Kewpie dolls, you'll find an Eskimo doll carved of walrus tusk and only 1.75 inches tall, a 1797 "penny" wooden doll, and an Egyptian doll that dates to 1200 B.C. There are dolls from around the world, including Swedish, Russian, and Portugese, as well as Hopi kachina dolls. Some quirky ones are dolls of the Dionne quintuplets and dolls representing the television Addams Family. Also part of the museum is the historic **Claflin–Richards House,** dating to 1660 and characteristic of an English house of that period. Last but not least, Wenham's nineteenth-century ice industry is chronicled. So famed for purity and long-lastingness was Wenham ice that it was shipped to India, the West Indies, and England; Queen Victoria served it at Buckingham Palace. The Wenham Museum is open from 10:00 A.M. to 4:00 P.M. weekdays and from 1:00 to 4:00 P.M. Saturday and Sunday. Admission is $4.00 for adults and $2.00 for children.

The **Ipswich River Wildlife Sanctuary** is Massachusetts Audubon's largest. The property is remote and wild: two thousand acres of meadow, swamp, ponds, drumlins, kettles, and eskers surrounding the Ipswich River. Highlights are an unusual rockery, waterfowl ponds, and an observation tower overlooking swamp and meadowland. One of the buildings has a long and narrow bird-viewing window high up from which you can see many birds at a profusion of feeders in the backyard. Programs include guided river float trips, maple sugaring, canoe rentals, cabin rental and camping on Perkins Island, and many nature programs for children. The sanctuary is located on Perkins Row in Topsfield, just off Route 97 east from Route 1. It's closed Mondays. There's a trail fee of $3.00 for adults and $2.00 for children. Call (978) 887–9264.

One of the most splendid estates in all of Massachusetts is on Argilla Road in Ipswich. This fifty-nine-room seaside mansion was built by Chicago industrialist Richard T. Crane, Jr., whose father made a fortune in plumbing valves and fittings. Crane succeeded his father as president in 1914 and also made the company famous for elegant bathroom fixtures in the 1920s, partly by advertising them in *National Geographic.* Built in 1927, **Castle Hill** was a summer home for Crane and his wife. Touring the mansion is like touring one of the great castles of Europe. A long drive winds up and up through the landscaped grounds, past the stone walls and balusters of a sunken Italian garden and a rose garden. The mansion's long, symmetrical lines reflect great seventeenth-century

English houses of the Stuart period. Inside, you find yourself staring up at 16-foot ceilings and elaborately carved ceiling moldings, marveling at serpentine marble fireplaces and crystal and brass chandeliers, and noticing such exquisite details as delft tiling, parquet floors, and sterling-silver bathroom fixtures. Bay windows in many rooms offer sweeping views of the barrier beach and the ocean down below and of the green lawns of the grounds. A particularly striking view is of the Grand Allée, which slopes down a wide path straight to the sea. Lined with spruce trees and stone garden statuary, the allée was the site of a casino used for summer parties and of a saltwater swimming pool, now filled in. One terraced lawn was formerly a bowling lawn; another held a classically designed boxwood maze.

Inside, the entrance rotunda offers an unusual example of circular architecture. Its round surfaces are covered with canvas painted with murals of Roman emperors, Corinthian columns, and the Crane children, Florence and Cornelius. You can see most of the house on the tour, from the 63-foot gallery to the dining room, kitchens, and guest and family bedrooms and bathrooms. The library was taken entirely from an English estate in Hertfordshire. Warm and rich wood paneling culminates in ornately carved fruits and flowers framing a doorway and several paintings, the work of famed seventeenth-century English craftsman Grinling Gibbons. Surrounding the bathtub in daughter Florence's bathroom is a striking mosaic of reverse-painted glass tiles in a black clipper-ship motif framed in silver. Mrs. Crane's bathroom was done entirely in green-and-white serpentine marble and *faux marbre*. The green marble was designed to make the bathwater look like seawater.

The house is open for public tours from 1:00 to 4:00 P.M. on Tuesdays from May through October. Tickets cost $5.00 for adults and $3.00 for children. Appointments can also be made for groups. Call (508) 356–4351 for information. Castle Hill also hosts summer concerts and other special programs on its beautiful grounds, events that sometimes include preliminary house tours. Picnicking on the Grand Allée before a summer concert is a popular activity. Visitors are welcome to stroll through the lovely grounds anytime there is not a private function.

Just below Castle Hill, at the foot of Argilla Road, is one of the North Shore's most magnificent beaches: *Crane Beach,* once part of the Crane estate. A white sandy beach stretches more than 4 miles, reaching down from a scenic sweep of dunes and marsh grasses and a view of the Ipswich River. There are bathhouses and a snack bar. Parking fees are $14 on weekends and $8.00 during the week. For information, call (508) 356–4354.

On your way back from the beach, be sure to stop at **Goodale Orchards** on the left, at 123 Argilla Road (978–356–5366). This is a great old-fashioned barn of a place, famous for its homemade cider doughnuts. Come fall, the doughnuts are washed down with cider, stocked in three antique white refrigerators. The barn rambles back forever, and its rafters are piled high with old wooden bushel baskets. It smells perennially of good things: homemade fruit pies, newly harvested berries, jams and jellies, stick candy, vegetables, and cut flowers. Children love the place for the hayrides and farm animals–the pig, goats, geese, ducks, chickens, and horses.

# Essex and Cape Ann

At the entrance to Cape Ann, the town of Essex is well known as an antiques capital. What is typically overlooked here is the **Essex Shipbuilding Museum,** though it is in the thick of the antiques shops, right on Main Street (Route 133). Into this small but fascinating museum are crammed a great number of artifacts and photos illustrating Essex's three-hundred-year shipbuilding history, during which more than four thousand ships were built. Essex became famous for its Chebacco Dogbody boat, a two-masted fishing boat designed to be built quickly to help replace New England's fishing fleet after it was destroyed by the British. There are models of schooners with beautiful linen sails, as well as many half-models of Essex-built fishing schooners from the Smithsonian collection in Washington, D.C. Half-models were used in boat design, their lines judged for speed and seaworthiness. Near a workbench with antique tools is an 1890s trunnel lathe, used to make trunnels (treenails, or wooden pegs). The appealing smells of oakum (tarred hemp) and pine pitch permeate the caulking exhibit. Everything for Essex ships was made in town: windlasses, blocks, pumps, sparks, cordage, anchors, sails, and riggings. Many Essex ships were built at the A. D. Story Shipyard, a five-minute walk from the museum. Museum hours are 10:00 A.M. to 5:00 P.M. Monday through Saturday. Tickets cost $4.00 for adults, $3.00 for seniors, and $2.50 for children, with a $10 maximum per family. Call (978) 768–7541.

Leaving from Essex, **Essex River Cruises** (800–748–3706) pass by all the harbor islands and along the back of the Plum Island wildlife reserve. **Hog Island** is where the movie *The Crucible* was filmed, and you can see one building from the set as you sail past. To see this island closer and learn the story of "Hollywood Meets the Trustees of Reservations" (the island's owner), take the boat-and-hay-wagon tour offered by the Trustees; *Hog Island Tours,* Trustees of Reservations; (508) 365–4351. Or rent a kayak from *ERBA Sea Kayaking* at the Essex Ship-building Museum and paddle there yourself; (800) KAYAK–04. You can explore the island on foot, but you must stay in the tracks so as not to disturb the wildlife. From its top, you can see all the way to the Maine coast on a clear day.

*Hammond Castle Museum* looks just like a real castle. Its stone battle-ments and towers, built right on the rocky shores of the Atlantic Ocean, house one of the most unusual private homes in America. The castle is a fitting monument to the man who built it, Dr. John Hays Hammond, Jr., America's second-greatest inventor, next to Thomas Edison. When he died in 1965, Hammond held 465 patents resulting from more than 800 inventions. He collected monuments all through Europe, such items as Roman tombstones, Renaissance furniture, and a medieval fireplace. To house it all, he built his castle in the 1920s.

Tours begin in the thirteenth-century-style Great Hall, whose 60-foot ceiling complements an 8,200-pipe organ, the largest organ in the world installed in a private home. You can hear a recording of the organ music. The walls surrounding the courtyard and pool are made of half-timbered shop facades from a fourteenth-century French village: a bakeshop, wine merchant, and butcher, complete with symbols for the illiterate. A church front holds Hammond's collection of Roman tomb-stones set into the wall. There's also a Renaissance dining room, along with Gothic and early American bedrooms. The lobby contains a list of Hammond's patents and exhibits some of his patent models. An "inven-tor's inventor," Hammond pioneered in radio, television, radar, and remote-control radio. He and his wife entertained Serge Koussevitzky, Helen Hayes, George Gershwin, Cole Porter, John D. Rockefeller, and Noël Coward, as well as Ethel and Lionel Barrymore, who staged read-ings of Shakespeare in the Great Hall. The museum is open from 9:00 A.M. to 6:00 P.M. daily from mid-June to mid-September, and then from 10:00 A.M. to 4:00 P.M. Thursday through Sunday. It is wise to call first on Saturdays because this is a popular spot for weddings. Hammond Cas-tle is located at 80 Hesperus Avenue, Gloucester; call (978) 283–7673 or (800) 649–1930 (in Massachusetts). Tickets cost $6.00 for adults and $4.00 for children. A wide array of programs are held year-round.

The marine heart and soul of Gloucester shows at the *Cape Ann His-torical Association,* starting with the nation's largest collection of paintings and drawings by Fitz Hugh Lane. A Gloucester native, Lane was the first American marine painter to win stature. His scenes of Gloucester Harbor and other shores in New England are full of light and sky. Decorative-arts exhibits include Queen Anne and Hepplewhite furniture. Upstairs are fisheries exhibits. Long oars, painted in bright colors and carried in the annual St. Peter's Fiesta, hang on the wall. A flake yard shows how fish was salted and dried years ago. Connected to the museum and part of the tour is an 1804 Federal-style sea captain's house, the **Captain Elias Davis House.** The museum is located at 27 Pleasant Street; call (978) 283–0455. Hours are 9:00 A.M. to 5:00 P.M. Tuesday through Saturday. Admission is $4.00 for adults, $3.50 seniors, and $2.50 students.

In Gloucester's fishing heyday, thousands of schooners fished the outer banks for cod and haddock. The nation's last active dory-fishing schooner was the **Adventure,** a two-masted knockabout built of sturdy oak and pine in 1926. On board this 121-foot ship, it's easy to picture yourself alongside Spencer Tracy in a scene from *Captains Courageous.* Topside, you can learn how the gaff-rigged sails are set and handle some lines. Take your turn at the large spoked wheel and feel the hollows in the deck worn by the feet of helmsmen over twenty-seven years. Down below, you'll see the galley, with its old-fashioned black iron stove and pump, the fo'c'sle, and the former fish holds, where the catch was kept on ice. The ship is open to the public on Saturday and at other times, so it is best to call ahead (978) 281–8079. Admission is $4.00 per person or $15 per family. On Sundays, the *Adventure* offers breakfast and afternoon chowder in the galley ($4.00 per person). The schooner is berthed on the Harbor Loop off Main Street in Gloucester, next to a white building with a sign that says GLOUCESTER MARINE RAILWAYS CORP.

*The Rudder,* at 73 Rocky Neck Avenue (978–283 7967), is a real institution, Gloucester's oldest restaurant. It's situated out on Rocky Neck, America's oldest art colony, and dinner or drinks here is a nice way to cap a day spent gallery hopping. Housed in a 175-year-old former fish-packing shed right on the water, the dining room is all dark wood and brass lanterns. An oceanfront porch opens up for summertime dining. The chief attraction is not so much the food, although the variety of seafood is well-prepared, as the "spontaneous entertainment" provided by its theatrically minded family owners. They are likely to flit about the dining room or accompany themselves in an impromptu number on the piano every night. A "celebrity wall" holds photos of famous guests: Liv Ullmann, Anthony Newley, Judy Garland. The ceiling is plastered with menus from restaurants around the world, collected by the owners' many globe-trotting friends.

Near the visitors center at the harbor waits *Moby Duck,* a Vietnam veteran landing craft now fitted for tours. Unlike most of these amphibious craft, this one is solid-hulled, so it can go into the ocean. It lumbers down the main street, onto the beach and into the sea, taking you through the little drawbridge that marks the northern entrance to the famous Inland Waterway. The trip up the Anisquam River to Lobster Cove, which costs $12 for adults, $10 for seniors and $8 for children, is uneventful but a cool and scenic trip for a summer afternoon. Reserve with Moby Duck Amphibious Tours; (508) 281–DUCK.

New England's cheapest harbor tours, on the *Annie* or the *Squam,* leave from the same wharf: For $1.00 you can ride to Rocky Neck, where artists' studios fill the tiny houses and waterfront buildings. It's a nice place for ambling. Or you can stay on the boat and ride on to Ten Pound Island, where there's a beach. Or you can go right back to Gloucester Harbor.

Out on Gloucester's exclusive Eastern Point is one of the most intriguing houses you'll ever see: ***Beauport.*** This rambling shingled-and-turreted house was built in 1907 by the daring interior designer Henry Davis Sleeper, who numbered among his clients Henry Francis du Pont, Joan Crawford, and Fredric March. Sleeper collected pieces of decorative art and then ran out of room to display them in his three-room house. He began adding on, and kept adding on, for more than twenty-six years, until his death in 1934. The final fantastic product has twenty-two roof levels and more than forty rooms. Without a guide, you could get lost wandering these cramped and dark little rooms that honeycomb throughout the house, occasionally opening on only a peek of a view of Gloucester Harbor. Sleeper built secret staircases, fake windows, and doors to nowhere. He indulged his every fancy. He built shrines to the American colonial past, honoring George Washington and Benjamin Franklin. The China Trade Room started as a medieval hall until Sleeper acquired some hand-painted eighteenth-century Chinese wallpaper. The wallpaper's large murals show village scenes in China. The Chinese theme is completed with a Chinese pagoda–shaped ceiling and a Buddha in the fireplace. The Octagon Room has eight sides and contains a collection of eight-sided antiques. A guest room called the Strawberry Hill Room is done with a strawberry theme, vaulted ceiling, and red-and-black lacquered wallpaper of elephants and camels. Beauport is at 75 Eastern Point Boulevard. (This is a private road but open to visitors to Beauport.) Admission for adults is $5.00; for children, $2.50. The house is open from 10:00 A.M. to 4:00 P.M. weekdays from May 15 through mid-September; thereafter, until October 15, it's also open on weekends. Call (978) 283–0800 for information.

When you arrive in Rockport, you'll find dozens of restaurants—but you can't get any more genuine than the ***Lobster Pool.*** You place your own order, serve yourself, and bus your own picnic table. Set right on the ocean's edge, the restaurant has many tables outside, for smashing views of lobster boats putting in, the rocky coast, and the pounding surf. Specialties are fresh, excellent lobster in the rough and fried and broiled seafoods, but there are also hamburgers and french fries. Save room for homemade desserts: strawberry shortcake, peach cobbler, and blueberry and apple pie. Open from 11:30 A.M. to 8:30 P.M., the Lobster Pool is on Route 127, just south of downtown Rockport; call (978) 546–7808.

We all have our curiosities. Elis Stenman of Rockport wanted to see how far you could push newspapers without destroying the print. Accordingly, he built a house out of them, starting in 1922, and the structure is still standing today—the **Paper House.** The two-room house has walls made of 215 thicknesses of newsprint and contains furniture made of rolled-up newspapers. You can still read the print under the shellac. A desk gives an account of Charles Lindbergh's historic flight. A grandfather clock made in 1932 contains papers from the capital cities of forty-eight states. The mantel is made of Sunday rotogravure sections. Stenman and his wife used the house and its furniture for four summers. The house is located at 52 Pigeon Hill Street. Take Route 127 north to Curtis Street; then follow signs to the Paper House. It's open daily from 10:00 A.M. to 5:00 P.M. July through October and can be seen by appointment in spring; call (978) 546–2629. Admission is $1.00 for adults and 50 cents for children.

At the northernmost tip of Cape Ann is an old quarry site that is now **Halibut Point State Park,** a small but special park. A film at the visitor center tells the story of how granite was king here for almost a hundred years. Paving blocks went to Boston, Philadelphia, New York, and Havana. Halibut Point granite blocks were used in Boston's Custom House tower, the Brooklyn Bridge, and the Holland Tunnel. A self-guided trail passes by the vestiges of quarrying and emerges on a stunning vantage point overlooking a quarry pool high up over the Atlantic Ocean. This is also a great place for bird-watching; hundreds of species have been sighted. Saturday morning guided tours are offered from 9:30 to 11:30 A.M. from late May to Columbus Day (a $2.00 parking fee is charged during these months). The visitor center is usually open from noon to 4:00 P.M., but this is indefinite because of staff cuts. Call (978) 546–2997.

If you'd like to stay at a place that's handy to Halibut Point, try the **Old Farm Inn,** right next door. A rambling old red farmhouse set way back behind a stone wall, the Old Farm Inn is a real farmhouse that dates to about 1799 and once housed granite workers from the Halibut Point quarry. At a distance from Rockport Center, it's a restful alternative to the crowds and noise of downtown Rockport. The country decor includes original gun-stock beams, handmade quilts, and braided rugs. Breakfast is served in a glassed-in sunroom overlooking the land-scaped grounds. For reservations, write the inn at 291 Granite Street, Rockport 01966, or call (978) 546–3237 (doubles $88–$125).

Another welcoming Cape Ann home port is the *Yankee Clipper Inn,* where we choose a second-floor room overlooking the village of Rockport, which can be seen across an expanse of waves breaking onto the granite ledges that line the shore. Whether or not you're lucky enough to get a room at the Clipper, you can enjoy its sophisticated dinner menu and the sea view from the dining room. The Yankee Clipper Inn has rooms beginning around $100 in high season, including a splendid breakfast. It is at 96 Granite Street, Rockport 01966; (978) 546–3407 or (800) 545–3699.

Within a five-minute walk of shops and harbor is the *Peg Leg Inn,* on Beach Street, whose public rooms are decorated with a fine collection of paintings by Tom Nicholas, a well-known artist who now lives in Rock-port. Guest rooms are well-decorated, and the chef has a winning way with seafood. A second building across the street has guestrooms over-looking the water; (800) 346–2352.

If you keep following Route 127 around the back side of Cape Ann, it goes to *Annisquam,* a remote village that was a fishing and boatbuild-ing center for more than two and a half centuries. Annisquam is tiny, with just a few narrow streets hemming the ocean, winding uphill and down. The people who live here have stately ocean views from their attractive Victorian shingled and wooden saltbox houses. The *Annisquam Yacht Club* is unusual, built out on the water on stilts. And the *old wooden footbridge* crossing Lobster Cove is a nice place to stroll and admire the cove.

# *Historic Boatbuilding Capitals*

P lum Island, which juts south more than 6 miles into the Atlantic, is the site of one of the best birding spots on the East Coast, the *Parker River National Wildlife Refuge,* one of the last undeveloped barrier beaches. More than three hundred species have been sighted here. The spectacular scenery encompasses five thousand acres of wide sandy beach, dunes, bogs, freshwater pools, and tidal marshes reaching into river and ocean. Boardwalks lead to the beach, and there are several

**Annisquam Footbridge**

nature trails, observation towers, and camera blinds. Because this is a very popular place, the best time to come is off-season. Another good reason to come off-season is that the beach is closed to people from April until July or August, to allow the endangered piping plover to nest and fledge its young undisturbed. The rest of the refuge is open for birding, biking, hiking, and nonbeach recreation. You'll find something happening and something to see every month. In November and December, you can watch migrating Canada and snow geese; January brings snowy owls; and you can pick wild beach plums and cranberries in September and October (within limits). Call (508) 465–5753 for information. Admission is $5.00 per car and $2.00 per pedestrian or bicyclist. Park headquarters is at the northern end of the island and is open from 8:00 A.M. to 4:30 P.M. weekdays. To get there, follow signs from Route 1A.

The city of Newburyport is one of the most attractive on the coast. Along High Street (Route 1A) stand dozens of sea captains' houses, ranging from Greek Revival and Federal to Georgian and Victorian, some with cupolas and widow's walks. Downtown, nineteenth-century brick commercial buildings in Market Square have been made into a handsome shopping and dining complex, gracefully accented with cobblestone sidewalks; black iron, gas-style streetlamps; and lots of trees and potted geraniums.

A hop, skip, and a jump away, at 25 Water Street, is the *Custom House Maritime Museum,* whose collections are beautifully set off in the classic 1835 Greek Revival granite structure. Its small rooms still have their original vaulted ceilings, brick floors, marble windowsills, and tall, wide windows. A cantilevered granite stairway leads to the second floor. Newburyport is the birthplace of the U.S. Coast Guard, and the first revenue cutters were built here by Newburyport shipwrights. The office of the collector of customs holds chests of Ceylon tea, barrels of rum, and lacquered boxes. There are antiques and oil portraits memorializing shipping families, as well as many other maritime memorabilia. The museum is open from 10:00 A.M. to 4:00 P.M. Monday, Tuesday, Thursday,

Friday, and Saturday and from 10:00 A.M. to 1:00 P.M. Wednesday and 1:00 to 4:00 P.M. on Sunday. Tickets cost $3.00 for adults, $2.00 for children and seniors, and $6.00 for families. Call (978) 462–8681.

The *Cushing House Museum* is the home of the Newburyport Historical Society, a National Historic Landmark, at 98 High Street. This fine Federal home belonged to the Cushing family, whose ships sailed under three generations of owners during Newburyport's golden era of shipping. Along with the furnished rooms, the house displays several outstanding collections, including fans and toys. The period gardens beside the house are in the process of restoration. The museum is open Tuesday through Friday 10:00 A.M. to 4:00 P.M. and Saturday 11:00 A.M. to 2:00 P.M., May through October. Admission is $4.00; (978) 462–2681.

The downtown streets seem lined by restaurants. Next door to each other on State Street are *Nasturtiums* and *Scandia Restaurant*. The former serves a varied selection of creative dinner entrees—pan-seared breast of duck with black raspberries; pesto-parmesan chicken; shell pasta stuffed with herbs, vegetables, and cheese—ranging from $10 to $18. It is also open for lunch Thursday through Sunday; (978) 463–4040. Entrees at Scandia include salmon served with lobster and artichokes and brie, and run from $14 to $18. Breakfast is served from 8:00 to 11:00 A.M. Friday through Sunday, featuring such tony dishes as orange-brandy French toast; (978) 462–6271. *Kathy Ann's Bakery,* at 350 Merrimack Street, is where locals head for breakfast; (978) 462–7415.

For a retro moment, stop at *Fowles,* just down the street, to sit at its old-fashioned marble soda fountain or in one of the original booths. Breakfast is served from 6:00 A.M. (6:30 on Sunday). Those who really wanted to run away to sea should continue downhill to browse in *Boat House Antiques and Books,* which sells everything from model boats and brass lanterns to scrimshaw and painted screens from the China Trade days.

On Inn Street, which is a pedestrian way running parallel to State, *Le Bistro* serves a cafe menu of hefty, creative sandwiches and salads, which in good weather you can enjoy at sidewalk tables overlooking a small park with a playground. It is open most days from 8:00 A.M. to 4:00 P.M., Sundays noon to 5:00 P.M.; (978) 465–7400.

Newburyport goes all out for the holidays, beginning with Santa's arrival by Coast Guard boat and the lighting of the giant *Christmas tree in Market Square.* For the whole month of December, the downtown and waterfront area is alive with music, street performers, bells, gleaming candles, and bright decorations. Shopkeepers welcome visitors with warming drinks and goodies, historic homes are open for tours, sailors in costume sing rollicking sea chanteys on street corners. Munch on hot roasted chestnuts, ride in a carriage, shop at craft shows and bazaars, listen to choral concerts and Christmas carols, or bring the kids to meet Santa's elves. The final event is First Night on December 31. For a complete schedule, call (978) 462–6680 or visit Newburyport's Web site at www.newburyport.chamber.net.

Hidden away from downtown Newburyport is *Maudslay State Park,* acquired in 1985. Once the private estate of a wealthy family, the property retains its beautifully landscaped grounds, carriage roads, and trails. Enormous rhododendrons rise over your head along the paths, as do centuries-old stands of laurel, one of New England's largest natural stands. Although the mansions are gone, there are still an allée of red oak, the stone foundations of greenhouses, and the foundations of a formal Italian garden and a rose garden. A walk through the woods brings you to a large clearing on a rise, offering a stunning view of the Merrimac River. Lots of special programs and arts performances take place in the park, including autumn hayrides and children's outdoor theater. In winter, cross-country skiing here is pleasant. The park is on Curzon's Mill Road. From Route 113 east, take a left onto Noble Street and follow the signs. Call (978) 465–7223.

High Street (Route 1–A) continues south to the historic town of Newbury, where the first settlers landed in 1635. They are buried in the *old cemetery,* about a quarter of a mile north of the Lower Green. A small sign on the roadside marks the spot, but when you step through the lilac hedge, you are miles from busy Route 1–A. Small stones without inscriptions mark early graves, but you will find dates from the 1600s and winged cherub stones from the time of the Revolution. You're also likely to see rabbits, as well as a herd of deer browsing in the field beyond.

Behind the cemetery, off Newman Road, is *Old Town Hill Reservation,* which includes a glacial drumlin rising 170 feet above the coastal marshes that was used as a mariner's landmark. Climb the trail, and from the top you can see Plum Island and Newburyport. You can also be eaten alive by voracious mosquitoes, so wear a good repellent. The first settlers spent the winter of their arrival in shelters they dug into the sides of this hill, with the open sides enclosed by saplings covered in thatch to protect them from the wind. Trails through the reservation cross Newman Road at several points, where you can access the marsh, meadows, and Little River, a tidal estuary. This and the little waterways through the marshes offer good canoeing. On the opposite side of Route 1–A at the Lower Green, follow signs to the landing place of the first settlers, where there is a stone marker and a good boat put-in on the Little River.

Sleepy little Amesbury is so far off the beaten path that few people come here. But they're missing *Lowell's Boat Shop,* which dates to 1793 and is still making handmade wooden boats on the original site. Although few others know it is here, wooden-boat fanatics from around the world seek it out. Now a National Historic Landmark, the shop was founded by the Lowell family, who owned and ran it for seven generations, until 1976. In 1793, Simeon Lowell found boats unseaworthy for the three-knot current at the mouth of the Merrimac River. He designed himself a boat that would not capsize and that would be rowable in the heavy surf: a double-ended lapstrake skiff with a raked transom. The world-famous design was called the Amesbury skiff, or dory. Thousands were made for Grand Banks schooners, the U.S. Life Saving Service (forerunner of the Coast Guard), the U.S. Army and Navy in World War II, and early nineteenth-century pleasure boaters.

The shop still looks as it did more than two hundred years ago, sitting right on the banks of the Merrimac River. Only a woodstove heats the wooden building, which smells of sawdust and spar varnish. Downstairs in the paint shop, paint drippings of centuries are so thick—some 7 inches deep—that the floor looks paved. Amesbury skiffs are still handmade exactly the way they were in 1793, of hand-cut white oak, mahogany, and pine. It takes almost two months to build a boat, and orders come from as far as California, Florida, and Africa. The shop holds classes in antique boatbuilding, woodworking, tool care, and making Windsor chairs. You can visit the shop during business hours—from 7:30 A.M. to 5:00 P.M. weekdays—if you call ahead, and by appointment on weekends. Lowell's Boat Shop is at 459 Main Street; call (978) 388–0162.

John Greenleaf Whittier lived in Amesbury for fifty-six years, until his death in 1892. The *Whittier Home* is entirely furnished with this Quaker poet and abolitionist's belongings and books. A white frame house with a picket fence, it has small, cozy rooms done in simple country style. Whittier, who never married, lived here with the female triumvirate of his mother, sister, and aunt. Memorabilia include the desk where he wrote his famous poem *Snow-Bound* and his newspaper-lined traveling case. The Garden Room, where Whittier did most of his writing, has his woodstove and divan in place, and the room's walls are full of pictures of his favorite writers. His boots stand on the floor, and his shawl and hat are draped on the rocker. The home, at 86 Friend Street, is open from 10:00 A.M. until the last tour at 3:15 P.M. Tuesday through Saturday, May 1 to October 31. Fees are $3.50 for adults and $1.00 for children. Call (978) 388–1337.

## MORE PLACES TO STAY ON THE NORTH SHORE

***Addison Choate Inn,***
49 Broadway,
Rockport 01966;
(978) 546–7543 or
(800) 245–7543.
Beautifully furnished
rooms in a historic bed-
and-breakfast, close to
downtown and the harbor.
Rooms from $85 off-sea-
son, $100 in summer.

***Pleasant Street Inn,***
17 Pleasant Street,
Rockport 01966;
(978) 546–2152 or
(800) 541–3915.
A hilltop Victorian close to
the center of town.

***Rocky Shore Inn
and Cottages,***
68 Marmion Way,
Rockport 01966;
(978) 546–3471 or
(800) 648–7733.
A former estate on the
shore, with gardens and a
spring-fed swimming pool.

***The Clark Currier Inn,***
45 Green Street,
Newburyport 01950;
(978) 465–8363.
The elegant Federal home
of a Newburyport ship-
builder, with antique features and furnishings,
Continental breakfast,
afternoon tea, and central
location, from $75 to $155.

## MORE PLACES TO EAT ON THE NORTH SHORE

***Stuzzi Tuscan Trattoria,***
114 Merrimack Street,
Newburyport;
(978) 465–3131.
Open for dinner only,
Tuesday through Sunday,
serving creative Italian
dishes.

***The Bayou,***
50 State Street,
Newburyport;
(978) 499–0428.
Creole and other flavors of
the Deep South, updated
for New England palates.

***David's,***
11 Brown Square,
Newburyport;
(978) 462–8077.
Eclectic "New American"
dishes, with childcare
provided while you dine.
Why didn't somebody
come up with this idea
before?

***Stripers Grille,*** at 175
Bridge Road in Salisbury, is
known for its low prices
and large quantities.

## WORTH SEEING ON THE NORTH SHORE

***Whale watching*** off Cape
Ann with Cape Ann Whale
Watch, (800) 877–5110, or
Captain Bill Whale Watch;
(800) 33–WHALE.

***Fishing, whale, or harbor
tours and sunset cruises***
leave from docks near
Newburyport's Waterfront
Park; whale watch
(978) 465–7165 or
(800) 848–1111, fishing
(978) 465–9885, harbor
tours and cruises (888)
975–1842.

## TO LEARN MORE ABOUT THE NORTH SHORE

Cape Ann Visitor's Center,
Gloucester;
(800) 649 6839

Newburyport Chamber of
Commerce,
29 State Street,
Newburyport 01950;
(978) 462–6680,
Web site: www.newbury-
port.chamber.net.

For complete travel information, contact the North
of Boston Convention and
Visitors Bureau, 12
Peabody Square, Peabody
01960; (800) 742–5306 or
(978) 977–7760.

# South Shore

Y ou might call Boston's "other" shore—the South Shore—a black hole. People tend to just drive through it on their way to Cape Cod. But that's a mistake. Snubbed as the least preferred of the three bedroom regions of greater Boston, the South Shore is a truly hidden area—except Plymouth, of course. Colonial shipbuilding and fishing villages stretch all along the coast from Hingham to Plymouth. Most still have the traditional look of a New England village, with the pretty saltbox and shingled houses they always had. Small-town life is remarkably well preserved in the distinctive downtowns of Cohasset, Duxbury, Scituate, and Hingham.

The beaches and coastline are so appealing that much of the South Shore became a resort area in the nineteenth century. Vacationers came by steamer to grand hotels in Hull. Wealthy Boston Irish politicos, including Mayor James Michael Curley, took to summering in Scituate, yielding its nickname of "the Irish Riviera." The inland countryside of the South Shore offers scenic vistas of pine forest, farmland, and the banks of the North River. Most of Massachusetts's cranberry crop grows on the South Shore, spreading its low-lying russet vines along the landscape for miles in Carver, Middleborough, and Plymouth.

## *Along Boston Harbor*

T hough tourists usually bypass Quincy, it's the only American city that was home to two U.S. presidents: John Adams and John Quincy Adams. You can see the family home of four generations of Adamses at the ***Adams National Historic Site.*** It's hard to picture this stately gray house surrounded by farmland, gardens, and orchards, as it was when John and his wife, Abigail, moved in, in 1788. While John pursued his duties in Washington, Abigail busied herself tending the farm and adding a new wing to the house. Family possessions give a deep sense of how loved and used the house was as a family seat. A good-luck horseshoe hangs over the door where Abigail placed it. The wing chair that John Adams died in is still there. Waterford crystal bowls in a china

# South Shore

*Massachusetts Bay*

*Quincy Bay*

1

93

**Quincy**

1

93

ALONG
BOSTON
HARBOR

3

**Weymouth**

3A

228

3

**Scituate**

123

COLONIAL
TOWNS

**Rockland**

139

123

27

3

**Brockton**

14

3A

28

18

27

24

106

58

**Plymouth**

3A

**Bridgewater**

3

18

105

*Plymouth Bay*

**Middleboro**

44

PILGRIM AND
CRANBERRY
COUNTRY

495

25

195

6

N

0                    10 mi

0                    10 km

**AUTHORS' FAVORITES ON THE SOUTH SHORE**

*U.S. Naval and Shipbuilding Museum*

*Cranberry harvest*

*Pilgrim Hall Museum*

closet are cracked because John Adams sprouted seeds in them. The lovely landscaped grounds hold formal gardens, lilacs with waist-thick trunks, and climbing wisteria. The site, at 135 Adams Street, is open daily from 9:00 A.M. to 5:00 P.M. April 19 to November 10. Call (617) 773–1177. Your $2.00 ticket also admits you to the nearby **Adams Birthplaces** on Franklin Street, where John Adams and John Quincy Adams were born.

The city of Quincy was one of the country's preeminent builders of navy ships for more than sixty years. The Fore River Shipyard opened at the turn of the century and operated until 1986. It lay dormant for nine years, but in 1995 the city opened the *U.S. Naval and Shipbuilding Museum* in the former yard, just south of downtown Quincy. The museum's center-piece is a 700-foot heavy cruiser that served as the Sixth Fleet's flagship in the Mediterranean, the USS *Salem*. Visitors can tour the machine shops, hospital, and crew's quarters, as well as the bridge and the command cen-ter. The museum grounds house the military archives for Massachusetts from the Revolutionary War up to the present day. Open from 10:00 A.M. to 4:00 P.M. daily, the museum charges $6.00 for adults and $4.00 for seniors and children. Call (617) 479–7900 for more information. The museum is off Wharf Avenue; to get there, from Route 3A south, bear right at the rotary just before the Fore River Bridge.

Just barely over the line from Quincy into North Braintree on Route 53, you'll have to look hard to spot the discreet sign for *Spazio* in a tiny strip of shops at 200 Quincy Avenue. You'd never look for a restaurant of this caliber in such an unlikely setting, but it's here, and enough people have found it to make reservations advisable. Begin with grilled quail stuffed with sausage and fresh thyme, served on a bed of caramelized vegetables and drizzled with a blend of port and plums. The last time we ate here, the daily special was a filet of salmon encrusted in potatoes and grilled, served over a ragout of fall vegetables, but each day brings new takes on the freshest locally caught seafood. Dessert might be a "simple" Mackin-tosh apple tart or an espresso cheesecake in chocolate graham crust topped with mocha. Inspiring chef/owner Michael Richardi are the pan-Mediterranean influences of Greek, Spanish, and North African foods on the cuisine of southern Italy, where he returns twice a year to "cook with friends." The restaurant is open daily from 5:00 to 10:00 P.M. Entrees are reasonably priced at $13 to $19. If you want to see a current menu, visit Michael's Web site at www.spazio's.com; (781) 849–1577.

Route 3A takes you the whole length of coastal South Shore. The first stop is Hingham, a colonial town whose **Main Street** (Route 228) Eleanor Roosevelt called "the most beautiful Main Street in America." This wide, tree-lined boulevard is an oasis of restored homes spanning three centuries. Downtown Hingham has a wealth of historic sights. Unique among them is the **Old Ship Church,** at 90 Main Street (617–749–1679), America's oldest continuously operating church, since 1681. It's one of the few Tudor-style structures left in New England. Ship's carpenters made its lofty ceiling like an upside-down ship's keel.

Just beyond Hingham Square, at 21 Lincoln Street, you'll find the **Old Ordinary,** once a seventeenth-century hostelry and now a museum of Hingham history. As a tavern, the Ordinary served an "ordinary meal of the day" to travelers. The taproom looks just as it did, with bar and wooden grille, wooden kegs, and copper tankards. An eighteenth-century parlor, kitchen, dining room, toolroom, and small library are furnished with period antiques. Upstairs, bedrooms display memorabilia of local families and rare silk mourning samplers. The museum is open from 1:30 to 4:30 P.M. mid-June to Labor Day. Admission is $3.00 for adults and $1.00 for children. For information, call the Hingham Historical Society at (617) 749–0013.

Across the street from the Old Ordinary is a small, green park with a **statue of Abraham Lincoln,** whose ancestor Samuel Lincoln hailed from Hingham. In the summer, ferries run from Hingham (board at the same dock where the Boston shuttle ferry leaves) to Georges Island, operated by Bay State Cruises; (617) 723–7800.

At lunchtime, make tracks for **The British Relief,** at 152 North Street in Hingham Square (617–749–7713). This is one of those homey eateries where everyone feels welcome. Housed in a redbrick storefront, the restaurant has comfortable wooden booths and tables and a massive carved oak table that seats ten. Outstanding breakfasts and lunches—including homemade muffins and coffee cakes, hearty homemade soups, salads, sandwiches, and desserts—are dished up cafeteria-style.

For a dinner you'll not soon forget, reserve a table at **Tosca,** just off the harbor at 14 North Street. Set in the warm brick and wood backdrop of a beautifully adapted granary, Tosca pays close attention to every detail, from the spacing and lighting of tables to the impeccable timing of dishes. In the fall you might be offered a first course of rabbit ragout over herbed gnocci, or tagliatelli with seared figs, Tuscan peppers, and duck braised with port; the flavors lie in layers, beginning with the perfume of figs and cinnamon so faint it takes a second bite to identify it.

# SOUTH SHORE

### ANNUAL EVENTS ON THE SOUTH SHORE

**Mid-August**

*Marshfield Fair,*
the oldest in Massachusetts.
(It's been held for more
than 130 years.);
(781) 834–6629.

**Late September**

*Chowda-Fest,*
Nantasket Beach, Hull, with
plenty of chowder to sample;
(781) 925–9980.

**Early October**

*Massachusetts Cranberry
Harvest Festival,*
Edaville Cranberry Bogs,
off Route 58 in South Carver,
has crafts, hayrides,
and country music;
(508) 295–5799.

**Late October**

*Halloween Tours,*
Plymouth, weave ghostly
stories into a tour of town,
with each participant
carrying a lantern;
(508) 747–4161
for reservations.

Pasta and risotto come in half-portions as a first course or an entree, and the risotto might be stirred with butternut squash and zucchini, creamy and moist, with pan-wilted pea vines; littleneck clams are served with fresh corn and a grilled lemon, beside potatoes mashed with tomatoes and spicy chorizo. These entrees are $18 to $25. It's hard to save room for dessert, but you will want to, especially if it's fresh figs with roquefort, wild honey, and glazed walnuts, or a granita of delicate white wine. In October we were served a whole roasted baby pumpkin filled with pumpkin crème broulet and a garnish of maple-flavored shortbread cookies in the shape of maple leaves. These frivolous inventions are the perfect note on which to end a meal. Chef Joe Simone enjoys food, and he's not happy unless you do too; (781) 740–0080.

Also in Hingham is one of the South Shore's nicest parks, **World's End.** Planned as a housing subdivision in the nineteenth century, World's End has wide allées designed by Frederick Law Olmsted. The paths sweep uphill to stunning views of the Boston skyline, especially at sunset. To get there, go straight through the rotary on Route 3A south onto Summer Street and turn left onto Martin's Lane. Call (978) 921–1944 or (781) 749–8956 for information. Admission is $4.00 for adults, and children are let in free. The park is open 9:00 A.M. to 8:00 P.M. on weekdays, 8:00 A.M. to 8:00 P.M. on weekends.

At the turn of the century, Hull was a stylish resort, complete with grand hotels and an amusement park with a roller coaster. Bathing-costumed vacationers sought summer relief on the miles of white sand and surf at Nantasket Beach, one of the largest beaches on the South Shore. In later decades, Hull deteriorated into a more honky-tonk atmosphere. But the town is once again metamorphosing into a sparkling place, spurred by its arts community.

One vestige of the amusement park that still charms is the vintage 1928 **Carousel under the Clock,** across the street from the beach in a wooden pavilion under an antique clock tower. A ride on the carousel is magic in summer. Infectious antique-pipe-organ music pumps away, the lights shine, and a breeze from the beach sweeps in through the open doors. Brightly painted horses and mermaid-bedecked chariots ferry you around in season. Call (781) 925–0472 for information.

Nantasket Avenue, Hull's main street, takes you out to the **Hull Lifesaving Museum,** an engaging place that re-creates the days of valiant surfmen and tragic shipwrecks. The bare wood walls of the station show the spartan surroundings the surfmen lived in a hundred years ago. They drilled every day, simulating capsizing accidents, practicing with the breeches buoy, and working on boat launchings and resuscitation techniques. You can tour the galley, an equipment room, and the bedroom of Joshua James, the station's first captain. Dedicating his life to rescues at sea after his mother and baby sister drowned at sea, James became the nation's most decorated lifesaver, rescuing more than 540 people from eighty-six wrecks. When this station opened in 1889, it was the first official lifesaving service in America. There are lots of memorabilia and photos to look at, as well as a breeches buoy and faking box. In the boathouse you can admire a hundred-year-old surfboat with 16-foot pulling oars. A ladder climbs up to the lookout tower. The museum, at 1117 Nantasket Avenue, is open Wednesday through Sunday from 10:00 A.M. to 5:00 P.M. in July and August and only on weekends and Monday holidays in the off-season. Admission is $2.00 for adults, $1.50 for seniors, and $1.00 for children over five. Call (781) 925–5433.

Up behind the Hull Lifesaving Museum, you can climb **Telegraph Hill,** the highest point on the South Shore, for a splendid view of Hull Harbor and the Atlantic Ocean. Though now it's covered with graffiti, the stone, Revolutionary War–era **Fort Revere** has the distinction of having been fired on by the British. Plans are still under way to clean up Fort Revere and make it into a waterfront park.

If you'd like to stay in a place where you can admire the views in Hull, choose the **Allerton House,** once a turn-of-the-century home, on Allerton Hill. From the top of this hill, you can see Boston Light, America's oldest lighthouse. The Victorian house has wonderful ocean views and a large

**Hull Lifesaving Museum**

wraparound porch for enjoying the breeze. Rooms are decorated with hand-painted furniture from the innkeeper's gift shop and watercolors by a local artist. The large living room features a massive fieldstone fireplace. Breakfast of fruit and French pastries is served either on the wide porch or in the dining room. It's just a two-minute walk down the hill from the inn to the beach. For reservations (doubles with private baths $85), write the inn at 15 Tierney Avenue, Hull 02045, or call (781) 925–4569.

An unusual restaurant find in this beach town is *Saporito's Florence Club Café,* at 11 Rockland Circle—a gourmet Italian restaurant where the food is so good that it lets the South Shore thumb its nose at Boston's North End. Well-disguised inside a beat-up, 1940 Italian club is a gardeny Florentine retreat done up in turquoise and peach. The mouthwatering food includes such intriguing appetizers as grilled *pizzettas*—perhaps topped with lamb, veal, sausage, red and yellow peppers, and feta—and swordfish Involtini with lemon, sesame, capers, and marinated white beans. Entrees of seafood, meats, and pastas in original sauces include black-olive pasta ragu with roasted peppers and red onions and baked goat cheese; and a veal chop with grappa, capers, anchovies, and cream. Saporito's is open for dinner only and is closed Mondays and Tuesdays; call (781) 925–3023.

# *Colonial Towns*

Newport has Ocean Drive. Cohasset has *Jerusalem Road.* This scenic drive winds between Route 228 and North Main Street along rocky coast and secluded beaches, past million-dollar houses perched perilously close to the sea. Offshore, the tall granite spire is *Minot's Light,* whose famous signal flashes (1–4–3), which has been traditionally interpreted as I–LOVE–YOU. To learn more about this historic light, whose predecessor was washed away in a terrible storm, go to the *Maritime Museum* maintained by the Cohasset Historical Society, right in the center of town. Its collections and photographs give a clear view of Cohasset in the glory days of sail and shipbuilding. This is one of three small museum buildings belonging to the society, each of which is worth a visit; (781) 383–0773.

Downtown Cohasset has a classic town green with a duck pond and white-steepled church. At the other end stands a tall granite church, Saint Stephen's. This church is home to the oldest running *carillon concert series* in North America, begun in 1924. Its fifty-seven-bell carillon, cast in England, is the largest in New England. Concerts by famous carillonneurs from all over the world are given Sundays at 6:00 P.M. from late June through August. Hearing a concert is a delightful way to spend a summer evening, perhaps also picnicking on the green lawn of Cohasset Common. Call (781) 383–1083 for a schedule.

A hop, skip, and a jump from Cohasset Common is a really nice take-out restaurant, **Strawberry Parfait,** at 2 Pleasant Street (781–383–9681). A green lawn with flower gardens holds a scattering of picnic tables where you can take your fried clams, burgers, lobster rolls, and ice cream. Around the corner is an excellent gallery—the **South Shore Art Center,** at 119 Ripley Road (781–383–2787)—that features the work of local artists. Founded in 1955, the South Shore Art Center sponsors the longest continuously operating art festival in the country, held each summer on Cohasset Common.

When you drive through downtown Scituate, you may be startled to see a fifteenth-century-Roman-style tower standing in the middle of a green near the library. It's the **Lawson Tower,** built at huge expense by Thomas Lawson, "the Copper King" of Wall Street. Lawson made a fortune in copper, only to be ruined in later life. The water tower stood on his large estate here, called Dreamwold, which had its own railroad and post office. He wanted to cloak the tower's utilitarian purpose. Now, Dreamwold is condos; however, in 1902 Lawson gave the water tower to the town, and it now plays carillon concerts in summer. At 153 feet tall, the tower is a landmark for ships at sea and offers a clear vista of the South Shore when you climb its steps. To see the tower, take a left off Route 3A south onto First Parish Road and drive up behind the First Parish Church. The tower is open for tours during the summer and by appointment through the Scituate Historical Society (781–545–1083 or 781–545–0474), as are several other sites.

One is the 1811 granite **Scituate Lighthouse,** out on Lighthouse Point at Lighthouse and Rebecca Roads. In the War of 1812, the keeper's quick-witted teenage daughters prevented the British from sacking the town. Seeing two barges approach in the harbor, they grabbed up a fife and drum and played with all their might, hiding behind some cedars. The British, thinking an entire Yankee regiment awaited, beat a hasty retreat. For this feat, the girls went down in history as "the Army of Two."

Front Street in Scituate bustles with interesting little shops, galleries, and restaurants and a working fishing fleet anchors at its northern end. At the **Quarterdeck,** 206 Front Street, you'll find a blend of wares so eclectic that they also caught the eye of Hollywood scouts choosing locations for *The Witches of Eastwick.* This little shop with windows on Scituate Harbor is crammed with antiques, imports, nautical items, and an impressive collection of historic postcards of local scenes.

Handy to Front Street is the **Allen House Bed & Breakfast,** a large white Victorian high on a hill overlooking the harbor. The house is nicely fitted out with richly patterned wallpapers and fabrics conveying an antique sensibility. Unusual antiques grace the dining room, large guest parlor, and four guest rooms, some with ocean views and two with private baths. Stupendous four-course breakfasts start off with coffee and juices, or mulled cider or hot cranberry cup in cold weather. Next, a fruit plate, then a hot entree. The meal ends with homemade muffins, popovers, and scones. If this doesn't fortify you enough, innkeepers Christine and Iain Gilmour enjoy serving a proper British cuppa in the afternoon, with cream and scones. These are the kind of innkeepers who, when they have no rooms available, will interrupt their dinner to find a B&B for travelers caught without a place to stay. Write the Gilmours at 18 Allen Place, Scituate 02066, or call (718) 545–8221 (doubles $99 to $199 in high season, $69 to $159 in low season).

The stretch of Route 3A between Scituate and Marshfield is one of the prettiest drives on the South Shore. The tidal marshes of the **North River** reach out for miles on both sides. The play of sunlight is an artist's dream and makes this road a joy to drive on. In a reverse scenario of pristine wilderness to industrial wasteland, the river's banks once shouldered dozens of shipyards and factories, now gone. More than a thousand ships were built here, including the brig *Beaver,* of Boston Tea Party fame, and the ship *Columbia,* the first to carry the Stars and Stripes around the world.

Just over the little bridge at the town line of Marshfield, you'll see **Mary's Boat Livery** (781–837–2322) on the right. You can rent a boat here for either day or a half-day and take it up the North River, an ideal way to see its scenic meanderings. Half-day rentals (under five hours) are $45, full-day $70, including oars, gas, and life vests.

Park on the right and put your lights on when you pull in to **Johnson's Drive-In,** and a carhop will come out and take your order for clam strip plates, made-to-order burgers and cheeseburgers, and homemade A&W draft root beer, mixed daily, just as it's been since 1957. Inside, you can sit at the soda fountain on the padded stools and admire old photos of how the place used to look in the fifties (not much different). The cash register doesn't go any higher than $5.00, so the waitress has to compute your check in increments of five. Johnson's is at 2105 Ocean Street (Route 139), right before Route 3A. Call (781) 834–9163.

In its day, the 1699 *Winslow House* was a mansion, as befit its owner, Judge Isaac Winslow, grandson of Plymouth Colony Governor Edward Winslow, the Pilgrim founder of Marshfield. The leading men of Plymouth Colony were entertained here, at formal teas and dinners. Although the house looks plain by our standards, its Jacobean staircase with acorn finials was a standout. Behind the Georgian paneling in the drawing room is a secret chamber where Tories reportedly hid. Daniel Webster had an estate in Marshfield for twenty years, and his law office was moved here; the office has letters and photos of Webster's. Also on the property are a blacksmith shop and a one-room schoolhouse. The Winslow House is open from 1:00 to 5:00 P.M. Wednesday through Sunday, mid-June through mid-October. Admission is $3.00 for adults and 50 cents for children. Call (781) 837–5753.

No matter what the season, it always smells like Thanksgiving at *Gerard Farm,* a family business for fifty years. The smell of roasting turkey and chicken fills the air at this wonderful shop that sells many kinds of homemade foods, with freshly roasted turkey its specialty. Where else can you get a thick turkey sandwich made with two kinds of bread, cranberry sauce, stuffing, and mayonnaise? Freezers stock frozen turkey pies ("all dark meat" and "all white meat"), turkey croquettes, roast turkeys, and turkey soup. The shop is at 1331 Ocean Street (Route 139). Call (781) 834–7682.

Marshfield has a particularly nice place to stay and enjoy the area, at *Beech Hill Bed & Breakfast*. This mid-1800s home has been restored and renovated over the years without losing its fine antique features, including a marble fireplace. The guestrooms are lushly decorated without being overdone, and all are bright and airy, with pale-colored walls. The gardens are beautiful, as are the yards of the surrounding homes in this quiet hillside neighborhood. A suite has a separate entrance, a kitchen, and a living room. The Bechtolds are excellent hosts, with a sense of humor. Their two golden retrievers are also hospitable, greeting guests like old friends and helping show them to their rooms. It's a pleasant place to come home to, and the rates are a happy surprise for this shore town, only $80 on weekends, $65 midweek. The suite is $95 and $120, with special rates for longer stays.

Each spring thousands of herring fight their way 16 miles from the ocean up the North River to spawn in freshwater ponds, as they have for centuries. The herring, also called alewives, were a vital source of food for the Pilgrims and the Indians. Colonists regulated fishing rights strictly, appointing a "herring superintendent" to oversee the harvesting and distribution of fish. Widows, spinsters, and other needy persons were given bushel baskets of fish. There are half a dozen points on the South Shore where you can watch the herring run. A good spot is **Herring Run Park** on Route 14 in Pembroke, which celebrates the herring run with an annual fish fry in late April. The herring are dipped from the brook with nets. A modern-day herring superintendent oversees the action while children wade in and fish with dip nets, bare hands, and anything else they can find. The fish are fried in big cast-iron skillets over an open grill and served with corn bread and baked beans. (Nona*fish*ionados can eat hot dogs.) For the date and other information, call the Plymouth County Development Council at (781) 826–3136 or (800) 231–1620.

# Pilgrim and Cranberry Country

The town of Duxbury was settled as early as 1625, by Pilgrims from the nearby Plymouth Colony. Among them were colonists with names that ring through history: Alden, Standish, Brewster. Although there is no evidence that John Alden had to win his wife, Priscilla, away from Myles Standish as Longfellow's famous poem recounts, the couple are known to have lived out their later years in a tiny house built in 1653. The **John Alden House** is cramped and dark and looks none too comfortable. Its low, rough plaster ceilings were made of crushed clam and oyster shells, and even the formal parlor has a stark look to it. Other features of the house are the cambered panels in the "best room" and the gun-stock beams in the bedchambers. The house, located at 105 Alden Street, off Route 3A, is open from 10:00 A.M. to 5:00 P.M. Monday through Saturday, 2:00 to 5:00 P.M. Sunday, from late June through September. Admission is $2.50 for adults and $1.00 for children. Call (617) 934–9092 for information.

Down the street from the Alden House is a much brighter, contemporary place: the **Art Complex Museum.** This small but intriguing museum was founded by Carl Weyerhaeuser—grandson of the founder of the lumber company of the same name—and his wife, Edith, as a home for their private collection. Much of it is Asian art, as well as Shaker and American works. There are semiannual showings of contemporary New England artists. A unique feature of the museum is an authentic Japanese teahouse designed in Kyoto; traditional Japanese tea ceremonies are conducted in the summer months. The museum, open from 1:00 to 4:00 P.M. Wednesday through Sunday, is at 189 Alden Street. Call (617) 934–6634.

When appetite calls, head for the home-style *Milepost Tavern Restaurant* (781–934–6801) on Route 3A. It's hard to explain how such an unadorned place can be so appealing, but there you are. Big factors are the friendly waitresses and good food. Besides homemade hearty soups and sandwiches, lunch specialties include baskets of fried clams and scallops or honey-dipped fried chicken, served with french fries. At dinner, you can choose from such standard, comforting offerings as chicken, veal, beef, and seafood, plus blackboard specials, priced from $13 to $16.

For dessert (or a luxurious breakfast), you can't beat *French Memories Bakery.* This bakery was founded by real French natives, who bake real French croissants and baguettes on the premises. They also create mouthwatering pastries that are colorful works of art: kiwi, strawberry, and apple tarts; chocolate mousse; brioches; and opera cake. The shop is at 459 Washington Street, next to Sweetser's General Store; call (781) 934–9020.

The town of Duxbury once had sixteen shipbuilders. The wealthiest of them, Ezra Weston and his son, Ezra Weston II, grew so rich that they both came to be called "King Caesar." In 1808, the son built a gorgeous, Federal-style mansion overlooking his wharves. The light-filled *King Caesar House* shows off exquisite woodwork and fanlight windows, as well as sweeping ocean views. One room displays treasures of the China Trade, such as Chinese writing implements and beautifully hand-painted fans. The two front parlors display rare French mural wallpapers. The many fine furnishings include a thirteen-light cabinet symbolic of the thirteen colonies, a 1795 girandole mirror, and Sandwich and cable glass. (Cable glass was made in a cable-shaped pattern to commemorate the laying of the first transatlantic cable from France to Duxbury in 1869.) The house, on King Caesar Road, is open from 1:00 to 4:00 P.M. on Wednesday through Sunday from early June through Labor Day and on Friday and Saturday in September. Admission is $4.00 for adults and 50 cents for children. Call (781) 934–6106.

If you follow King Caesar Road out to Duxbury Beach, you'll pass over the *Powder Point Bridge,* the longest wooden bridge on the eastern seaboard. (Some say the longest in the nation.) About 2,200 feet long, it was first built in 1892 and was then rebuilt after it burned in 1985. Cars are welcome to cross this wide span, which offers a pretty view of a little inlet just before Duxbury Beach. The bridge is favored by fishermen, the inlet by sailboarders. Duxbury Beach is a grand stretch of sand 6 miles long that faces the open Atlantic. It's one of the few South Shore beaches open to the public.

NEW ENGLAND'S LARGEST BREAKFAST MENU trumpets the sign at *Persy's Place* in Kingston. Indeed, you might spend all morning perusing the offerings: sixteen egg dishes; twelve kinds of omelettes, including lobster, *chourico,* and "build-your-own"; and almost everything else your breakfast fancy might desire, from asparagus to rainbow trout, from finnan haddie to SOS (uh, chipped beef on toast). Persy's hews to Yankee traditions with fish cakes, corned beef hash, Boston baked beans, and grilled corn bread (outstanding). Four generations of the Heston family (the youngest is "growing as fast as she can") serve breakfast all day long. The small dining rooms with wooden booths are so homey that they feel like your living room. An outdoor deck opens in nice weather. Next door, the owners run a small country store that sells hand-painted wooden decorations and the like. Persy's Place is at 117 Main Street (Route 3A), just south of exit 9 from Route 3. Call (781) 585–5464.

So much "Pilgrimiana" is awash in Plymouth that the *Mayflower* couldn't possibly carry it all back to England. Busloads of people from all over the world come to see Plymouth Rock enshrined in its odd mausoleum, Plimoth Plantation, and the *Mayflower II,* flooding the waterfront and its schlocky shops and restaurants.

In the midst of this theme-park atmosphere, one place stands out: *Pilgrim Hall Museum,* behind its pillared facade at 75 Court Street, is the oldest museum in America, founded in 1824, and has the largest collection of possessions of the first settlers. It is fascinating for the personal look it gives of the everyday life of the Pilgrims, through their letters and belongings. Here also is the skeleton of *Sparrow-Hawk,* a rare ship built in the 1600s, the wreck of which was found off Chatham Bar in 1863. The museum is open daily, February through December; (508) 747–1620.

If you're on Pilgrim overload, you might try a whale watch. As big as the whale-watching business has grown in Gloucester and Provincetown, few people know you can sail from Plymouth. Head over to Town Wharf, where you'll find *Capt. John Boats,* which from April through October runs four-hour whale-watching cruises to Stellwagen Bank, the whales' feeding ground. These boats have a high success rate and have spotted finback, humpback, right, and minke whales, among other kinds. Cruises cost $24 for adults and $15 for children. Call (508) 746–2643 or

(800) 242–AHOY in Massachusetts. Capt. John Boats also runs harbor tours, cruises to Provincetown, and deep-sea fishing charters.

Massachusetts grows roughly half the country's cranberries right here on the South Shore. In the fall, the landscape blazes with bogs in crimson. Locals routinely see the *cranberry harvest* in progress as they drive along the country roads of Plymouth, Carver, Middleborough, and Wareham. The harvest is big business and is well promoted—bus tours arrive en masse. Still, watching the colorful harvest is a great way to spend a crisp, sunny fall day, and one that will prompt you to reach for the camera. The wet-harvesting method first floods bogs and then uses water reels like giant eggbeaters to loosen the berries from the vines so that they float to the surface. The huge sea of red berries contrasts vibrantly with the deep blue of the water. Enriching the tones of this picture, workers wearing yellow hip-waders corral the berries. Then a hose vacuums them up into a truck. Harvesting goes on from about Labor Day to late October or early November. You'll pass several bogs on Route 44 west through Plymouth, down Seven Hills Road, and out Federal Furnace Road. Or drive out Routes 106 or 58.

You might want to sample some cranberry wine on your tour. If so, turn in to the *Plymouth Colony Winery* (508–747–3334), on Pinewood Road in Plymouth, a left off Route 44 west. Housed in an 1890 cranberry-screening house, the winery also makes blueberry, raspberry, peach, and grape wines.

To learn all there is to know about cranberries, stop in at the *Cranberry World Visitors Center,* on the waterfront in Plymouth—the country's only museum devoted to cranberries. Exhibits illustrate cranberry history and trace harvesting methods and tools, from antique wooden scoops to modern ways. The cranberry bouncer, designed years ago, is still used to test ripeness by how high berries bounce. The free museum, on Water Street, is open May 1 to November 30, from 9:30 A.M. to 5:00 P.M. daily. Call (508) 747–2350.

Way out in the sticks among the cranberry bogs is one of the finest restaurants on the South Shore—the *Crane Brook Tea Room.* When Emperor-to-be Akihito visited Massachusetts, this is where he dined. In a former iron foundry and cranberry-screening house overlooking a tranquil pond, the restaurant has transformed its rustic origins into a place of elegance and graciousness. The darkly romantic, living-room-size foyer invites you to rest amid armchairs and a glowing woodstove. An exquisitely created menu changes daily, based on the freshest and best seasonal ingredients. Special appetizers might include shrimp and black-bean cakes, or coastal Cape Cod mussels poached in a broth of white wine curry, cilantro, and garlic. For dinner entrees, you might choose from grilled rainbow trout in a brown butter sauce with red cabbage, grilled polenta, walnut, and parsley, or a roasted breast of duck with an orange-apricot-ginger glaze, red-wine-poached pear, and frisée. Entrees are priced from $24 to $32. Desserts are made to order. The Crane Brook Tea Room, located on Tremont Street in South Carver, is closed Monday and Tuesday; call (508) 866–3235.

There's a lot to see at the *Middleborough Historical Museum.* You might start with the collection of Tom Thumb memorabilia, collected from General and Mrs. Tom Thumb's Middleborough house, built to their miniature size. The pair, who toured with P. T. Barnum, received gifts from queens, emperors, and kings. Also among the memorabilia are Tom's pipe and smoking stand, along with miniature clothing. The museum also has eighteenth- and nineteenth-century museum houses (historic homes that may be toured), antique vehicles, a blacksmith shop, and many period vignettes, such as a country store, an old-time print shop, and a straw-hat works. Nineteenth-century wedding gowns, antique children's toys, and Indian artifacts are on exhibit as well. The museum is located on Jackson Street, off Route 105, behind the police station. Hours are from 1:00 to 4:00 P.M. Wednesday through Sunday in July, August, and the first two weekends in September and by appointment. Admission is $2.00 for adults and $1.00 for students. Call (508) 947–1969.

Middleborough is a pleasant town convenient to all parts of the South Shore but without the overcrowding of the waterfront towns. Two B&Bs here make it a particularly good place to settle in. In the center of town, next to the impressive domed town hall, is the 1831 *Zachariah Eddy House*, a well-restored Victorian home with unusual architectural details. The upstairs bath, for instance, with the stained glass window set in an alcove was once the private chapel of the original builders. Rooms are very nicely furnished; we especially like the Copperbeech Room, which has a window seat and a half-domed ceiling. One small room is decorated with vintage hats. Plan to arrive in time to enjoy the large porch set in a shaded yard, with a view of the town hall through the trees. On warm mornings, your breakfast table will be set up out here. Off-season rates are $65 to $85, high season $85 to $125. The B&B is at 51 South Main Street, Middleborough 02346; (508) 946–0016.

In contrast to this history and downtown setting, *On Cranberry Pond Bed and Breakfast* is in the open countryside and occupies a beautiful new home, built especially to welcome overnight guests. The setting overlooks a cranberry bog and a pond, with birds to watch, walking trails, and bicycles, and a skating pond in the winter. Guest rooms are large and nicely decorated, with thoughtful touches such as plenty of closet shelves and good-quality soaps. Breakfast is likely to include a baked cranberry French toast, in keeping with the setting. Several comfortable parlors provide places to read or sit, and a flower-surrounded deck is a great place to sit and watch the cranberries grow. Although the setting is peaceful and quiet, On Cranberry Pond is easy to find, about a mile off Route 44 and close to I–495. Rates begin at $75 and range up to $140 for the suite with private living room and whirlpool bath. On Cranberry Pond is at 43 Fuller Street, Middleborough 02346; (508) 946–0768.

Middleborough is just south of Bridgewater, a town thick with interesting stops. Route 18 north all the way to East Bridgewater is lined with antiques shops—small stores in old houses filled with an agreeable clutter of furniture and collectibles. Look particularly for *Antiques at Forge Pond* and *Ye Old Tyme Shoppe.*

Where Route 18 meets Route 106 west, you'll find a post office that has stood its ground since 1861. The *Elmwood Post Office* was commissioned by Abraham Lincoln. The Elmwood section of Bridgewater was the birthplace of the shoe industry, and a tannery was built here as early as 1650. Lincoln ordered the post office so that the village could ship badly needed shoes to the Union army. The post office stands in a small, white-columned building, taking up only a tiny corner for its ancient black window grille and old-fashioned metal mailboxes with brass combination dials. Behind the grille is an old, slant-topped wooden desk, and hanging above the desk is a framed picture of Lincoln. The post office shares its floor space with an antiques shop. Postmistress Sally Flagg Aldrich represents the fourth generation in her family to manage the post office.

Elmwood was once called Joppa, after the biblical city. The *Joppa Grill* (508–378–3510), a vintage country restaurant that dates to 1926, honors that name. From its striped canvas awnings to the old wooden tables and winged booths, the restaurant is virtually unchanged. As they have for decades, faithful regulars flock here for all-homemade food at affordable prices and complimentary appetizers of Joppa sticks—fried dough sprinkled with brown and confectionery sugars. The strongly traditional lunch and dinner menus include grilled cheese sandwiches, lobster sandwiches, chef's salads, broiled ham steak, lamb chops, pork chops, fried clams, and fried chicken; deep-dish apple pie and grapenut pudding are featured for dessert. Full (three-course)

**Elmwood Post Office**

meals rarely exceed $19. The Joppa Grill is on Route 18 north, 1 block up from where Route 106 bends east.

Another country restaurant, in Hanson, is an excellent place to go any time of day, for any reason: breakfast, coffee, dessert, snacks, lunch, dinner—you name it. At ***Phil's Family Restaurant*** (781–294–8147), truckers and construction workers—who have always known how to eat well and cheaply at the same time—perennially hunker down at the counter and in the orange-and-blue Formica booths. Everything is homemade from recipes contributed by family, friends, and customers. If you can't find something here you like, your mother didn't raise you right. Breakfast, served all day, ranges from steak and eggs to blueberry pancakes and "build-your-own" omelettes. At lunch and dinner, there are forty kinds of sandwiches (counting burgers and hot dogs), plus dishes like meat loaf, chicken Parmesan, and liver and onions. The all-homemade desserts, numbering thirty-two, claim some originals as well as traditions: Betty's chocolate macaroon pie, French silk pie, apple crisp, and strawberry shortcake. The largesse extends to a bakery counter that sells enormous muffins, pies, cookies, and brownies. Phil's is located at 1357 Main Street (Route 27), west of Route 58.

## MORE PLACES TO STAY ON THE SOUTH SHORE

*The John Carver Inn,*
25 Summer Street,
Plymouth 02360;
(508) 746–7100 or
(800) 274–1620.
Standard motel with
special fall packages that
include admission to local
attractions. Rooms from
$85 in season.

*Foxglove Cottage,*
101 Sandwich Road,
Plymouth,
an 1820s Cape with
antiques; reserve through
DestINNations at
(800) 333–4667.

*Pilgrim Sands Motel,*
150 Warren Avenue
(Route 3A),
Plymouth 02360;
(508) 747–0900 or
(800) 729–SAND.
Rooms from $60 off-
season, $100 in summer,
with a private beach for
guests.

## MORE PLACES TO EAT ON THE SOUTH SHORE

*The Barker Tavern,*
21 Barker Road,
Scituate;
(781) 545–6533.
The tavern was built in
1634, and it seems to shine
most brightly with classic
dishes like the swordfish,
which melts in your mouth.
Entrees around $20.

*Iguana's,*
170 Water St.,
Plymouth;
(508) 747–4000.
Standard south-of-the-
border fare with burritos
and enchiladas blends with
char-broiled steaks, ribs,
and chicken. Dinner
entrees are $9 to $13.

*Cafe Nanina,*
14 Union Street,
Plymouth;
(508) 747–4503.
Out of the maddening
crowds of Pilgrim-town,
this Italian oasis serves
stylish entrees ($15–$20)
in a nice setting over-
looking the water.

## WORTH SEEING ON THE SOUTH SHORE

*Plimoth Plantation,*
Plymouth, is a re-creation
of the village where the
Pilgrims lived. Here
costumed interpreters
enact their lives in the early
1600s, even speaking in the
dialect of the times;
(508) 746–1622.

*Mayflower II,* Plymouth;
(508) 746–1622

## TO LEARN MORE ABOUT THE SOUTH SHORE

Contact the Plymouth
County Convention and
Visitors Bureau, Box 1620,
Pembroke 02359;
(781) 826–3136,
E-mail info@plymouth-
1620.com.

# Cape Cod and the Islands

Although Cape Cod is the site of the most legendary summer traffic jams in the state of Massachusetts, there must be something here to see or there would be no lines.

Many sneer that overcrowding and tacky development have ruined the Cape. Untrue. Yes, whole towns have surrendered to strip malls, T-shirt shops, and fast-food and factory outlets. But pockets of untouched beauty endure: landscapes of windswept salt marshes and weathered houses, windmills and lighthouses, beach roses and dunes. A good 40 miles of coastline is preserved as the Cape Cod National Seashore, and its majestic beaches look just as wild now as they did years ago, when Henry David Thoreau, and, later, Eugene O'Neill walked in the sands. And the Cape's northern, bay side still harbors serene villages of sea captains' houses.

Shaped like a giant bent arm, Cape Cod juts into the Atlantic Ocean, with Bourne at its "shoulder," Chatham at the "elbow," and Provincetown way out at the "fist," the northeast tip. The landscape gets wilder as you head out toward the very end, the place of fabled 100-foot dunes, wide-open beaches, and acres of waving grasses. For some reason, the "shoulder" is known as the Upper Cape and the tip as the Lower Cape (also the Outer Cape). In between is the commercialized Mid-Cape.

The Cape's two island neighbors, Martha's Vineyard and Nantucket, are distinctly different from each other, despite their common whaling heritage. Martha's Vineyard is much larger and has a more varied terrain. Diminutive Nantucket is less touristy and is a wilder place of rolling moors.

The Cape and the Islands are lovelier in the off-season. The summertime hordes trample almost every acre of the Cape and disgorge from ferries and cruise ships onto the Islands. Though fall and spring are no longer quite the secret they were, they're much more tranquil times to visit. The surge of tourism dies down to a low roar, and the natives regain their friendlier selves, bolstered by resuming their small-town rhythms.

# Cape Cod
# and the Islands

Provincetown

OUTER
CAPE

6

Cape Cod
Bay

Cape Cod
Canal

6

Sandwich

6

MID-CAPE

6

28

South
Yarmouth

Chatham

UPPER CAPE

28

28

Hyannis

Buzzards
Bay

Falmouth

Nantucket
Sound

Elizabeth Islands

Oak Bluffs

Vineyard Sound

MARTHA'S
VINEYARD

Menemsha

NANTUCKET

Muskeget
Channel

Nantucket

N

0          10 mi
0          10 km

AUTHORS' FAVORITES ON CAPE COD AND THE ISLANDS

*Cape Cod National Seashore*

*Whale Watching*

*Cycling on Nantucket*

# Upper Cape

**B**efore you even get to the Cape, there are things to see. Most people don't give the Cape Cod Canal a second thought, except for how fast they can get over the bridges in heavy traffic. But those two graceful steel bridges, the **Sagamore Bridge** and the **Bourne Bridge,** won a national award for "most beautiful steel bridges" when they were completed in 1935. From them, you can see for miles over the Upper Cape and watch the sun flooding across the 500-foot-wide expanse, the widest sea-level canal in the world. There is a constant parade of boats and ships in the waterway; some twenty thousand a year pass through it, making it one of the world's busiest canals. Myles Standish first suggested a canal here in 1623, but it took until 1914 to get the 17-mile-long route built. The U.S. Army Corps of Engineers oversees the canal and maintains a popular visitors center in Buzzards Bay. But few people stop into the *reception area* at the administration building just down the road (508–759–4431).

The white wooden building sits hard by the banks of the canal, dwarfed by the towering legs of the Bourne Bridge. Two red-and-yellow tugs ride at anchor nearby. In the marine traffic controller's office, you can see a large diorama of the canal and watch the controller at work behind a massive bank of computer monitors, radios, and closed-circuit television screens. You'll hear the crackling broadcasts of approaching ships too. A slide show explains how the traffic control system works. The visitor reception area is open from 9:00 A.M. to 4:00 P.M. weekdays. From the Sagamore rotary, follow signs for Buzzards Bay to Main Street. Turn left at the first set of traffic lights onto Academy Drive.

The Corps also sponsors nature walks, bike trips, campfire programs, and similar events in the canal area. Two 8-mile *service roads* paralleling the canal are nice, flat terrain for bicycling and offer views unseen by drivers. The roads are accessible from more than half a dozen points on the mainland or on the Cape. Mainland parking spots include behind the Friendly Ice Cream Shop off the Sagamore Bridge rotary, at Herring Run on Route 6 between the rotary and Buzzards Bay, and at Scusset Beach. You might bike out to Scusset Beach, a long, sandy strip with bathhouses and a snack stand, for the afternoon. On the Cape side, you can park at Freezer Road at Sandwich Marina or at Monument Beach–Pocasset. (Head east from the Bourne Bridge rotary and turn left at the sign.)

If you'd like an even-better view of the canal, take a narrated sight-seeing cruise along it, perhaps by moonlight or sunset or accompanied by some rousing jazz music. *Cape Cod Canal Cruises* (508–295–3883) runs two- and three-hour daily cruises from Onset Bay, spring through fall. Steaming along on a two-hundred-passenger boat with an observation deck, you'll see such historic places as the site of President Grover Cleveland's summer mansion, Gray Gables. Rates for adults range from $7.00 to $12.00; children under 12 are free on day cruises.

By taking the Bourne Bridge over the canal and onto Route 28, you can make a loop tour of the Cape's chunky "shoulder." The first stop is Bourne, where there is a jewel of a little museum, the *Aptucxet Trading Post.* This primitive-looking building is a replica of the first trading post in English-speaking North America. It stood here in 1627 and was built by the Pilgrims for trade with the Dutch and Indians. But the post looks and is authentic in many ways. The inside is fitted out with wooden barrels of tobacco, furs hanging on the wall, and wooden scales. It's easy to picture Pilgrims and Indians trading together here. Traders used wampum, bits of shells that were America's first form of currency. Some architectural details are seventeenth-century, such as beams, wide-planked flooring, and leaded-glass diamond-pane windows.

Glass cases hold seventeenth-century potsherds, Indian arrowheads, and stone tools and wampum found on the site. Also on the grounds are President Cleveland's Victorian summer railroad station for arriving guests and a replica of an eighteenth-century saltworks with rolling roofs. There are picnic tables on the wooded grounds. The post is open from May through Columbus Day, 10:00 A.M. to 4:30 P.M. Tuesday through Saturday and 2:00 to 4:30 P.M. on Sunday. The museum also opens Mondays in July and August. Admission is $2.50 for adults, $2.00 for seniors, and $1.00 for children. Call (508) 759–9487. To get to the museum, turn right after crossing the Bourne Bridge and go 1 mile to a cemetery on the left; then turn right under a white railroad underpass onto Aptucxet Road, which jogs right. A windmill stands at the entrance.

Because it lies in its own little corner of the Cape, far from busy Route 6, Falmouth is often bypassed by those intent on "doing the Cape" from end to end. Route 28 goes through the center of the village, which still retains its green surrounded by fine homes, and a pleasant compact business district known as the Queen's Buyway, along with a harbor filled with pleasure craft. Here you can sign on for cruises and fishing trips, choosing among several boats including the sailing schooner *Liberté*; (508) 548–2626 or (800) 734–0088.

Facing the green is the *Julia Wood House,* a Federal home built in 1790 and decorated with furniture from that period. It is open from

## ANNUAL EVENTS ON CAPE COD AND THE ISLANDS

**Late April**

*Daffodil Festival, Nantucket, when the island is abloom with spring bulbs, and activities from bird-watching to picnics welcome visitors; (508) 228–1700.*

**Mid-May**

*Cape Cod Maritime Week, at various locations, offers lighthouse tours, cruises, visits to historic ships and homes, walking tours, and a variety of other sea-related activities; (508) 888–1233, www.capecodcommission.org.*

**Late June**

*Annual Portuguese Festival, Province-town, with food, music, dancing, and the Blessing of the Fleet; (508) 487–3424.*

**Early August**

*Irish Festival, Otis Air National Guard Base, Bourne; (800) 526–8532.*

**Mid-August**

*Annual Sandcastle and Sculpture Day, Jetties Beach, Nantucket, open to islanders and visitors; (508) 693–5380.*

**Early September**

*Annual Bourne Scallop Festival, Buzzards Bay Park, brings crafts, entertainment, and, of course, scallops; (508) 759–6965.*

**Mid-September**

*Tivoli Day, Circuit Avenue, Oak Bluffs, Martha's Vineyard, with art, music, and food; (508) 696–7643.*

**Early December**

*Christmas-by-the-Sea Weekend, Falmouth, brings food, music, bazaars, lighthouse tours, and a parade; (508) 548–8500 or (800) 526–8532.*

2:00 to 5:00 P.M. Wednesday through Sunday from mid-June to mid-September. Admission is $3.00 for adults, 50 cents for children. You can stroll along the brick-and-flagstone paths of the lovely boxwood-bordered garden anytime, but it is especially nice in May when the azaleas are in bloom or in June when the roses are at their best; just walk in through the front gate. Adjacent in two other buildings are a collection of sailor art and other maritime antiquities and a barnful of old farming tools; (508) 548–4857.

Hidden away from downtown Falmouth on a country road is **Peach Tree Circle Farm,** a blend of farm stand, bakery, cafe, and garden shop. Housed in a rustic, gray, clapboard house with yellow-and-white-striped awnings, Peach Tree Circle feels cozy and welcoming inside with its warm country style. An open barn-board ceiling is hung with dried flowers and herbs. Antique bottles and cans line the shelves, and pictures of wild birds decorate the walls. In cold weather, a wood-burning stove warms the shop. A small restaurant serves up homemade chicken pie, quiches, sandwiches, soup of the day, dill rolls, and desserts from its bakery. I recommend the magic squares: bars made with chocolate chips and coconut. In summer, cafe tables are moved outside to the deck. At the farm stand, you can purchase all kinds of goodies: teas, jams and jellies, sauces, marinades, and fresh produce. Peach Tree Circle (508–548–2354) is at 881 Old Palmer Avenue in West Falmouth, off Route 28.

Continuing south on Route 28, turn left onto Route 151 in Falmouth. Just off 151, you'll find a wildlife sanctuary that's full of Christmas spirit year-round—the *Ashumet Holly Reservation and Wildlife Sanctuary.* Here grows the largest native holly collection in New England—eight species and sixty-five varieties. They're all identified along a nature trail surrounding a grassy pond. A walk here is a wonderful discovery of holly's endless variety beyond the familiar red berry. Some hollies are trees, towering 20 or 30 feet tall; others bear orange or black berries. Berries turn color in late October, lingering through March unless robins and squirrels eat them all. Fragrant wreaths and swags of greenery are sold at Christmastime. A barn swallow colony nests in the barn May through August. The sanctuary, at 286 Ashumet Road in East Falmouth (508–563–6390), is open from dawn to dusk. Trail fees are $3.00 for adults and $2.00 for seniors and children.

Before you get to Woods Hole, off Route 28 and via a right turn onto Quisset Harbor Road is a lovely little sanctuary, the *Cornelia Carey Sanctuary.* (Locals call it "the Knob.") The road winds around picturesque Quisset Harbor and its fishing boats before coming to a dead end. Where a sign announces PRIVATE ROAD, there's a fence with a turnstile in front of a large house. Walk through the turnstile and over a stone-fortified causeway. A small wooded area of red cedar and oak opens up to a bare, grassy promontory high up, offering views of Buzzards Bay and the Elizabeth Islands. The Salt Pond Areas Bird Sanctuaries owns the land; call (508) 548–0703 (in the offices of Ermine Lovell Real Estate) for information.

You can take a trolley from Falmouth to Woods Hole, where there is very limited public parking. For a schedule, or to buy a pass or discounted tokens, contact the Falmouth Chamber of Commerce; (508) 548–8500 or (800) 526–8532.

The *Woods Hole Oceanographic Institution,* the largest independent oceanographic laboratory in the world, seems to dominate the village of Woods Hole on its water-surrounded little corner of Falmouth. The Exhibit Center and Gift Shop are at 15 School Street, open Monday through Saturday 10:00 A.M. to 4:30 P.M. and Sunday noon to 4:30 P.M. from Memorial Day to Labor Day; Tuesday through Saturday in May, September, and October; and only Friday and Saturday the rest of the year. Here you will find displays and hands-on exhibits about the deep-diving research station *Alvin* and other vehicles that explore the ocean depths. You can also see a video about the institution and another about *Alvin* and the discovery of the wreck of the *Titanic.* Guided walking tours of the WHOI, as the institution is called locally, leave at 10:00 A.M. and 1:30 P.M. on summer weekdays from the Information Center at 93 Water Street. You'll get a tour of the facilities, including the pier, where you may have a close-up look at the institution's research vessel *Atlantis,* and other areas of the campus not usually open to the public. Tours are free, but you must have a reservation; (508) 289–2252.

The *National Marine Fisheries Service Aquarium* on Albatross Street is also free, open from mid-June through mid-September, daily 10:00 A.M. to 4:00 P.M. The rest of the year, it is open the same hours on week-days only. Be there at 11:00 A.M. or 3:00 P.M. to see the seals fed, but you can watch the seals even when the facility is closed; (508) 495–2001.

The *Woods Hole Historical Museum*, on Woods Hole Road as you enter town, is open Tuesday through Saturday from mid-June to mid-September, 10:00 A.M. to 4:00 P.M. Along with the displays of local history at the Bradley House, it has a Small Boat Museum and conducts walking tours of the village at 4:00 P.M. on Tuesdays. Admission is free; (508) 548–7270.

*Fishmonger Cafe* overlooks the water (as does nearly everything in Woods Hole) right at the drawbridge. Dinner entrees include mussels Borracho—steamed in beer with green chilis, onion, and garlic—and are priced from $11 to $19 (for the seafood platter). Sandwiches and lunch specials are in the $6.00 range.

Following Route 28 from Falmouth to Mashpee, you will pass the Visitors Center of the *Waquoit Bay National Estuarine Research Reserve*. This reserve includes a beach, a state park recreation area, an island with ten campsites, an upland forest tract, salt ponds, barrier beaches, dunes, and open water along 15 miles of shoreline. The center often has evening programs and interpretive walks; (508) 457–0495.

At the southern shore of Mashpee, about 2 miles from the intersection of Great Neck Road and Great Oak Road, is *South Cape Beach State Park,* part of the Estuarine Reserve, with miles of beach and a $2.00 parking fee. While it is filled with sunbathers on nice summer days, the rest of the time, it is quiet, the preserve of the piping plover and surf fishing enthusiasts. Great Flat Pond Trail begins near the parking lot, a level walking path that leads through this shore environment.

On the way to the state park, you will pass *Mashpee National Wildlife Refuge* and the *Jehu Pond Conservation Area,* with more walking trails. A wide bike lane borders the road here, and you can rent bikes from Corner Cycle, 115 Palmer Avenue, near the Village Green in Falmouth; (508) 540–4195.

Falmouth has several very good places to eat, including the one that is often credited with stepping up the culinary pace for the entire Cape. *The Regatta of Falmouth-by-the-Sea*, overlooking the water at Falmouth Harbor, serves a pricey-but-worth-it lunch and dinner in the summer season only; (508) 548–5400.

Don't mistake *The Quarterdeck* for the pub it looks like from the street. From the engaging greeting at the door to the lively waitstaff, the service is personal and very well-informed, which is good because you will find some dishes here that require a detailed description. The menu is innovative and eclectic, with subtle Portuguese influences in the chef's handling of seafood and pork—as well as in the wine list. Start with the likes of smoked salmon cheesecake or grilled portabella on a bed of tender spring greens, then move on to salmon Oscar with crabmeat, asparagus, and bernaise, or pork tenderloin marinated in port and rubbed with rosemary. The decor is backlit stained glass and nooks filled with seaport antiques. Dinner of chef's specials for two, with a bottle of good Dão and the tip, barely comes to $50. The restaurant also serves lunch daily, at 164 Main Street close to the Village Green in Falmouth; (508) 548–9900.

Another place we really like is *Peking Palace.* This is not just another Chinese restaurant in a resort town. While there are plenty of Cantonese and Szechuan dishes on the menu, the chef really shines with the Mandarin specialties: crown chicken with macadamia nuts and black mushrooms, mango chicken, or shrimp served in a sweet tomato sauce with walnuts. Entrees are between $9.00 and $12.00, and the restaurant is open daily from 11:30 A.M. to 2:00 A.M., at 452 Main Street in Falmouth; (508) 540–8204.

Immediately after Route 28 passes Route 130 heading east in Cotuit, you'll see a red colonial building on the left, the *Cahoon Museum of American Art.* The setting of this small but gemlike museum heightens the flavor of its engaging collections. Once a tavern and stagecoach stop, the house was built in 1775. The six galleries have original low plaster ceilings, wide-planked floors, nineteenth-century stenciled walls and floorboards, and period wooden furniture. These serenely antique surroundings give the feeling that the paintings hang in a private home. Primitive artists Ralph and Martha Cahoon bought the house for their studio in the 1940s. The museum opened in 1984, with the Cahoons' paintings as the heart of the permanent collection. Ralph was fond of painting mermaids, posing them whimsically in Cape settings of ocean, lighthouses, and ships. These paintings just have to bring a smile to your face, as you see mermaids cavorting in hot-air balloons shaped like fish and birds, or doing their laundry using a whale for a washboard. Also on exhibit are some of the largest and most gorgeous sailors' valentines I've ever seen, set in gold-framed, octagonal shadow boxes. These beautiful pieces, traditionally bought in the West Indies by sailors for their wives and sweethearts, were made of hundreds of tiny pink, white, and purple seashells formed into patterns of flowers and other elaborate designs. The collection also includes the work of primitive itinerant portrait painters, marine artists, Hudson River landscape artists, and American impressionist painters. The museum is open from 10:00 A.M. to 4:00 P.M. Tuesday through Saturday and is closed from January to March. Call (508) 428–7581. Admission is free.

Leaving Cotuit, take Route 130 north to the town of Sandwich. This attractive, colonial-looking village is famous for its Sandwich Glass Museum, among other sites ranged around its attractive village green and pond. Just off the green, at 1 Water Street, Britishers Mike and Mary Bell have re-created a British tearoom, the **Dunbar House** (508–833–2485). Warmly paneled with dark wood and thickly hung with antique prints and paintings, the dining room exudes restfulness as classical music plays. Blackboard specials might include a rich cream-of-chicken soup, chicken savory, and a traditional ploughman's lunch of cheeses, fruits, and French bread. Cream tea and scones accompany all. An enormous dessert table overflows with the most indulgent English desserts, among them Queen Anne cake and English toffee cake. There's also a gift shop here that sells British books and collectibles, specialty foods, quilts, and decoys. The tearoom is open from 11:00 A.M. to 4:30 P.M. daily; the shop from 10:00 A.M. to 5:00 P.M., hours that are extended in the summer.

Over in East Sandwich, you'll find the **Green Briar Jam Kitchen and Nature Center,** where they still make jam the way they have since 1903. If you tour the kitchen, you'll feel as if you've stepped into your grandmother's kitchen. Copper counters line the blue-and-white expanse and sunny windows brim with pink geraniums. A many-burnered, 1920 cast-iron gas stove runs the length of the kitchen, flanked by a Hoosier cabinet and big wooden barrels of sugar. During a jam-making class, steam rises in your face, releasing the delicious smells of warm fruit. The classes are given year-round. A gift shop sells more than a hundred kinds of homemade jams, jellies, and preserves, from popular strawberry, raspberry, and blueberry to beach-plum jellies and marmalades. In the fall and winter, the kitchen makes cranberry conserve, tomato relish, and mincemeat.

A Sandwich woman, Ida Putnam, started the Green Briar Jam Kitchen, using many recipes from her friend Fannie Merritt Farmer's famous cookbook. Naturalist and author Thornton Burgess roamed the jam kitchen's woods as a boy, later basing his *Old Briar-Patch* and *Smiling Pool* on spots he found there. The Green Briar Jam Kitchen and Nature Center, at 6 Discovery Hill Road in East Sandwich, gives tours from 10:00 A.M. to 5:00 P.M. weekdays; call (508) 888–6870.

# Mid-Cape

A gorgeous barrier beach called **Sandy Neck** stretches over the town line between Sandwich and Barnstable. Calmer than the pounding surf of the Cape Cod National Seashore, this beach is backed by lots of dunes and beach grasses. Hiking trails wind through the dunes. Alas, the days of walking on dunes are virtually gone; fragile dunes easily erode underfoot, and if you walk on the dunes, you'll be asked to leave. But you can't hurt the view. To reach Sandy Neck, turn left on Sandy Neck Road off Route 6A. It costs $8.00 to park on weekends from Memorial Day until July 4; then the fee is charged daily until Labor Day. The small parking lot fills up rapidly on weekends, holidays, and hot days. For information, call the gatehouse at (508) 362–8306. If you'd like a view of the splendid **Great Marshes** on Sandy

## Run, Alewives, Run

*E*ach spring thousands of alewives, the silver-sided herring abundant all along the Atlantic Coast, return to freshwater ponds to spawn. Before the Cape was settled, these fish used natural waterways for their migration, jumping falls and working their way up rapids, and in some places, they still do. But in others, where dams, the canal, or even natural changes to the landscape have interfered, engineers have created artificial watery staircases

for the alewives to climb. In April or early May, you can watch these fish at Herring Pond, off Herring Pond Road in Bournedale (the part of town on the mainland side of the canal), which you can reach from Route 6, about a mile south of the rotary, or at Stoney Brook Herring Run in Brewster, by the Stoney Brook Grist Mill. In Harwich, you'll find another constructed run in the Conservation area next to Bell's Neck Road, off Depot Road.

Neck's south side, drive a little farther east on Route 6A and turn left onto either Bone Hill Road or Millway in Barnstable. In season, a $10 parking fee is charged until 4:00 P.M. Parking is then free until closing at 9:00 P.M.

Just off Route 6A on Route 149 in the center of Barnstable Village is a store that's more museum than store—the *Barnstable Stove Shop* (508–362–9913). Rusting hulks of stoves line the drive up to the weathered old barn that serves as showroom. Proudly gleaming with the shiny new faces given them by owner Doug Pacheco stand several dozen antique cast-iron stoves. The potbellied stoves, parlor stoves, and sturdy kitchen ranges are so beautifully restored that they look brand-new. A Glenwood parlor stove bears intricate scrollwork over almost every square inch and sports a 1-foot-tall fancy chrome finial. Hundreds more are in storage or under repair. Since the owner is often off scavenging for more stoves, it's best to call for an appointment.

Behind the low, shingled *St. Mary's Episcopal Church,* on Route 6A in Barnstable, is an astonishing series of gardens, where you may wander through roses set around a well, past brilliant red azaleas, along a streambank swathed in ferns, or in walled terrace gardens reminiscent of ancient monasteries. A unique brick garden house shelters benches, stone pools provide focal points, and polychrome saints gaze placidly over the bright beds of flowers. Come at any time during the growing season, since the gardens are designed to bloom in sequence, from dogwood to asters. The garden is free, but a donation box is there if you wish to help with its upkeep.

As you travel east on the Cape, it's much more fun and scenic to take the windier Route 6A—the *Cranberry Highway*—than to go barreling along Route 6, the Mid-Cape Highway, which reveals almost nothing along the way. Route 6A passes right through the main streets of three attractive northside villages: Barnstable, Yarmouthport, and Brewster, lined with old sea captains' houses, general stores, and inns and restaurants. You might particularly poke about the antiques shops in Barnstable Village, taking time to stop into the *Trayser Memorial Museum* of local history, located in the handsome old brick customhouse.

By the time you get to Hyannis, you've hit some of the worst the Cape has to offer. Lots of commercialism and strip malls densely pack this area. Thousands of tourists come hoping to catch a glimpse of the Kennedys, who for years have had their family compound in Hyannisport. There had never been a place for Kennedy fans to visit until 1992, when the Hyannis Chamber of Commerce opened the *John F. Kennedy Hyannis Museum* at 397 Main Street, in the Old Town Hall. Large black-and-white and color photographs as well as videos show the young Kennedy family swimming and boating off Hyannisport and JFK walking his solitary miles along the beach, as he did during his presidency. Despite the small size of the museum's collection, it's a memorable visit. It is open daily from 10:00 A.M. until the last visitors are admitted at 3:30 P.M. The museum closes at 4:00 P.M. After mid-October, it opens Wednesday through Saturday from 10:00 A.M. to 4:00 P.M. Tickets cost $3.00 for adults and admission is free for children. For information, call (508) 790–3077.

While in town, potato-chip junkies may want to visit some premium chips at their source. *Cape Cod Potato Chips,* which are sold all over New England, gives free factory tours Monday through Friday from 9:00 A.M. to 5:00 P.M. Take Independence Drive off Route 132 to find the factory, where chips are still made the old-fashioned way; (508) 775–3206.

There were once so many sea captains' houses along Main Street in Yarmouth that it was known as "the Captains' Mile." A number have been turned into inns. One of the nicest is the *Captain Farris House,* an 1845 Greek Revival home in South Yarmouth set peacefully just two blocks from the Bass River. Two acres of lawn surround the large, white house trimmed with plum-colored shutters and a huge wraparound veranda set with Adirondack chairs and settees. The house blends an antique sensibility with such modern-day luxuries as all-new bathrooms and Jacuzzis. Guest rooms are decorated in such exquisitely chosen colors as muted rust, silver, and gold overglazes, soothing to the eye and softened by yards and yards of damask draperies. The eight rooms, plus two in another house, are decorated with a mix of antique and contemporary pieces, and some have private decks or private entrances. A central open-air courtyard with a small fountain and flowers makes a lovely setting for breakfast and lunch. A formal parlor with an antique baby grand and a small library are also available for guest use. The innkeeper creates his own menus around the seasons, starting breakfast with fresh juices and fresh fruits, then serving a hot entree. Past creations have included cornmeal pancakes with strawberry-rhubarb sauce and whipped cream, and a turkey hash flavored with garlic and rosemary and topped with poached eggs. For reservations. contact DestINNations, P.O. Box 1173, Osterville 02655–1076; (800) 333–4667 or (508) 428–5600 (doubles $85–$175; suites $115–$225).

Those who find restaurants altogether too much fuss will feel right at home at *Jack's Outback Restaurant,* at 161 Hallet Street in Yarmouthport (508–362–6690). Handwritten signs announce: THE FOOD IS GOOD, BUT THE SERVIS STINKS! and IF THERE'S A BIG LINE, USE YOUR BRANE, GO AWAY!

Jack's has none of your traditional restaurant amenities such as menus or service. You have to write up your own order, get your own coffee and silverware, and bus your own table. Offerings of the day are handwritten on a corkboard. When you walk in, you'll see a blue counter with stools; it overlooks the open kitchen, where most days you can see Jack at the griddle—he's the one with frizzled gray hair and a checked flannel shirt. His expertly cooked breakfasts include bacon and eggs, toast, and Belgian waffles. Lunches run to sandwiches and salads, including macaroni salad; quiches; and homemade soups. Tips are received in a big bowl marked, "Don't Forget the Widows and Orphans," and the arrival of each tip is heralded by a special-effects hammer that makes crashing and breaking sounds.

To get there, look for a store called Design Works in a small complex of shops on Route 6A east. Turn right into the driveway next to it and drive around behind the shops, where you'll see a gray-and-white building with pink flamingos out front.

In West Dennis, overlooking its own breakwater-protected beach, *The Lighthouse Inn* is a family-owned country inn with accommodations in shingled cottages and the main house. Although it's far from dowdy, it has that warm, relaxing aura of old-fashioned beach resort hotels, where families stayed for weeks at a time, with its wicker-furnished library and sunporch and large bright dining room. On the property are a working lighthouse, tennis courts, lawn games, and a heated pool, although the sea water is warm here. The inn is family-friendly, with an InnKids program of daily activities and a supervised kids' dining room for parents who would rather dine alone and later. Rooms with breakfast begin at $90 per person, plus $20 if the five-course dinner is included. Children's rates begin at $35, including dinner. This is a no-tipping property. In summer, the dining room is open to the public for lunch and dinner, with dinner entrees beginning at $14. The Lighthouse Inn, West Dennis 02670–0128; (508) 398-2244, fax (508) 398-5658, www.lighthouseinn.com.

Biking enthusiasts should definitely try their wheels on the *Cape Cod Rail Trail* bike path, a 22-mile stretch from Dennis to Wellfleet that follows the old right of way of the Penn Central Railroad. The easy, flat terrain passes some lovely scenery: stands of cedar and scrub pine, horse farms, cranberry bogs, salt marshes, beaches, and kettle ponds. Despite the Rail Trail's popularity, this is still one of the great things to do on the Cape. One of the nicest things about the Rail Trail is that you can use it to bike to the beaches along the way, thereby escaping the parking aggravation.

You can join the trail almost anywhere you like and can bike for as long as you want. Access is from more than a dozen points, clearly marked by signs on Routes 6 and 6A. The southerly trailhead is at a parking lot on Route 134, just south of Route 6 in South Dennis; the northern end comes out in Wellfleet. There are plenty of take-out stands, ice-cream shops, rest rooms, and bike-rental shops along the way. For information about the Rail Trail, call Nickerson State Park at (508) 896–3491. A good trail guide is *The Cape Cod Bike Book,* by William E. Peace ($2.50), available at the Salt Pond Visitors Center of the Cape Cod National Seashore and many Cape bookshops.

Only half a mile from the Rail Trail in South Dennis, the **Captain Nickerson Inn** offers hospitable accommodations in an 1879 Queen Anne Victorian house built by a sea captain. The inn is located on a quiet country road in the historic district. White wicker rockers invite you to sit and relax on the wide front porch. Handsome flowered wallpapers, parquet floors, and period antiques grace the living room, dining room, and guest rooms, all named after the captain's ships. Bedrooms have white-iron, brass, and four-poster beds. There's a backyard play area with swing set that children are welcome to share with the innkeepers' young children. The full breakfast you are offered might feature eggs, pancakes, french toast, or perhaps a blueberry crepe with whipped cream. For reservations, contact DestINNations, P.O. Box 1173, Osterville 02655–1076: (800) 333–4667 or (508) 428–5600 (doubles $60–$90).

Even closer to the trail, where it crosses Route 6A in Brewster, is **Cobie's,** which has been serving up fried clams, lobster rolls, and ice cream since 1948. The crabmeat salad roll is filled with chunks of snow crab meat, for $5.95 the last time we tucked into one. On Sunday Cobie's serves a fisherman's platter of clams, scallops, shrimp, and cod for $12.95. Take your plate to a picnic table on the deck or in the shaded pavilion. This is the kind of old-fashioned quality roadside stand you thought had given way everywhere to fast-food chains. Open from 11:00 A.M. to 9:00 P.M. daily May through Labor Day, at 3260 Main Street (Route 6A), Brewster; (508) 896–7021.

Cobie's is within easy cycling distance of **Nickerson State Park,** a vast tract—nearly 2,000 acres—of rolling upland forest surrounding eight ponds that are unique because no brooks or streams feed them. These are "kettle ponds," created when melting glaciers left large chunks of ice behind more than 10,000 years ago, when Cape Cod was formed as a ridge of terminal glacial moraine. The ponds provide canoeing, swimming, fishing, and birding opportunities, and the rest of the park has paved cycling paths, hiking trails, and more than 400 campsites, divided among eight campgrounds. Most sites can be reserved in advance (508– 896–4615), but 165 are not reservable. These are distributed each morning at a 10:00 A.M. site call, which may involve a wait of several days. Park attendants can usually predict when you take your number how many days you will have to wait for a space, so you don't have to be there every morning. The park is open year-round, with winter camping allowed. Campsites are $6.00 or $7.00 depending on size and location; (508) 896–3491.

The town of Brewster has several museums spread out along Route 6A. The first you'll come to is the absolute best place to learn about the outdoor wonders of the Cape: the *Cape Cod Museum of Natural History.* A small shingled building surrounded by beach roses and salt marsh, the museum was founded in 1954 as a children's museum. Exhibits are still interpreted with children in mind. Children can pick up seashells and whale bones, play a birdsong identification game, and put on their own animal puppet shows. Many native Cape birds and animals are displayed in an engaging manner. Nature trails lead through woodland and out to a barrier beach. There are picnic tables outside the museum, which offers all kinds of excellent natural-history programs year-round. Located at 869 Main Street, the museum is open from 9:30 A.M. to 4:30 P.M. Monday through Saturday and from 12:30 to 4:30 P.M. on Sunday. Tickets cost $5.00 for adults and $2.00 for children ages 5 to 12. Call (508) 896–3867 or (800) 479–3867.

Throughout the year, the museum sponsors walks, canoe and kayak explorations, birding trips, boat excursions with naturalists, special programs on nature topics, art classes, and field trips to outstanding natural destinations in the state. These are geared to a variety of ages. Some are free with admission; others involve nominal fees.

*South Trail* begins across Route 6A from the museum, traversing upland woods, a salt marsh, and an unusual forest of beech. From April through June, Stony Brook, which follows part of the trail, is a run for alewives returning to freshwater to spawn. Expect to see ospreys along parts of this trail during nesting season. *Wing Island Trail* also begins at the museum, crossing an upland forest of pitch pines and a boardwalk across a salt marsh before arriving at a barrier beach. Near the beach is a unique sassafras grove, and in a field, you will find a recently built solar calendar of standing stones, demonstrating how modern concepts of time measurement grew from ancient astronomic calendars.

A short distance east on Route 6A lies the **New England Fire and History Museum** (508–896–5711). This museum is a collection of small-town buildings set around a little green, with a children's play area in the middle. You'll find a big barn, a blacksmith shop, the Union Fire Company (once under the direction of Benjamin Franklin), and an 1890 apothecary shop. The barn houses early hand-pulled and horse-drawn fire engines, with huge spoked wheels, leather buckets, and handsome brass bells and lanterns. A lighted diorama re-creates the famous 1871 Chicago fire, complete with clanging bells and smoke. Downstairs is the world's only 1929 Mercedes-Benz fire engine, as well as a collection of fire hats donated by the late Boston Pops conductor Arthur Fiedler, who loved fire trucks. Hours are 10:00 A.M. to 4:00 P.M. weekdays from mid-May through Columbus Day, when the museum closes for the season. Tickets cost $5.00 for adults, $4.50 for seniors, and $2.50 for children ages five to twelve.

Another family-oriented Brewster stop is the **Bassett Wild Animal Farm** (508–896–3224), a rustic sort of combination small zoo and farm. It's especially fun in the spring for children to see the new baby animals, which might include fox kits, goat kids, chicks, and goslings. The white-tailed deer are so tame that they wag their tails like dogs when you approach with food pellets. In a large fenced area, you can mingle freely with the ducks, sheep, goats, pigs, and rabbits. You'll also meet a crow named Irving that says "Oh, boy!" There are more-unusual animals too: a ring-tailed lemur from Madagascar, zebu cattle from India, and a South American green-wing macaw. In the pastures out back are pony rides and hayrides, and there are picnic tables in the shade. The animal farm is on Tubman Road, marked by a green sign on Route 137. Admission is $5.75 for adults and $4.00 for children. Hours are 10:00 A.M. to 5:00 P.M. daily, mid-May through mid-September, with the last admission at 4:20 P.M.

# Outer Cape

Chatham juts out at the Cape's elbow and so is almost surrounded by water, giving it some of the most spectacular views and nicest beaches on the entire Cape. To admire the view, drive out Shore Road along the ocean's edge, winding up at the Chatham Lighthouse.

One of a pair of twin lighthouses, built together so mariners could distinguish this point from the single lighthouse at Truro, Chatham Light was built in 1877. The other, which stood 100 feet to the north, was later moved to Nauset. During **Maritime Week,** in mid-May, this and other lighthouses are open for tours. For more information on lighthouse tours and the week's other activities, contact the Cape Cod Commission at (508) 888–1233 or visit its Web site at www.capecodcommission.org.

Although Chatham may sometimes seem like a preserve for the Cape's old-money gentility, it's a real town, with an active fishing fleet. To see the boats and watch them unload their catch, arrive in the afternoon at the *Chatham Fish Pier* on Shore Road. From late May throughout summer and fall, you can buy very fresh seafood right here on the wharf, at *Nickerson's Fish and Lobster Market.* Be sure to notice the attractive sculpture of fish, crustacea, and mollusks at the top of the landing, entitled *The Provider,* created by Sig Purwin and dedicated to the fishing industry.

There's so much in Chatham that you could spend a week here and not do everything. Of the half-dozen historic landmarks, a good place to start is with the oldest.

A treasure trove for learning about Chatham's history is tucked away in a solitary wood-framed house, the *Old Atwood House.* Five generations of a sea captain's family lived here, from about 1752. Nineteenth-century pieces and memorabilia fill the parlor, borning room, keeping room, music room, and kitchen with a fireplace. A whole gallery is full of portraits of Chatham sea captains. Among those seafarers were Captain Isaac White, who made a record, 120-day New York-to-Shanghai run on his clipper ship *Independent,* and Captain Oliver Eldredge, hired as a cook for eight men at the age of nine.

Black-and-white photographs show historic local scenes: the railroad depot, the coastline, and Twin Lights. There are lots of maritime artifacts too, such as a bottle of real whale oil. One room showcases hundreds of seashells on glass shelves, shining pink and white in the sunlight. Another room is devoted to noted Cape Cod author Joseph C. Lincoln. A barn in back displays the realistic murals of Alice Stallknecht Wight, each portraying Chatham townspeople and religious themes, such as Christ preaching from a dory. All this costs only $3.00 admission ($1.00 for students). The Old Atwood House is located at 347 Stage Harbor Road, about three-fourths of a mile from the rotary at the Congregational Church on Route 28. The museum is open from 1:00 to 4:00 P.M. Tuesday through Friday from mid-June through September.

Only a little "newer" is the *Old Grist Mill*, off Shattuck Place, which was built in 1797. The wind-powered mill ground corn for early residents when wind speeds were 20 to 25 miles an hour—or higher with a little reefing of the sails on the huge sweeping arms.

Every summer Friday night, **brass band concerts** unfold in Kate Gould Park on Main Street, a decades-long tradition whose pleasure is undimmed by the thousands who come. People spread out on blankets and lawn chairs and bring their babies, dogs, popcorn, and coolers. Lights dramatize the gleaming white bandstand and snappy red uniforms. The band plays old favorites, inviting the audience to sing along, do the bunny hop, and waltz. These evenings take on a magical quality as dusk falls, with floating clouds of brightly colored balloons and children waving glow-in-the-dark light sticks.

Chatham is one of the rare "walking" towns left on the Cape, a place where you can stroll among the shops and browse the restaurant menus in a pleasant village setting. Restaurants are almost all privately owned—only one franchise eatery is in town—and you will find a wide variety here. To learn the season's dining news, we always stop to chat with the chef/owner at **Amara's Italian Deli and Pastry Shop,** at 637B Main Street, almost hidden on the ground floor behind the CVS drugstore. This bright cafe is redolent with good things baking, and with the aromas of espresso and capuccino. Pastries are irresistible, and the bread is real Italian, with a crunchy bite. Custom-made subs can include the usual or the unusual, such as roasted vegetables and chicken cutlet. An antipasto bar, Sicilian pizza and gelato round out the menu, available every day from May through Columbus Day from 10:00 A.M. to 10:00 P.M.; (508) 945–5777. Amara's faces a large parking lot (with public rest rooms), accessible from Main Street or from Stage Harbor Road, a good place to park while you wander around town.

The screen door slams often with the many arrivals at **Marion's Pie Shop,** a family bakery for more than forty years on the west side of town, at 2022 Main Street (508–432–9439). Everything is made from scratch. Irresistible smells emanate from freshly baked cinnamon rolls and hand-cut doughnuts, cranberry nut and zucchini-pineapple breads, and old-fashioned two-crust pies such as apple, peach, and blueberry. Chicken and clam pies make great take-home dinners.

At the very tip of Chatham, past the lighthouse, you'll find **Monomoy National Wildlife Refuge,** on Morris Island (508–945–0594). Its two barrier islands, North Monomoy Island and South Monomoy Island, were once a single 7-mile-long island that was split in two by the blizzard of 1978. These starkly beautiful islands are splendid spots for birding and hiking. Their wild, windswept terrain includes tidal flats and salt marshes, thickets and dunes, and inspiring ocean vistas from every angle. The sea winds will clear your brain cells thoroughly of any city anxieties. Thousands of birds use the islands as a staging area, and close to three hundred species have been spotted here. The many shorebirds include marbled godwits, piping plovers, oystercatchers, whimbrels, and terns.

The only access to Monomoy is by private boat or guided tour. Two groups lead day trips: the Wellfleet Bay Wildlife Sanctuary (508–349–2615) and the Cape Cod Museum of Natural History (508–896–3867). Wellfleet Bay offers half-day or all-day trips year-round, most frequently in summer, ranging in price from $30 to $65, and $25 for seal cruises. To get a current list of trip dates and prices, write Wellfleet Bay Wildlife Sanctuary, P.O. Box 236, South Wellfleet 02663. The Cape Cod Museum of Natural History runs trips from May through October. A special overnight trip ($130) goes to South Monomoy Island, where you'll sleep in the nineteenth-century lighthouse and keeper's cottage. The price includes the boat ride, dinner and breakfast, and a natural-ist's interpretation. For a current brochure and prices, write the Cape Cod Museum of Natural History, Drawer R, Route 6A, Brewster 02631.

Orleans is certainly not off the beaten path for avian tourists: Close to 300 species visit every year, and more live here as year-round residents. To see many of them, head for Nauset Beach. In June and July, you can visit one of the state's largest colonies of least terns, north of the beach, and west of them is Nauset Marsh and New Island, nesting ground for common terns, American oyster catchers, and black skimmers. Come here in August and September and you will see thousands upon thou-sands of shore birds migrating southward. If you visit in October or November, walk south along the beach to Pochet Island, where you may be rewarded for your long walk with sightings of hawks and owls. Return for a windy walk in the middle of winter to see eiders, scoters, and harlequin ducks.

During beach season, **Nauset Beach,** one of the Cape's finest and longest, charges $8.00 per car ($5.00 on weekends between Memorial Day and mid-June) for all-day parking, but if you are renting a cottage in Orleans, you can get a weekly pass for $25 or a seasonal one for $65. If you are staying elsewhere, a week's parking is $30. Many local lodg-ings have discount coupons for their guests. At the entrance to the beach are rest rooms and changing rooms with showers, as well as a snack bar. You can rent umbrellas here too, half-price after 2:00 P.M. The beach and all facilities are wheelchair accessible; (508) 240–3775.

On the way to the beach you will pass the often-overlooked **Meeting House and Museum** of the Orleans Historical Society, at 3 River Road, where it intersects with Main Street. Among the usual collections of local historical items are a number of Native American stone tools and weapons, and artifacts from a German U-boat attack off Nauset during World War I. Here also are artifacts from the shipwrecked *Sparrowhawk,* which you will have seen if you visited the Pilgrim Hall Museum in Plymouth. The museum is open in July and August on Tuesday, Thursday, and Saturday mornings and Wednesday and Friday afternoons. For off-season hours, which vary, call (508) 240–1329.

The Historical Society also maintains the *Jonathan Young Windmill,* dating from the 1700s, in Cove Park, overlooking Town Cove, not far from the rotary intersection of Routes 6 and 6A.

Orleans is a town that's chockablock with restaurants and shops. Two of the nicest stores, although they're no secrets, are right on Route 6A. The *Birdwatcher's General Store* (508–255–6974) is a bird-watcher's dream-come-true. Never in one store will you see so many birding items, from field guides, binoculars, feeders, and fountains to prints, note cards, paintings, and posters. *Tree's Place* (508–255–1330) is an art gallery and crafts showroom in one. Fine regional paintings are on exhibit, while the shop has some lovely, high-quality goods, including pottery, jewelry, decorator ceramic tiles, art glass, and Russian lacquerware boxes.

For morning coffee and pastries, you can't find anyplace better than the *Cottage Street Bakery,* at Routes 6A and 28. This tiny shop is filled with the warm smells of freshly baked European pastries and gourmet coffee blends. Among its innumerable enticing wares are French pastries, Danish, walnut rye bread, lemon poppyseed muffins, and cranberry scones. An antique Hoosier cabinet displays the bakery's very own cookbook, which you can purchase. Call (508) 255–2821.

Before you leave Orleans, step into the *French Cable Station Museum,* at the corner of Cove Road and Route 28, built in 1890 to house the extension of the transatlantic cable from France to Eastham. A jumble of original equipment lies piled on tables in several rooms, and there are also historic photos of the cable being laid. The curators demonstrate how a cable message was translated from wavy lines to letters. News of the wreck of the paddle steamer *Portland* on the Cape was telegraphed from Orleans to France and then to Boston via New York because all phone lines were down in a winter storm. News of Lindbergh's landing in Paris arrived here first. During World War I, the cable station was guarded by marines because General Pershing's orders were routed from Orleans to France. The museum is open in July and August from 1:00 to 4:00 P.M. daily except Sunday, and weekends in September. Admission is free, but donations are accepted. Call (508) 240–1735.

Main Street in Orleans becomes Rock Harbor Road when it crosses Route 6, and leads to historic **Rock Harbor,** now a habitat for shellfish, birds, and fish, and a place to walk on the sandflats at low tide. But it was once a very busy port for packet ships sailing out of Boston. A ten-ton sloop sailed this route as early as 1808, soon joined by others carrying passengers and freight between the city and the Cape. Here on December 19, 1814, the local militia repulsed a British landing party from the HMS *Newcastle,* whose purpose was to burn the village and its vessels. Rock Harbor is on the Cape Cod bike trail, which uses Rock Harbor Road through this section. You can rent bicycles in Orleans at **Bayside Bikes-n-Boards,** 9 Cove Road (508–240–2323) or from **Orleans Cycle,** 26 Main Street; (508) 255–9115.

Although there are plenty of upscale restaurants in Orleans, fishermen can feel right at home at **Captain Cass Rock Harbor Seafood,** on Rock Harbor Road (no phone), which is open June through October. Strung with buoys and nets, the restaurant looks like an old fishing shack, and you should be able to spill anything on its tables covered with black-and-white-checkered oilcloth or on its battered wooden floor. Lobster rolls ("no filler") are its specialty, along with fish, clam, and scallop plates. The restaurant is open for lunch and dinner.

Thousands of people visit the **Salt Pond Visitors Center of Cape Cod National Seashore** (508–255–3421), and you'll see why when you come. Wall-high windows offer striking vistas of Salt Pond and the surrounding coastline. The museum here is beautifully conceived and presented. There are excellent color photos of many native animals and birds, plus exhibits on such local industries as fishing, cranberrying, and whaling. The bookstore has a wide selection of field guides and natural-history books, and the slide shows about Cape history and geography are well worth watching. Several nature trails lead off from the visitor center. Despite the many visitors, most don't bother to sign up for the great variety of interpretive programs here, held daily in summer. You might follow in the footsteps of Henry David Thoreau, visit some retired lighthouses, or see a shellfishing demonstration. Another tour takes you to the **Captain Edward Penniman House,** an unusually ornate home built in 1867 for a New Bedford whaling captain. Of French Second Empire style, it features a mansard roof, an octagonal cupola, and an arch made of whalebone jaws framing its entrance.

When you see the sign on Route 6 for Wellfleet Center, take a left at the light onto Commercial Street. A short distance down on the left will be a small wooden footbridge crossing a salt marsh. The bridge is known as

*Uncle Tim's Bridge.* It offers a wonderful vista of Wellfleet's coastal scenery: a tidal creek, a wooded rise, and Wellfleet harbor to the south.

Wellfleet is called "the Art Gallery Town" because there are so many *galleries* here, almost two dozen. They're clustered on Main Street or within a few blocks, and so you can make a nice walking tour of them. Artists in every medium are represented, and you'll see the work of nationally known Cape artists as well as foreign artists. A popular tradition on many Saturday nights is attending cocktail party openings at which you can meet the artists. Strolling about to these openings on a warm summer night is a wonderful way to spend the evening. For a guide to the galleries, write the Wellfleet Art Galleries Association, P.O. Box 916, South Wellfleet 02667.

Many people like to top off their gallery tours with dinner at one of the number of excellent and sophisticated—also expensive—restaurants in town. A restaurant that is neither expensive nor sophisticated is the *Bayside Lobster Hutt* (508–349–6333), at the foot of Commercial Street, a 150-year-old former oyster shack on the waterfront. You'll know you're there when you see a man in a dory on the roof hauling up a giant lobster in a net. Service here is cafeteria-style, the floor is concrete, and you sit at communal picnic tables. But you can get some of the best and freshest lobster-in-the-rough you'll ever eat, plus fish-and-chips, fried clams, shrimp, swordfish, and bluefish.

Right across the parking lot from the Bayside Lobster Hutt is a romantic, dessert-only alfresco restaurant called *Just Dessert.* Its white lattice and blue-and-white awnings look out on a sweeping view of sea grass and lagoon and weathered old shipwrecks. With the breeze blowing on a summer evening, dessert here is an experience. Choices range from simple to fancy: ice cream and sundaes, freshly baked hazelnut torte, and tropical lemon cake. The restaurant also serves coffee and pastries in the morning. Call the Bayside Lobster Hutt (508–349–6333) for information.

For breakfast and lunch, a local favorite is *The Lighthouse,* right on Main Street (508–349–3681). The Lighthouse is always busy with customers who know where to find a good and freshly cooked breakfast with good coffee to match, served at comfortable wooden tables.

While you're driving along Main Street, you'll see the pretty blue cupola of the First Congregational Church. In the church steeple is the only *town clock* in the world that strikes on ship's time (four bells, six bells, and eight bells, just as in *Moby-Dick*).

The *Wellfleet Bay Wildlife Sanctuary* (508–349–2615) is one of Mass-

**Bayside Lobster Hutt**

achusetts Audubon's largest and most active. Its thousand acres of pristine salt marsh, woods, fields, and brooks are fine places to wander, on 5 miles of nature trails. The program offerings are rich and of wide appeal. Besides birding and botany walks, there are canoe trips, sunset and whale-watching cruises, and family hikes. A three-hour cruise to Nauset Marsh takes you to the setting of *The Outermost House,* Henry Beston's book about a year spent living alone among the dunes. Nauset Marsh is also home to thousands of shorebirds and Massachusetts's largest tern colony. Hardy souls will love the wintertime cruises from January to April to see harbor and gray seals. Thousands of these playful-looking mammals winter off the Massachusetts coast. Reservations are required. Wellfleet Bay is on West Road, just off Route 6.

*Truro* is the quintessential Outer Cape. You could drive through it without knowing you were here. Rural and remote, Truro is not much more than a stretch of dunes. In the dunes are shacks where solitary writers and artists once sought inspiration, among them Harry Remp and Eugene O'Neill. Cape Cod narrows so much at this point that you can see water on both sides. Some of the Cape's earliest cabin colonies, built in the 1920s and 1930s, still stand in Truro along Route 6A. Truro has the smallest population of any Cape town, only about 1,600. A tiny town center holds little more than a post office and store, the Cobb Library, and the Blacksmith Shop restaurant, once the workplace of Truro's only blacksmith. Not many people come to Truro. And that's how the natives like it.

For a scenic drive, take Depot Road off Route 6A north to Mill Pond Road, which becomes Old County Road. Old County Road's windswept hills and ridges are called "the Hogsbacks" because they looked like animals in a pen to the early settlers. Edward Hopper once had a studio off Old County Road.

Follow Route 6A north again and turn right onto South Highland Road, which will bring you to Lighthouse Road, the entrance to the *Highland Light.* This handsome black-and-white lighthouse is the Cape's oldest, built in 1797 and rebuilt in 1857. An overlook of the beach below will show you the same views that Thoreau described on his visits here in the mid-1800s. Storm erosion threatens Highland Light with toppling right into the sea, and efforts are under way to raise money to move it back from the shoreline.

A newly opened bed-and-breakfast in Truro is also Cape Cod's first vineyard, *South Hollow Vineyards.* Its five green acres were a horse and dairy farm for 150 years—one of the last working farms on the Outer Cape. Arriving here presents a peaceful vista of an 1836 white Federal farmhouse draped by a towering elm tree and surrounded by terraces of grapevines. Guest rooms, decks, and a sunny, flagstone breakfast room of many windows all overlook the vineyards. Innkeepers Judy Wimer and Kathy Gregrow have planted three kinds of French grapes and plan to bottle the wine themselves. Kathy, who grew up on a farm in upstate New York, drives the tractor at planting time. Kathy and Judy have collected many pieces of antique winemaking equipment and placed them around the inn, including a 100-year-old crusher-destemmer, a 150-year-old wine press, and barrels, corkscrews, and bottles. The collection will eventually become a small museum. The house's antique wooden beams and hand-cut nails can still be seen, but rooms are decorated in gorgeously rich colors such as burgundy and deep green, with brass accents and four-posters. For reservations, contact DestINNations, P.O. Box 1173, Osterville 02655–1076; (800) 333–4667 or (508) 428–5600 (doubles $65–$85).

## Righteousness Is Next to . . .

*A plaque on Cornhill Road in Truro commemorates the first theft recorded in Massachusetts, and explains the name of the road. It recounts that Myles Standish and his scouting party, on November 16, 1620, found seed corn that had been buried there by Indians, and they promptly carried off a basketful. Later, they looked for and found similar mounds under which the corn was buried, for a total of about ten bushels. The Pilgrims were glad to have this vital food, but history doesn't mention whether the Indians who had stored it and depended on it were equally pleased.*

"Off the beaten path in Provincetown" is an oxymoron. Summer crowds jam this resort town so densely that people walk twelve abreast on Commercial Street. Still, P'town is a carnival of variety and audacity, its alternative lifestyles and dozens of galleries, boutiques, sophisticated restaurants, nightclubs, and arts offerings serving as a magnet for the masses. There's no other place like it in all of Massachusetts.

Provincetown is farther from the beaten path before Memorial Day and in the glorious fall days of September and October. While some of the lodgings and businesses are open only in the height of summer, many do remain open and are crowd-free in the off-season.

The lively arts scene and live-and-let-live attitude are Provincetown's two key draws, and both are found in abundance along Commercial Street, a long and crowded promenade that hugs the inner shore. On the east end especially are a multitude of galleries, displaying everything from the exquisite to the truly strange. At night, look toward the west end of the street for small clubs and cafes with live music. Performance times and dates vary, and places open and close, so you'll have to rely on local advice and your own explorations. Once we found a small club where we heard some of the best live jazz singing since Ella Fitzgerald. Keep your ears and mind open and you'll probably find something you like.

If the energy required on Commercial Street wears you down, drive out to **Race Point,** which never disappoints. The narrow road out to the lighthouse winds through dunes and hillsides covered with waving grasses and wind-beaten scrub. You can smell the salt heavy in the air and feel the cleansing wind in your face. In any season, no matter what the weather, Race Point is starkly wild and beautiful. Thoreau, who made a walking tour of the Cape in 1849, wrote that "a man may stand there and put all America behind him." So you may.

A look at an aerial photograph of Provincetown and the end of the Cape shows the violence with which the Atlantic Ocean beats this exposed pile of sand. Huge wind-driven mounds of sand lie like gigantic waves about to wash over the eastern beaches. Fortunately for visitors, this violence is less visible from footpath level, where the terrain is a lot more inviting than threatening. These fragile, windblown dunes were once favored places for crude cabins where locals retired in summer.

The best way to appreciate the work of the wind and water is from the air. **Willy's Air Tour** combines the thrill of air exploration with a rare chance to fly in a vintage craft. Willy's 1930 Stinson Detroiter was among the earliest to transport passengers. The big yellow plane has a great wooden propeller and an engine that sticks out the front with all its cylinders showing. Its large windows and its stability make it the perfect way to see the dynamics of the end of the Cape. Climb aboard at Provincetown Municipal Airport, but it's best to make reservations; (508) 487–0240.

Another thing that never disappoints is **whale watching.** Seeing these gentle giants up close is a moving experience—one you'll never forget. Cruises go to Stellwagen Bank, the whales' feeding ground. A number of cruise lines dot the wharves, but the Dolphin Fleet boats are staffed by scientists from the Center for Coastal Studies, experts in whale research. The Dolphin Fleet pioneered whale watching on the East Coast. The scientists have identified and named several hundred humpback whales. Scientist-led cruises are sensitive to the whales' behavior and are less likely to disturb the creatures' feeding or breeding activities. The Dolphin Fleet offers nine cruises a day, from April through October, leaving from MacMillan Wharf. Advance reservations are advised in summer, especially on weekends. Fares are $18 for adults and $15 for children in the summer; they drop by $1.00 in spring and fall. Call (800) 826–9300 or (508) 349–1900.

The hook at the Cape's end forms Provincetown Bay, sheltered from the rougher waters. *Flyer's Boat Rental, Inc,* at 131–A Commercial Street, on the western end near the Coast Guard wharf, has a wide range of craft to get you out onto its waters. Our favorite is the plastic sea kayak, of basic design. It's a wonderful way to scout along the harbor, skim the beaches, and explore the outer reaches of the sandy arm as far as the lighthouse. Bear in mind that you should wear a bathing suit, since these little kayaks have self-draining holes in the hull and you will get wet. The cost is $25 a half day, $40 a day. Flyer's also has Sunfish, 16-foot powered skiffs, and traditional and racing sailboats. Sailing lessons are also available; (508) 487–0898 or (800) 750–0898.

The terrain at the end of the Cape is essentially flat, with an occasional hillock rising no more than 20 feet or so. A landscape like that begs to be explored by bicycle, even for those who don't cycle regularly. *Provincetown Bikes* has two locations, one at 42 Bradford Street and the other at 306 Commercial Street; (508) 487–8294. The shops can fix you up with good broad-tired bikes that work well in the sand, and also have helmets and other gear—and can service your own bike if you brought one. *Arnold's,* 329 Commercial Street, (508–487–0844) also has bikes for rent.

Cycle out to *Herring Cove Beach* to pick up the bike trail on the north end of the parking lot. It will take you along Race Point, and you can follow it along the shore through the dunes to Race Point Road. Go to the end of the road and the beach, then return to town either by the same route or via Race Point Road, Conwell Street, Arch Street, and Commercial Street.

That tall tower you've been seeing across the bay during your travels on the Cape is the *Pilgrim Monument and Provincetown Museum,* a tribute to the Pilgrims, who actually landed first in Provincetown in November 1620, not in Plymouth. Dedicated in 1910, the monument is the tallest all-granite structure in the United States, at 252 feet tall. You can climb to the top for an unparalleled view of Cape Cod and the distant Boston skyline. Outside the monument are seven acres of grounds, where you may bring a picnic. Adjacent to its base is a museum with exhibits about the Pilgrims, the *Mayflower,* and Provincetown's early fishing and whaling history, including a captain's cabin from a whaling ship. The museum also holds specimens of birds and polar bears brought back by Admiral Donald MacMillan, for whom MacMillan Wharf is named. To get to the monument, take the Shankpainter Road exit from Route 6, make an immediate left, and then take the next right onto High Pole Hill. The monument is open daily from 9:00 A.M. to 9:00 P.M. July through September, and from 9:00 A.M. to 5:00 P.M. April through June. Admission is $5.00 for adults and teens and $3.00 for children over four. Call (800) 247–1620 or (508) 487–1310.

You can learn more about Provincetown history at the *Provincetown Heritage Museum,* at 356 Commercial Street. Housed in a former Methodist church built in 1860, the Heritage Museum has varied exhibits on Provincetown maritime, artistic, and literary history, including a model of the famous fishing schooner *Rose Dorothea,* fishing artifacts, and paintings by many artists who worked in Provincetown. There's also a re-creation of the dune shack used by poet Harry Kemp. The museum is open from 10:00 A.M. to 6:00 P.M. daily. Admission is $3.00 over age 12; call (508) 487–7098.

Beachcombers should head for *Long Point,* a low spit of sandy beaches and dunes. This desolate wind- and sea-whipped place was part of the town settlement at one time until its residents had a better idea and floated their houses across the harbor to safer moorings in the present town. You can catch a water shuttle to Long Point from Flyer's Boat Rental or you can walk, following Commercial Street along the waterfront to the end, then crossing the stone breakwater that protects the sensitive marshlands at the inside corner of the harbor. The beach here offers the best chance to find handsome small multicolored seashells and to watch the many varieties of seabirds that live on and migrate through these shores.

P'town is a restaurant mecca, and some of the Cape's finest eateries are here. There is such a wide choice that it's impossible to single out the most remarkable ones. Here are a couple of personal favorites.

*Ciro and Sal's,* at 4 Kiley Court, off 430 Commercial Street (508–487–0049), is a wonderful bastion from the early days of P'town's unknown beginnings as an artists' colony. Founded by two artists in the early 1950s, Ciro and Sal's was opened in a dirt-floor basement down an alley, with nail kegs for seats, a stove found at the town dump, and fishermen and artists as its first customers. Today, you're more likely to find tourists in the majority, but the rough wooden beams hung with straw-covered Chianti bottles remain the same, as does the excellent Italian cuisine. It opens at 6:00 P.M., and you'll need a reservation.

A terrific breakfast spot is the *Cafe Edwige,* at 333 Commercial Street (508–487–2008). It's an airy, upstairs loft space with light woods and paintings by local artists. Creative pancakes and omelettes are specialties, as are pastries and fruit and yogurt dishes.

# Martha's Vineyard

Closer to the mainland than Nantucket, Martha's Vineyard is only forty-five minutes by ferry from Woods Hole. For information, call the Woods Hole, Martha's Vineyard, and Nantucket Steamship Authority (508–771–4000), which services both islands. (Summer car reservations must be made months in advance.)

The ferry fare to Martha's Vineyard from Woods Hole is $5.00 for adults, $2.50 for children, $3.00 for bikes and $47 for a car. Or you can reach the island at Oak Bluffs from New Bedford via the passenger ferry *Scha-monchi,* which makes four crossings a day from mid-May to mid-October. The fares are higher—$17 for an adult—than on the Steamship Authority ferry from Woods Hole, but if you are traveling from the Providence or southern Massachusetts areas, it saves a lot of driving. Once on the island, you can rent a bike at any of a number of places close to either ferry landing, or take a Yellow Line bus on its circuit from Vineyard Haven to Oak Bluffs and Edgartown, via the beach road.

The mass of tourists descend on Vineyard Haven, where the Woods Hole ferry docks. They also converge on Oak Bluffs, to see the Flying Horses Carousel—the nation's oldest—the nineteenth-century gingerbread cottages, and the open-air Methodist Tabernacle. The rest of the island is generally less crowded. Shuttle buses service Martha's Vineyard in summer. If you have a sturdy pair of legs, you can bike about—the island is 20 miles long and 10 miles wide.

A short distance from the ferry terminal is an island institution, the **Black Dog Tavern,** at Beach Street Extension (508–693–9223), with a seaside porch dining room. Local seafood dishes, meats, and freshly baked breads and desserts from its own bakery are offered.

Off the southeast corner of Martha's Vineyard, the island of **Chappaquiddick** embraces some of the remotest and wildest territory on the island, reachable only by four-wheel drive. From Edgartown, take the **Chappy On-Time Ferry,** which holds only three or four cars and takes less than two minutes to cross the inlet. A few miles down the Chappaquiddick Road, the second dirt road you come to forks left. Follow it, and you'll find **Mytoi,** a Japanese-style garden of several acres with a small pond, wooden footbridge, and several acres of blooming plants and trees nestled in a pine grove. Mytoi is a Trustees of Reservation property; admission is free.

Continuing down the Chappaquiddick Road to School Road and then to Wasque Road brings you to **Wasque Reservation,** a two-hundred-acre reserve owned by the Trustees of Reservations. Wasque edges the Atlantic in a landscape of heath and dunes. There's a gatehouse and a lot where you can park and walk to the beach and nature trails. Hooking four miles northward from Wasque, **Cape Poge** is a wind-ripped barrier beach reachable only with a four-wheel drive vehicle. At its tip stands the Cape Poge Light. Admission to Wasque costs $3.00 per car and $3.00 per pedestrian or bicyclist. For information, call (508) 693–7662.

For more places to walk and enjoy the quiet natural areas of the island, pick up a copy of *Vineyard Visitor,* a free publication of the *Martha's Vineyard Times.* A handy pullout centerfold shows individual trail maps for 14 walking paths located on Land Bank properties throughout the island.

Tiny downtown Edgartown is crammed with resort amenities: boutiques, restaurants, and ice-cream stands. Yet just two blocks up, the resort roar quiets to streets of white sea captains' houses with neat green or black shutters and white picket fences.

Away from the crush of the village yet close enough to walk to is the **Captain Dexter House,** a sea captain's house built in the 1840s that is now a seventeen-room inn. This large home is spacious and rambling, with long halls leading to guest rooms everywhere: upstairs, down-stairs, in a side wing, off the parlor. All are warmly decorated with flowered wallpapers, canopied four-posters, and antiques. Much of the house is still intact: paneled slate blue wainscoting, a Rumford-design marble fireplace, and working fireplaces in the guest rooms. There's lots of space to choose from for relaxing, from a wicker-furnished sitting room to a formal parlor with matching sofas and the handsome dining room where breakfast is served. Breakfast features such home-baked goodies as lemon bread and coffee cake, lots of fresh fruits, orange juice, and coffee. For reservations, contact DestINNations, P.O. Box 1173, Osterville 02655–1076; (800) 333–4667 or (508) 428–5600 (doubles $65–$180).

As you tour Martha's Vineyard, it may surprise you to see a white-tailed deer or a wild turkey cross the road. But the island is a great haven for wildlife, and one of its most stunning achievements is the osprey-nesting program. You can see the 40-foot poles erected as nesting platforms for these huge birds at the *Felix Neck Wildlife Sanctuary* (508–627–4850) on the Edgartown–Vineyard Haven Road. From two breeding pairs in 1971, their numbers had grown by 1990 to almost eighty pairs; in 1989 the osprey was removed from the list of endangered species, the first one in Massachusetts removed because of recovery. There's also a small museum here as well as nature trails.

Another place to enjoy the out-of-doors—and a more-remote pre-serve—is *Cedar Tree Neck.* A car-disabling dirt road leads to a tiny parking lot where a short wooded trail takes you to the beach. An almost-constant wind has twisted the trees into intriguingly blasted-looking shapes. Finally you come upon a peaceful vista of sandy beach, dunes, and bayberry circling a lagoon—especially nice at sunset. Take Indian Hill Road off State Road several miles west of Vineyard Haven.

Quintessential Martha's Vineyard is expressed by the *Field Gallery,* an art gallery in a field in the center of West Tisbury. Some twenty larger-than-life dancing white figures inhabit the lawn, looking slightly Picas-soesque with their thick, rounded limbs and curving forms. There are a massive chicken with a tiny head, a figure blowing a trumpet, a hatted figure with a little dog, and a colonial figure on horseback. The sculptures are the work of island artist Tom Maley, who exhibits the work of others in the adjacent gallery. The Field Gallery is such an island institution that people like to get married here.

Also in West Tisbury, on Stoney Hill Road, is *Chicama Vineyards,* which takes advantage of the island's unique warm autumn and mild winter to grow European wine grapes. You can take a tour in the afternoon from Memorial Day to Columbus Day, or visit the shop for a tasting year-round. Days and hours vary widely with the season, so it's best to call ahead or pick up the vineyard's brochure on the boat; (508) 693–0309.

A surprising amount of Martha's Vineyard is farmland. Goats, sheep, cows, vegetables, and fruits are husbanded by entrepreneurs who like island living as much as their independence. Llamas and miniature donkeys are raised at *Takemmy Farm* (508-693-2486), one of only a handful of llama farms in New England, on State Road in Vineyard Haven. The farm also produces and sells honey, mulch, hay, and yarn, and offers animal visits from 1:00 to 5:00 P.M. daily except Sunday; the charge is $3.00 per carload.

The *Allen Farm* on South Road in Chilmark has been a family farm since the seventeenth century, and Allens still run it, these days keeping a herd of some 150 New Zealand sheep. The wool goes into gorgeous hand-knit sweaters of a comforting weight, as well as scarves, hats, blankets, and shawls—all sold in a sunny gift shop behind a neat stone wall. Call (508) 645–9064.

The road to *Menemsha* winds through field and forest and ends abruptly at a stone wall that could pitch you right into the sea. In this miniature fishing village with a tiny harbor are more boats than houses. The village has a post office, a fish market, a restaurant, and a gas station, and that's about it. A small beach facing due west is a popular spot for celebrating the sunset, one of the few places on the East Coast where the sun sinks into the sea. (Key West, stand aside.)

While busloads of tourists tramp along the path to the *Gay Head Cliffs,* these spectacular white-chalk cliffs should not be missed. They run for 1 mile along the coast, with a dramatic backdrop of russet-colored beach vegetation and the stout, handsome brick spire of the Gay Head Light. The cliffs were the country's first registered National Natural Landmark.

Passengers arriving from New Bedford will disembark in Vineyard Haven, a tad more down-to-earth than the somewhat-precious Oak Bluffs. A right turn from the landing leads to an island institution, *The Scottish Bakehouse.* The bakery offers breakfast, lunch, or teatime goodies with a Highland flavor, including scones, buttery shortbread, and meatpies, along with fresh-baked bread and other baked goods. It's open Thursday through Tuesday from 8:00 A.M. to 5:00 P.M., at 977 State Road; (508) 693–1873.

# Nantucket

N antucket is somehow even more an island than Martha's Vineyard. Isolated 20 or so miles at sea, it's two and a half hours by ferry from the mainland. If you get stranded by a winter gale (and people do), you're really stranded. Because of its flat terrain and smaller size—16 miles long by 6 miles wide—the island is manageable on a bike, which will get you outside the crowded town of Nantucket. There are also buses and taxis.

You can bring your own bike on the ferry or rent one when you arrive from Young's Bicycle Shop at 6 Broad Street; (508) 228–1151. You can also get a free map here with streets and cycling paths. Be sure to observe the one-way street signs, since you are considered a vehicle when on two wheels, and will be ticketed. If you must go the wrong way, do it as a pedestrian. Cobblestones make some streets in town uncomfortable for road bikes.

It's a lot faster to fly to Nantucket than to take the ferry: a twenty-minute flight from Hyannis. Cape Air flies more than ten times a day to Nantucket, as well as to Martha's Vineyard and Boston, and from Boston to Provincetown. Call (800) 352–0712 for reservations and departure times. The planes are small enough for a baby to offer his bottle to the pilot, but the oversea route gives you an aerial view of Nantucket that shows what is meant by "the little gray lady of the sea." From the air, all the houses look gray against the subdued landscape of heathered moors.

Maria Mitchell was the nation's first woman astronomer. The king of Denmark awarded her a gold medal in 1847 when she discovered a comet. She was born in a typical Quaker house built in 1790, a two-story dwelling with weathered shingles on Vestal Street. Now it's the *Maria Mitchell Science Center and Birthplace.* The small rooms of the family home have plain plaster walls and some Mitchell family memorabilia. Adjacent to the birthplace are a science library and natural-history museum containing native flora and fauna and offering nature walks; in summer, Wednesday nights are "star nights" at the nearby Loines Observatory. The birthplace and museum are open from 10:00 A.M. to 4:00 P.M. Tuesday through Saturday, mid-June through August. Admission is $3.00 for adults and $1.50 for children. (A pass covering the birthplace and the museum is available for $5.00 for adults and $2.00 for children.) Call (508) 228–9198.

An often-overlooked spot a short distance from town is the *Nantucket Lifesaving Museum,* a replica of the 1874 lifesaving station. Years ago, shoal-bound Nantucket harvested so many wrecks that it was called "the Graveyard of the Atlantic." A newspaper clipping recounts the dramatic 1829 rescue of the crew of the *H. P. Kirkham,* 15 miles offshore in a winter storm. Sepia-toned old photos show other wrecks and a horse-drawn lifeboat on the beach. Quarter-boards hang on the walls—ships' wooden nameplates with gold letters and elaborately carved floral designs. The museum is 2.5 miles out on Polpis Road, on the left by a marsh. It's easy to miss by car, but on a bike you'll quickly spot the white stone marker with the museum's name at the entrance. Hours are 9:30 A.M. to 4:30 P.M. daily, June 15 to September 15. Entrance costs $1.50.

Nantucket Harbor is enclosed by a giant fishhook of sand that encompasses some 18 miles of shoreline, the ***Coskata-Coatue Wildlife Refuge.*** These miles and miles of barrier beach are open country of salt marsh and tidal creeks, pine and holly, and clam flats. Coskata-Coatue is home to a vast array of wildlife and birds, among them snowy owls, eiders, herons, and egrets. Rare and endangered least terns and piping plovers nest on the beach. The refuge is much favored for surf casting, picnicking, and bird-watching. You can drive to its entrance out the Wauwinet Road, but from there you'll either have to walk or use four-wheel drive. From the gatehouse, it's a 1-mile hike to the beach. For information, call (508) 228–0006.

Despite this island's tiny size, fully one-third of it has been set aside as open space by the Nantucket Conservation Foundation and the Nantucket Land Bank. Their actions ensure that the island's fragile beauty will be protected from the heavy pressures of tourism and development. One such property is ***Sanford Farm,*** a great place for hiking, out on Madaket Road. Out Polpis Road, just past the Wauwinet Road turnoff, is the ***Windswept Cranberry Bog,*** a small working bog where you can watch the harvest in season. For a map of land bank properties, write the Nantucket Land Bank Commission, 18 Broad Street, Nantucket 02554, or call (508) 228–7240. The Nantucket Conservation Foundation, at 118 Cliff Road, Nantucket 02554 (508–228–2884), sells a guide to its properties for $3.00.

A scattering of quaint, interesting villages dots the island. Siasconset, called *'Sconset* for short, began as a fishing village of one-room shacks in the seventeenth century. Sconset's tiny, weathered cottages cluster together like a dollhouse village, festooned with rambling roses—a pretty sight in summer. There's a nice public beach but few conveniences besides a gas station, market, and post office. Nonetheless, the island's best restaurant, Chanticleer (508–257–6231), is here, serving classic French cuisine in a rose-covered cottage. (It's closed in winter.)

Nantucket has dozens of restaurants and, in general, better restaurants than Martha's Vineyard. In Nantucket town, there's a restaurant on every block, and the only hard part is choosing one. Here are a few you might try.

The **Brotherhood of Thieves,** at 23 Broad Street (no phone), has a tavernlike atmosphere, with dark woods, romantic lighting, and the warmth of a fireplace. People willingly stand in line for its burgers, sandwiches almost too thick to eat, and curly shoestring fries, served on pewter plates. At dinner there are grilled fish dishes and steaks as well.

Far fewer people think to dine just outside the village, despite the fact that it is much easier to get a table and only a few minutes away by cab. An excellent choice at 2 Bayberry Court in Nantucket Commons is the **Caffee Bella Vista,** an intimate Italian restaurant with a welcoming warm pink decor. Its terra-cotta tiled floors, outdoor patio, and trompe l'oeil rose trellises put you in a continental frame of mind for the cuisine to follow. Appetizers start you off, with deep-fried calamari or oysters Perrone, among other choices. Entrees include linguini alla carbonara, or alla vongole, fettuccine Alfredo, vitello alla Milanese, and scampi alla griglia. Meals are complemented by freshly baked bread with an olive paste spread, fresh salads, and homemade soups. Desserts include tiramisu and chocolate-chip cannoli. For reservations, call (508) 228–8766.

For a quick coffee and snack in town, stop into the **Espresso Cafe,** at 40 Main Street (508–228–6930), where a self-service counter dispenses great home baked cookies, breads, and desserts to go, with espresso and cappuccino. There's also a good selection of homemade soups and unusual sandwiches, such as grilled gouda with apple chutney on egg-dipped bread. In season, you can sit out on the garden patio.

While you're on Nantucket, you'll most likely want to tour the island's excellent bike paths. One inn that includes a fleet of blue bicycles with its guest room rates is the inn at **Eighteen Gardner Street,** an 1835 sea captain's house at a quiet remove from the noise of downtown. The Colonial-style house has weathered shingles, a friendship staircase, and a rooftop balcony. Inside are high-ceilinged rooms with raised paneling, tall windows, and wide pine floors, all comfortably furnished with antiques, period reproductions, and lots of mahogany and Oriental-style rugs. The guest rooms feature carved four-posters, and some have working fireplaces. Innkeeper Roger Schmidt is a fount of knowledge about his island and can tell you where to take your children to feed the ducks, where to find a small and hidden beach, and how to shop Nantucket's expensive boutiques in the off-season. Breakfast here is far better than average, particularly the apple sweetcakes: a hot pancake with fresh apple compote in the middle (also made with blueberries or strawberries). For reservations, contact DestINNations, P.O. Box 1173, Osterville 02655–1076; (800) 333–4667 or (508) 428–5600 (double $65–$300).

To experience the setting in which successful island captains and shipbuilders lived a century and a half ago, book into the **Jared Coffin House,** at 29 Broad Street, a short walk straight ahead from the ferry landing. The main house has been supplemented by several others of equal (or greater) architectural and historic distinction, where you will find fine paneling, antiques, large rooms, and the hospitable touch of luxury. Those traveling alone will appreciate the modestly priced single rooms here, a rarity in most inns; (508) 228–2405 or (800) 248–2405 or through DestINNations at (800) 333–4667.

**MORE PLACES TO STAY ON CAPE COD AND THE ISLANDS**

*The Dan'l Webster Inn,*
149 Main Street,
Sandwich 02563;
(508) 888–3622 or
(800) 444–3566.
A modern inn with traditional furnishings—canopy beds, wing chairs, fireplaces.

*The Belfry Inne,*
8 Jarves Street,
Sandwich 02563;
through DestINNations at
(800) 333–4667.
A stunningly maintained Victorian where individual features—balconies, deep tubs, fireplaces, skylights—make each room unique.

*Shoreway Acres Resort Inn,*
Shore Street,
Falmouth 02541–0907;
(508) 540–3000 or
(800) 352–7100,
fax (508) 540–9337.
Refreshingly priced for the Cape, with rooms under $100 even in high season, under $50 off season, often including Continental breakfast.

*Admiralty Inn,*
51 Teaticket Highway
(Route 28),
Falmouth 02541;
(508) 548–4240 or
(800) 341–5700,
fax (508) 457–0535.
You'll have to drive (or bike) to town or beach, but it's a good base with high-season motel rooms around $100.

*The Wedgewood Inn,*
83 Main Street (Route 6A),
Yarmouthport;
(508) 362–5157 or
through DestINNations at
(800) 333–4667.
An 1812 Greek Revival-style inn, with Federal accents, it has working fireplaces in most rooms, canopy beds, antique furnishings, and thoughtful touches.

*Blueberry Manor,*
438 Main Street
(Route 6A),
Yarmouthport; through
DestINNations at
(800) 333–4667.
A classic 1700s captain's house "modernized" in the following century, furnished in antiques, with rooms from under $100 to $150.

For bed-and-breakfast lodgings in Orleans, contact Orleans Bed & Breakfast Associates; (508) 255–3824, representing more than sixty locations.

**The Whalewalk Inn,**
220 Bridge Road,
Eastham;
(508) 255–0617.
Upscale property with
country antiques, fine
linens, and soft colors, and
a garden where you can
breakfast in the summer.

**The Over Look Inn,**
3085 County Road
(Route 6),
Eastham;
(508) 255–1886 or
(800) 356–1121
or through DestINNations
at (800) 333–4667.
An eccentric Victorian
mansion with Scottish
breakfasts and great
gardens; rates begin
under $100.

**Provincetown Inn,**
1 Commercial Street,
Provincetown 02657;
(508) 487–9500 or
(800) 924–5388.
It may look tired from the
outside, but its hospitable
owners are not. At the end
of town, it's away from the
crowds and within walking
distance of the lighthouse.

**The Ship's Inn,**
18 Kennebec Avenue,
Oak Bluffs,
Martha's Vineyard 02557;
(508) 693–2760.
Close to the ferry landing,
with private baths and
bright rooms, some with
private entrances, at
$60–$145 in summer.

**The Look Inn,**
13 Look Street,
Vineyard Haven 02568;
(508) 693–6893.
In a restored farmhouse
dating to 1806, this B&B is
casual, with shared baths
and Continental breakfasts
at $125 per room in
summer.

**The Pineapple Inn,**
10 Hussey Street,
Nantucket;
through DestINNations at
(800) 333–4667.
A captain's mansion built
in 1838 and furnished with
period antiques, marble
baths, and goosedown
comforters.

**MORE PLACES TO EAT
ON CAPE COD AND
THE ISLANDS**

**Marina's Eatery,**
67 Thad Ellis Road,
Brewster.
Three meals a day in high
season, only dinner the rest
of the year, in what may be
the Cape's only Greek
restaurant;
(508) 896–4457.

**The Sea Grille,**
31 Sea Street,
Harwichport;
(508) 432–4745.
Very contemporary Ameri-
can cuisine, inventive and
quite reasonably priced for
its quality, with entrees at
$13–$22.

**Andiamo Cafe,**
2653 Main Street
(Route 28),
South Chatham;
(508) 432–1807.
Casual evening dining with
an Italian/European menu.

**Vining's Bistro,**
upstairs in the Wheeler
Building,
595 Main Street,
Chatham;
(508) 945–5033.
Imaginative dinners with
excellent salads, wood-
grilled chicken, and
sauteed vegetable and
pasta combinations. Dinner
only, from 5:30 P.M.

**Pate's Restaurant,**
1260 Route 28,
Chatham (toward
Barnstable);
(508) 945–9777.
The lamb chops, cooked
over an open-hearth grill,
are outstanding, as is the
Caesar salad; open daily
from 5:30 P.M.

**The Cheese Corner,**
56 Main Street,
Orleans;
(508) 255–1699.
Sandwiches on good bread,
along with soups, chowder,
and salads to eat there or
carry out.

**Martin House,**
157 Commercial Street,
Provincetown;
(508) 487–1327.
Don't be misled by the
antiquity of the house;
the food is as up-to-date
as you'll find. Entrees
from $16.

**The Boatslip,**
161 Commercial Street,
Provincetown;
(508) 487–4200.
Informal with a good
seafood selection and
accommodating staff.

**Harry's Homemade
Ice Cream,**
on the pier,
Provincetown.
The name says it all—
except how good the ice
cream is.

**Zapotec,**
Kennebec Avenue,
Oak Bluffs,
Martha's Vineyard;
(508) 693–6800.
Southwestern and Mexican
dishes blend with innova
tive combos in the South-
west style. Most entrees are
$15–$16; children's menu
at $6.00.

**The SeaGrille,**
45 Sparks Avenue,
Nantucket;
(508) 325–5700.
Known for its Nantucket
bouillabaisse and other
seafood dishes, moderately
priced.

WORTH SEEING ON CAPE
COD AND THE ISLANDS

**Sandwich Glass Museum,**
Route 130,
Sandwich;
(508) 888–0251.
Demonstrations of glass
production and a collection
of the famous Sandwich
glass made here in the
1800s.

**Heritage Plantation,**
Grove and Pine streets,
Sandwich; (508) 888–3300.
A museum village of Amer-
icana, including a Shaker
barn, carousel, antique
cars, and military displays.

**Whaling Museum,**
Broad Street,
Nantucket;
(508) 228–1736.
The lifeblood of the island
was whaling, and it was
this industry that built the
fine homes you see here;
the museum chronicles this
rich past.

**Cruises, whale watching,**
and **fishing** trips aboard
any number of boats,
including:

- Hyannis Whale Watcher
  Cruises, Barnstable Harbor; (508) 362–6088 or
  (800) 287–0374.

- The schooner *Freya*,
  Northside Marina, East
  Dennis; (508) 385–4399.

- Hyannisport Harbor
  Cruises, Ocean Street
  Dock, Hyannis;
  (508) 778–2600.

- Cape Cod Canal Cruises,
  Town Pier, Onset Center;
  (508) 295–3883.

TO LEARN MORE ABOUT
CAPE COD AND THE ISLANDS

Cape Cod Chamber of
Commerce,
P.O. Box 1001,
Hyannis 02664–1001;
(508) 362–3225.

Falmouth Chamber of
Commerce,
20 Academy Lane;
(508) 548–8500 or
(800) 526–8532,
Web site www.falmouth–
capecod.com.

Martha's Vineyard
Chamber of Commerce,
Beach Road,
P.O. Box 1698,
Vineyard Haven 02568;
(508) 693–0085

Nantucket Island
Chamber of Commerce,
Pacific Club Building,
Nantucket 02554;
(508) 228–1700.

Orleans Chamber
of Commerce;
(508) 255–1386 or
(800) 865–1386,
E–mail
capecod–orleans.com,
Web site
www.capecod–orleans.com.

Provincetown Chamber of
Commerce,
307 Commercial Street;
(508) 487–3424,
fax (508) 487–8966,
Web site www.ptowncham-
ber.com, E-mail:
info@ptownchamber.com.

# Southeastern Massachusetts

Southeastern Massachusetts, or Bristol County, holds some of the prettiest and most unspoiled territory in the state. Tucked into a corner between Rhode Island and Plymouth, it encompasses miles and miles of farmland, where quiet cornfields line both sides of the road. Small rural towns like Dighton, Rehoboth, and Berkley appear as little surprises here and there.

The coastal villages east of New Bedford are picturesque gems. Founded mostly by shipbuilders, they're proud of their history and have preserved it well. These villages became favored summer resorts for residents of New York and Boston, among them Oliver Wendell Holmes, who summered in Mattapoisett. In Marion, you can still see the great Victorian summer homes erected along a long waterfront avenue, with broad acres of lawns.

The most high-profile cities are Fall River and New Bedford. Both have prestigious pasts. Fall River led the world in textile production in the nineteenth century, and many of its old mill buildings now serve as offices and shops. New Bedford was one of the greatest whaling ports in the world and today has a lingering flavor of whaling's heyday in its historic district's cobblestoned streets and gas-style lamps.

## Northern Bristol County

As you walk or drive about North Easton, it's a little startling to see Gothic behemoths of stone, complete with gargoyles, looming from every corner. Altogether, there are five **buildings designed by Henry Hobson Richardson,** as well as nine landscapings by Frederick Law Olmsted, three Augustus Saint-Gaudens sculptures, two John La Farge stained-glass windows, and three National Historic districts—such wealth that architects come from Chicago and Australia just to see it.

How did it happen? It all goes back to Oliver Ames, who founded the world's largest shovel company here in the early 1800s. By 1850, more than 60 percent of all the world's shovels were Ames shovels. During the

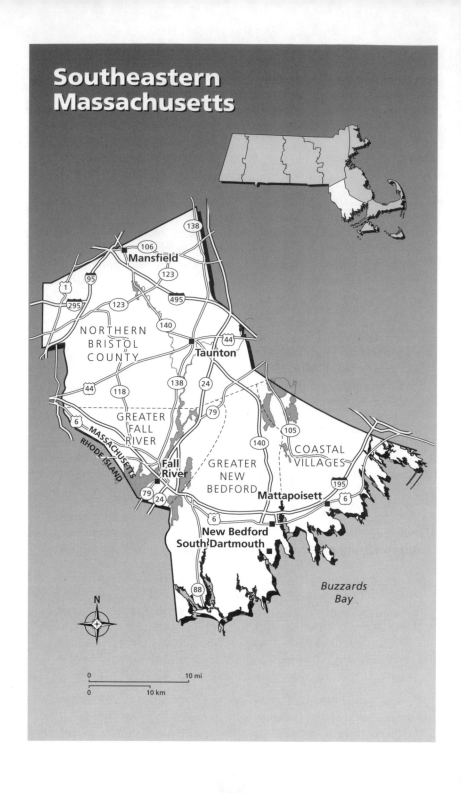

# Southeastern Massachusetts

Mansfield

NORTHERN
BRISTOL
COUNTY

Taunton

GREATER
FALL
RIVER

MASSACHUSETTS
RHODE ISLAND

Fall
River

GREATER
NEW
BEDFORD

COASTAL
VILLAGES

Mattapoisett

New Bedford
South Dartmouth

Buzzards
Bay

N

0          10 mi
0          10 km

Civil War, President Lincoln personally asked Oliver Ames to supply the Union army with his shovels. Ames's descendants subsequently shoveled the profits into elaborate mansions and civic gifts, commissioning Richardson. One such building is the **Old Colony Railroad Station,** on Mechanic Street, which serves as a town history museum. Here you can get a walking/driving–tour map. The towering **Oakes Ames Memorial Hall** and the **Oliver Ames Free Library** on Center Street are also HHR creations. Besides these larger structures, Richardson designed the stone **Gate Lodge** and shingled **Gardener's Cottage.** The museum is open from 2:00 to 4:00 P.M. the second Sunday of every month. For information, write the Easton Historical Society, P.O. Box 3, North Easton 02356, or call the curator at (508) 238–3143.

Across the banks of the Taunton River to the east is a large rock with ancient inscriptions on it—a curiosity whose origins have mystified scientists for three centuries. It's displayed under glass in a small, white pavilion in **Dighton Rock State Park** in Berkley. The faded characters are definitely there, kind of pointy and hieroglyphic-looking. But who wrote them? More than twenty theories have been advanced. The front-runners, explained in large panels, are that the marks originated from American Indians, Phoenicians, Vikings, or Portuguese explorers. The park overlooks the Taunton River, with picnic tables in the shade. It is open from 8:00 A.M. to 6:00 P.M. daily in the summer; call (508) 644–5522. To get to there, take exit 10 from Route 24 and follow the signs.

Hidden away in Attleboro is a wonderful family destination called **Capron Park Zoo.** The zoo here is small, but it has some exotic animals from Asia, Africa, Australia, and New Zealand. A small rain-forest exhibit is complete with waterfall, artificial fog, and recorded jungle sounds. There's a playground for the kids, green lawns with picnic tables, and a lovely rose garden. The park is on Route 123 off Interstate 95 at exit 3. It's open from 10:00 A.M. to 4:00 P.M. weekdays and from 10:00 A.M. to 5:30 P.M. weekends. Admission is $2.00 for adults and 50 cents for visitors ages twelve to eighteen; (508) 222–3047.

# *Greater Fall River*

Although it's one of the outstanding maritime attractions of New England's coast, we've never had to stand in line to see any of the ships in **Battleship Cove.** The showpiece is the battleship USS *Massachusetts,* sister ship to the USS *Arizona,* and once home to 2,300 servicemen. You can tour the ship and get lost quite easily—it's longer than two football fields and as tall as a nine-story building—and stop for a cheeseburger, sandwich, or fish and chips in the Officer's Ward-room restaurant. The ship, scheduled for scrapping in 1962, was saved by its former crew members as the state's memorial to those who lost their lives in World War II. Also in the cove are a destroyer, a submarine (contrast the cramped quarters here with those on the huge battleship), a Japanese "special attack" boat, a "Huey" helicopter from the Vietnam War, and two PT boats; (508) 678–1100 or (800) 533–3194.

Fall River lost its lead as a textile producer to low-cost southern labor. The story of the city's great rise and fall in prosperity is told at the **Fall River Heritage State Park,** designed to look like an old mill in an eight-acre waterfront setting. From a farm village, the city grew rapidly to more than a hundred mills, and production easily outstripped that of competitors Lawrence and Lowell. Poignant black-and-white pho-tographs show the immigrant mill workers, many of whom were chil-dren. A slide show tells the moving history of the many ethnic groups who powered the mills. The park is at 200 Davol Street West, next to Battleship Cove. It is open from 9:00 A.M. to 8:00 P.M. daily from the first Sunday in May through the first Sunday in November. Winter hours are 10:00 A.M. to 4:00 P.M. daily. Call (508) 675–5759.

One block away from the Heritage Park is the **Marine Museum at Fall River.** In its heyday, Fall River was a major port of call for steamship liners on the Fall River Line, which operated from 1847 to 1937. Float-ing palaces with every luxury onboard carried vacationers from New York and Boston. On view in this museum are many mementos of this age, including steamship china and chairs and a chandelier. A 28-foot model of the *Titanic* was used in the 1952 movie about the disaster. There are also *Titanic* artifacts and memorabilia. The museum is at 70 Water Street. Summer hours are 9:00 A.M. to 5:00 P.M. Monday through Friday and noon to 5:00 P.M. weekends. In winter, hours are 9:00 A.M. to 4:00 P.M. Wednesday through Friday and noon to 4:00 P.M. weekends. Tickets cost $4.00 for adults, $3.50 for seniors, and $3.00 for children. Call (508) 674–3533.

Among the many ethnic groups of mill workers were large waves of Portuguese and Polish, who left a lasting imprint on the city. The Por-tuguese have a home-front stronghold on **Columbia Street,** complete with eight-sided cobblestones and black iron lampposts. Old women in black with lace mantillas walk along with bowed heads; laundry hangs between the triple-decker houses, and the street is redolent with Por-tuguese bakeries, fish markets, coffee shops, and restaurants. The heart

# SOUTHEASTERN MASSACHUSETTS

**ANNUAL EVENTS IN SOUTHEASTERN MASSACHUSETTS**

**Early May**
*Annual Maritime Heritage Festival,* New Bedford, includes classes on boat building, knotwork, and even the carving of figureheads; (508) 997–0046.

**Early August**
*Fall River Celebrates America,* with a food fair, fireworks, and a parade of ships; (508) 676–8226.

of the street is *Chaves Market* (508–672–7821), where almost every customer speaks in the lilting tones of Portuguese. You can buy almost anything Portuguese here: octopus, conch shells, chourico, sugar-coated almonds, *vinho verde,* Portuguese cookies and sweet bread, paella pans, and porcelain samovars and centerpieces.

You could not find a more low-key place to get good Polish food than the **Ukrainian Home** restaurant (popularly called "the Uke"). Situated downstairs in a beat-up old yellow-brick building that saw better days before you were born, it has a grottolike darkness punctuated only by red and green ship's running lights and neon fish. It's been a fishermen's haunt since the 1950s, and their stuffed fish hang on the walls. A long menu of Polish and Ukrainian delicacies includes cabbage soup, *golumbki,* pirogi, kielbasa, and stuffed cabbage rolls, along with chourico sandwiches, priced from $7.00 to $13.00. The Uke is at 482 Globe Street; call (508) 672–9677.

To enjoy a true *scenic drive,* exit Route 6 at Route 88, follow it south to Kirby Road, and begin a driving tour that makes a natural loop around the east branch of the Westport River, taking you to Dartmouth. Along the way, you'll see farms with silver silos, stone walls, pastureland sloping to the sea, and several great finds in country restaurants. (Pick one for lunch.) Turn right on Kirby Road, and then turn left onto Main Road, which brings you through the center of Westport, past its town hall and Quaker Meeting House. Main Road becomes Westport Point Road as it approaches Westport Point Village, an enclave as quaint as its seafaring origins. On a little warren of tiny streets rise eighteenth- and nineteenth-century sea captains' houses, all dated and identified with signs (WILLIAM AND SAMUEL BRIGHTMAN, MARINERS, CA. 1788/1830; ABNER SISSON, HOUSEWRIGHT, CA. 1841).

Go back up to Drift Road on the right and take it over to Route 88 south. Just after the bridge over the inlet, the first right brings you to a little joint called *Jerome's Moby Dick Sandwich Shop.* In this brick bunker with blue picnic tables outside and a little counter and some tables inside, you can get great lobster, baked fish, and spaghetti, among other things. Route 88 ends just before *Horseneck Beach,* a spectacular stretch fronting the ocean on a narrow peninsula at the mouth of the Westport River. Leave the peninsula via East Beach Road, which brings you east of the river to Horseneck Road. Up on the left, with a panoramic view of sweeping pastureland that stretches unbroken down to the sea, is *The Bayside,* at 1253 Horseneck Road (508–636–5882), another great country restaurant. This one bills itself as "the best dinky little restaurant in the Commonwealth." And dinky it is—you can traverse its narrow dining room in two steps. Wide windows let you admire the view. Everything is "made from scratch," from sandwiches and burgers with hand-cut french fries to pan-fried smelts, and homemade pies.

Bordering the east branch of the Westport River, *Westport Rivers Vineyard and Winery* is New England's largest vinifera vineyard. On 110 acres of farmland, this small, family-run business grows grapes similar to those in France's Burgundy region. Among the wines produced are chardonnay, pinot blanc, Riesling, and sparkling wines. The winery and tasting rooms are housed in a renovated dairy barn and a Victorian farmhouse. The tasting room and art gallery are open from noon to 5:00 P.M. daily. Tours are given about every half-hour on the weekends. For information, call (508) 636–3423. To get there, follow Horseneck Road north and turn left onto Hix Bridge Road; the winery is at number 417.

# *Greater New Bedford*

From Horseneck Road, turn right onto Slade Corner Road, which brings you into the historic little village of Russells Mills, a neighborhood of South Dartmouth. In the center of the village, on Russells Mills Road, you'll find *Davoll's General Store* (508–636–4530), a local provisioner that dates to 1793.

If you backtrack from Russells Mills Road and go left onto Rock O' Dundee Road, it will bring you to Potomska Road and the *Lloyd Center for Environmental Studies.* This is really a hidden jewel. Set on the picturesque Slocums River estuary, its coastal-zone habitat makes it an amateur naturalist's and birder's paradise. You can wander the salt marshes, swamps, and forests on a handful of nature trails. On the research building's third floor, an observation deck gives lordly views of the estuarine lowlands, Buzzards Bay, and the Elizabeth Islands. Inside are casual, low-key exhibits on native wildlife and water pollution, along with the skeleton of a pilot whale. Beautiful photographs show the river and species of birds and butterflies. Downstairs is a roomful of aquariums and a tide-pool tank. A wide variety of educational and natural-history-oriented programs are offered. The center is at 430 Potomska Road; call (508) 990–0505. Hours are 9:00 A.M. to 5:00 P.M. daily except Monday (the grounds are open daily).

Continuing out on the neck of land that is Dartmouth, follow Little River Road to Smith Neck Road and turn left for three more interesting stops. On your right, at the sign for Round Hill Condominiums, look down toward the ocean. You'll see a rambling **stone mansion** that was built by the son of Hetty Green, the fabled "Witch of Wall Street." Heiress to a New Bedford whaling-and-shipping family fortune, she shrewdly invested her way to one of the largest personal fortunes in the country by the turn of the century. Hetty was a miserly sort who dressed in tattered black rags. She was so miserly, in fact, that when her son broke his leg, she refused him a doctor, and he became crippled for life. Perhaps partly for revenge, the son and his sister spent their mother's money into the ground. Building the mansion, which rivals those of Newport, certainly helped. Now, it's condominiums. You can also see it from Round Hill Beach in the off-season (October to May), when you can drive down the condominium access road to the beach.

Just up the road a piece on the left, you'll come to a giant brown wooden milk bottle with yellow-and-white awnings. It's **Salvador's Icecream,** a vintage lunch stand built in 1936. Now it dispenses cones, dishes, sundaes, burgers, linguica, and grinders at the edge of a pasture with grazing sheep. The stand is at 460 Smith Neck Road; call (508) 994–4193. It's open daily Easter to Columbus Day.

Smith Neck was named after Captain John Smith, who explored this location and owned land here in 1665. Some of that land belongs to a Smith descendant, Sally Brownell, who has opened her home as a bed-and-breakfast inn called **Salt Marsh Farm.** It was a working farm in the 1800s, and today the two hundred-year-old Federal farmhouse wears a patina of being well used. The wide-planked floorboards creak a bit, and you may have to stoop to get through the low, narrow doorways. Old etchings and paintings adorn the walls, and handmade flowered quilts grace the rooms. The innkeeper grows her own raspberries, blueberries, melons, and apples, as well as vegetables and herbs. Hens provide freshly laid eggs. All of these find their way onto the breakfast menu. A special aspect of this inn is the nature trail that winds through its ninety acres of hay fields, forest, salt meadows, and tidal marshes. Write Brownell at 322 Smith Neck Road, South Dartmouth 02748, or call (508) 992–0980 (two doubles, each with private bath, $75–$90).

Smith Neck Road ends at Gulf Road. If you take a right, you'll wind up in the village of Padanaram. But a short detour left will bring you to the **Children's Museum,** an unusual resource in a town this small. It's housed in an antique barn, with weathered silos still attached. "Please touch" is the message here, on two floors of hands-on exhibits. Everything is bright, cheerful, and colorful, from the balloons on the ceiling to the aquarium built into a fuchsia-and-green arcade. Play areas galore fill both floors, among them a crawling tube, a model car, and cutouts of fairy-tale characters that kids can put their faces in. Outside you can enjoy nature trails and picnic tables. The museum is at 276 Gulf Road; call (508) 993–3361 for information. Hours are from 10:00 A.M. to 5:00 P.M. Monday through Saturday and from 1:00 to 5:00 P.M. Sunday in the summer; times are slightly reduced in the winter, but the museum is open holidays then. Admission is $3.75.

The village of **Padanaram** is so sprightly and chic that you'll ask what it's doing in an old Yankee boatbuilding town. Padanaram is home to the world-famous wooden yacht company Concordia, and yachtspeople from all over the globe put in to port. Along two tiny blocks of Elm Street cluster some fine shops and restaurants that make for a nice stroll. Among the wares are Icelandic sweaters, dollhouses, antiques, handcrafted furniture, and china and gifts.

At dinnertime, a favored haunt is the **Bridge Street Cafe,** at 10A Bridge Street (508–994–7200). The menu features knockout dishes of soft-shell crabs, grilled and barbecued seafoods and meats, and nightly prix fixe specials. Lunch offers grilled seafood, homemade soups, salads, and sandwiches. The dining room is done in a contemporary style with mahogany tables, cherry chairs, and green screens. An outdoor deck above the dining room offers glimpses of the harbor. Entrees range from $9.00 to $21.00.

**Worden's,** at 7 Water Street, serves up a sumptuous menu of creative dishes based on ingredients fresh from the sea and from local farms. Stephen Worden not only creates interesting menus for the restaurant but also conducts cooking classes here to share his skills. Sign up to learn and expect to be well-fed in the process. Open for lunch and dinner; (508) 999–4505.

Despite the claims of other New England ports to whaling fame, New Bedford stands as the city of whaling heritage par excellence. Now that New Bedford has a more industrialized downtown, it's hard to picture just how vital whaling was. But by the 1840s, New Bedford was one of America's largest whaling ports and employed ten thousand seamen. Many Portuguese came to whale and fish, and today their descendants make up half the city—the largest Portuguese population in Massa-chusetts. Herman Melville, who has made sure we will never forget the days of whaling, described New Bedford in *Moby-Dick* as a place of "brave houses and flowery gardens." New Bedford today has the largest fishing fleet on the East Coast. The fleet ties up on the waterfront, just below the original cobblestoned section of the city, now a historic district. While the northern part of the city is heavily Portuguese, the southern section is home to a large Hispanic population.

New Bedford's busy working waterfront is the scene of much activity and more kinds of ships than you're likely to see in any one place anywhere else. You can take a walking tour of the waterfront called **Dock Walk,** starting from the **New Bedford Waterfront Visitors Center,** at Pier 3 just off MacArthur Drive (508–979–1745 or 800–508–5353), where you can pick up a brochure or join a guided tour. Besides Coast Guard cutters, scallopers, and draggers, ships on the tour include the *Lightship New Bedford,* a sixty-five-year-old red-and-white Coast Guard lightship with two masts and double lights, one of only seventeen remaining lightships. Lightships helped ships find land where lighthouses could not be built. Two more historic ships are the schooner *Ernestina,* a 101-year-old Gloucester fishing vessel, and the 1925 coastal steamer *Nobska,* the last of its kind. Plans are under way to refurbish the *Nobska* for coastal cruises.

There are two small vest-pocket parks on the piers, one honoring a Norwegian immigrant, Rasmus Tonnessen, who came to New Bedford in 1929 and founded New Bedford Ship Supply, a major supplier to fishermen that still operates today. In **Tonnessen Park** stands an unusual bronze statue of a sea god holding a cod and sturgeon. Winding all the way around the 10-foot base are creatures of the seven seas: a giant clam, a swordfish, a dolphin, an eel, a starfish, a sea turtle, a rock crab, and others. The statue honors fishermen lost at sea. The tour also points out an ice company, fish-processing plants where fishing boats are unloaded by "lumpers," and the **Bourne Counting House,** a granite building that dates to 1848 and was owned by a wealthy whaling investor. Dock Walk guided tours leave the visitors center daily at 10:00 A.M. and 2:30 P.M. in July and August.

Also on the Dock Walk is the ferry M. V. *Alert,* which leaves Pier 3 for **Cuttyhunk Island** daily in summer and less often in spring and fall (call 508–992–1432). Cuttyhunk is the westernmost of the Elizabeth Islands, most of which are privately owned by the Forbes family. This is the only island in the chain you can visit. A handful of people live on tiny Cuttyhunk, and there is only one store. Once you land, you'll be surprised by the quiet, since few vehicles survive out here. Narrow village lanes wind uphill past weathered cottages and stone walls. A long, paved path lined with stone walls like a European rampart leads to the summit, which offers a stunning view of the harbor, Buzzards Bay, and the nearby islands. Cuttyhunk is a lovely, unspoiled place, with small, secluded beaches and acres of windswept grasses and bayberry.

Just across the street from the waterfront in New Bedford, surrounding Union Street, begins the cobblestoned historic district. Opposite each other stand the two most important whaling attractions. Established in 1907, the **New Bedford Whaling Museum,** at 18 Johnnycake Hill, is the largest museum in the United States devoted to whaling. On display in its many galleries are items depicting every aspect of the industry—from tools and harpoons, logbooks and journals, figureheads and quarterboards to the giant skeleton of a humpback whale and a half-scale model of the whaleship *Lagoda* that you can climb aboard. The scrimshaw pieces include a sled made with ivory runners, a birdcage, and many kitchen tools with ivory handles. An exhibit of Herman Melville memorabilia illustrates the whaling experiences that formed the basis of his famous novels; it includes a 1930 edition of *Moby-Dick* illustrated by Rockwell Kent and an original 1851 edition of the novel. Marine paintings show nineteenth-century harbor scenes, famous whaling ships, dramatic chases, and whales biting dories in half. The museum is open year-round from 9:00 A.M. to 5:00 P.M. daily, from 1:00 to 5:00 P.M. Sunday, and Thursday until 10:00 P.M., with additional 9:00 A.M. openings on Sundays in July and August. Admission is $3.00 for children ages six to fourteen, $3.50 for seniors, and $4.50 for others. Call (508) 997–0046.

Melville visited the **Seamen's Bethel,** at 15 Johnnycake Hill, and described it in *Moby-Dick*. His pew is labeled. A somber place, the bethel is most famous for its prow-shaped pulpit. Marble cenotaphs memorializing men lost at sea line the walls and galleries. The bethel is still used today, and you may even chance on a Portuguese wedding.

From its original waterfront blocks, New Bedford spread south and west in the nineteenth century, with shipowners and whaling investors building their houses south of Union Street, which runs straight up from the waterfront. Sadly, few of these houses remain in an unaltered state. But there could not be a more shining incarnation than the **Rotch-Jones-Duff House & Garden Museum,** at 396 County Street, a few blocks west of the historic district. The architect Richard Upjohn designed this house in 1834 for William Rotch, Jr., a prominent whaling merchant. Later, another whaling merchant owned it. The house stands out as one of the nation's finest examples of the Greek Revival style. The interior reflects the owners' histories via period antiques from the mid-nineteenth century into the twentieth. You wander from Victorian parlors with Italian-marble fireplaces and gold-leaf mirrors to Rotch's opulent Greek Revival sitting room. Other house appointments include silk linens, eighteenth-century furniture, and a collection of Faberge-style eggs made by Mrs. Duff. The grounds showcase a wildflower walk, a dogwood allée, and a boxwood parterre garden with pink, white, and red roses. In summer, concerts of acoustic music are held on the grounds. From Memorial Day through September, the house is open for tours from 10:00 A.M. to 4:00 P.M. Tuesday through Saturday and from 1:00 to 4:00 P.M. Sunday. Off-season hours are from 9:30 A.M. to 5:00 P.M. Tuesday through Friday or from 11:00 A.M. to 3:00 P.M. Saturdays by appointment. Admission is $4.00; call (508) 997–1401.

Acushnet Avenue runs through the heart of the Portuguese North End. Lining the street are dozens of Portuguese shops, restaurants, and bakeries. To sample some Portuguese pastries, stop in at **Lydia's Bakery,** at 1656 Acushnet Avenue (508–992–1711), where you may choose from more than fifty varieties. Just off Acushnet Avenue, **Antonio's,** at 267 Coggeshall Street (508–990–3636), serves up such traditional Portuguese dishes as shrimp Mozambique, with huge, handmade Portuguese rolls to sop up the garlic sauce. Other dishes include *cacoila,* meat stews, seafood casseroles, and grilled meats, all served with ample portions of rice and roast potatoes, priced from $5.00 to $22.00.

Seamen's Bethel, New Bedford

If you love to shop for good food and want nothing but the best, stop in at the **Gourmet Outlet,** at 2301 Purchase Street (508–999–6408), which sells the freshest and best food from around the world. The Gourmet Outlet buys winter truffles from France, cold-pressed olive oils from Italy and Spain, some dozen kinds of olives, and all kinds of cheeses, pâtés, chocolates, coffees, Oriental foods—too many to list. Shelves of fresh raspberries, blueberries, edible nasturtiums and pansies, Portobello mushrooms, baby arugula, corn, lettuces, potatoes, and peppers tempt the senses. Buying specialty foods from all over the globe and wholesaling worldwide to the finest restaurants and chefs, the Gourmet Outlet makes up custom orders for its regulars, such as a pound of rose petals or an order of apricot-honey jam. The wholesale outlet has a retail showroom where you can shop for these goodies from 10:00 A.M. to 6:00 P.M. Wednesday through Friday and from 9:00 A.M. to 3:00 P.M. on Saturday.

In the south end of the city, tucked away in a residential area, the **Lisbon Sausage Company** makes its own smoked *linguica, chourico,* and other meats, which it wholesales around the country. You can buy the meat, too, at prices that compare quite favorably to the supermarket. As soon as you walk through the black wrought-iron gates, the pungent, spicy smells of sausage hit your nose. Behind the metal counter, through a glass wall, you can see white-coated workers hanging up yards and yards of freshly made sausage loops. The store, at 433 South Second Street, is open from 7:00 A.M. to 3:30 P.M. Monday through Friday and from 8:00 to 11:00 A.M. Saturday. Call (508) 993–7645. Mail orders are also taken.

Right across the harbor from New Bedford is **Fairhaven,** an often-overlooked place. Fairhaven flourished in the eighteenth century as a shipbuilding town, supplying whaling ships to the burgeoning trade from New Bedford. The original settlement area, called Poverty Point, consists of several blocks centered on West, Cherry, and Oxford streets, situated off Main Street north of Route 6. Many weathered old houses of the ship chandlers, merchants, and shipwrights of that time still stand. One is now the **Edgewater Bed & Breakfast,** originally built in the 1760s by a merchant who supplied the whaling and shipbuilding industries, and added onto in the 1880s. The Edgewater sits on a point of land overlooking the New Bedford Harbor scene. The water views from inside the house are splendidly set off by large, arched windows with inviting window seats. At night, the harbor lights make a pretty picture too. Rooms in the newer part of the house are larger and have nice antique touches, such as patterned wallpaper, a pencil four-poster, and a claw-foot bathtub. Two suites have working fireplaces. Rooms in the older section are smaller and more cramped, but nice too. Each has a private bath. Write the inn at 2 Oxford Street, Fairhaven 02719, or call (508) 997–5512 (doubles $70–$95, with breakfast).

A **walking tour of Poverty Point** takes you to some of the old whaling houses and turns up several interesting historical sites, such as where Joshua Slocum, the first man to circumnavigate the globe solo, set sail in 1895. (Edgewater innkeeper Kathy Reed has brochures describing the walking tour.) Elsewhere in Fairhaven are architectural treasures given to the town by millionaire Henry Huttleston Rogers. One is the

*Unitarian Memorial Church,* one of the finest examples of English Gothic architecture in America.

## Coastal Villages

Mattapoisett was famous the world over for its whaling ships and built ships of all kinds for more than a century, with six shipyards lining the waterfront. Mattapoisett men made the ship *Acushnet,* on which Melville crewed in 1840. *Mattapoisett's waterfront* is quiet now. But it's an attractive one, and a few wood-and-shingled eighteenth- and nineteenth-century houses still stand along narrow little Water Street. All have neatly lettered black-and-white signs identifying the owner and date, including the 1798 carpenter's shop and the 1832 block shop. A small, green park, Shipyard Park, looks out on the harbor.

Town history is on view at the *Mattapoisett Historical Society Museum and Carriage House,* 1 block up at 5 Church Street (508–758–2844). The museum is housed in an 1821 church with pews and pulpits, an interesting backdrop. The collection, mostly donated by town residents, varies strikingly. Sea captains brought back such exotic things as Pacific seashells, silk and feather fans from many countries, a Chinese lacquered writing desk, and two painted and gilded glasses used by Napoleon on Saint Helena. Military memorabilia span the Revolutionary War, the Civil War, and the War of 1812. Up on the balconies ranges a collection of dolls and toys, period furniture, and a stand full of antique canes, many with ivory tops. An attached building holds antique vehicles and farm tools, among them carriages and buggies, the town's first water wagon, a corn sheller, a bean winnower, a cranberry separator, and a corn chopper. The museum is open from 1:00 to 4:30 P.M. Tuesday through Saturday, July 5 to August 31. Admission is $2.00 for adults and 50 cents for children.

On Route 105 in Marion, north of Mattapoisett, you'll find *The Wave,* a family restaurant in more ways than one: It's a family business with a family-oriented menu and atmosphere. "We don't say we're a gourmet restaurant," the owners are quick to point out, in a refreshing bit of honesty, but they do serve good, reliable seafood and Italian dinners at prices that won't break the piggy bank. Go for the chowder first; it's not thickened to cream-sauce consistency, and it's full of clams. Open 7:00 A.M. to 11:00 P.M. daily; (508) 748–2986.

Continuing east along the coast brings you to Wareham. The first stop here, at 8 Elm Street, is the *Tremont Nail Company* (508–291–7871), the nation's oldest nail factory, listed on the National Register of Historic Places. Using hundred-year-old nail machines, the company still makes old-fashioned nails from cut sheets of high-carbon steel, rolled and tempered. Cut nails can penetrate any wood without splitting it and have better holding power than conventional nails. The company was founded in 1819, and the current mill dates to 1848. Although there are no tours, you can stand on a wooden platform and look in the windows any weekday from 7:30 A.M. to 5:00 P.M. while you listen to the rumbling and chugging of the nail-cutting machines. The mill is still warmed by a few potbellied stoves. The full line of nails is sold across the street in the **Old Company Store,** formerly the cooper shop. Nails, running from a 3/4-inch clout nail to an 8-inch boat spike, include rosehead, clinch, fine finish, and wrought-head. The store also sells Colonial-style hardware, paints, gifts, jellies, crackers, and penny candy. A film explains the company history and a little bit about nailmaking. Outside the factory is a herring run. Call (508) 295–0038 for information.

The village of Onset within the town of Wareham runs along the waterfront, passing sandy beaches and quiet vistas. If you'd like to stay awhile here, you can book a room in a turn-of-the-century Victorian estate set right on the beach, the **Onset Pointe Inn.** The mansion has seven antiques-filled guest rooms, all with private bath, and unparalleled ocean views. Wicker pieces and Adirondack chairs invite you to lounge on the sun porch or private beach, or in a gazebo on the lawn. Breakfast offers juices, fruit salad, all kinds of muffins and bagels, and the delicious Portuguese sweet bread. For reservations, contact the inn at 9 Eagle Way, Onset 02558; (508) 295–8442 (doubles $40–$150).

Before leaving Wareham, take a tour of its lovely **Victorian waterfront** at Onset Bay, along West and South boulevards, which lead onto Onset Avenue and take you to the town pier. Enormous Victorian summer cottages festooned with turrets and gables appear along this stretch, the sidewalk accented by black iron lampposts and cobblestoned sidewalks; a small park with a gazebo reaches up the hill. At the town pier is a ramshackle restaurant that is the essence of summer, painted all in white and with an outdoor deck over the water. It serves ice cream and hot dogs and is called **Kenny's of Onset Bay.** Right next to Kenny's on the town pier is a booth selling tickets for the cruises of the Cape Cod Canal that leave from here. (See the preceding chapter.)

### MORE PLACES TO STAY IN SOUTHEASTERN MASSACHUSETTS

**Hampton Inn,**
53 Old Bedford Road,
Westport 02790;
(508) 675–8500.
Well-kept rooms with refrigerators, irons, twenty-four-hour coffee, doubles from $70.

Independent lodgings are few in this area, but several budget chains, including Day's Inn and Comfort Inn, have good properties nearby.

### MORE PLACES TO EAT IN SOUTHEASTERN MASSACHUSETTS

**Cup of the Bay Cafe,**
3 West Central Avenue,
Onset;
(508) 295–3527.
Despite a name that conjures up ambiguous images of salty coffee, this cafe serves up a well-brewed cup, plus pastries, soups, and vegetarian sandwiches.

**Davy's Locker,**
1480 East Rodney French Boulevard,
New Bedford;
(508) 992–7359.
Popular with locals for its ample plates of fresh seafood, Davy's is open every day from 11:00 A.M. to 11:00 P.M.

**Puerini's Pasta Factory,**
1 Ace Street, Fall River;
(508) 678–1030.
As it says, it's a pasta factory, and you can get just about any kind served at lunch Monday through Saturday and dinner Wednesday through Saturday; entrees are about $10.

**Sagres Restaurant,**
181 Columbia Street,
Fall River;
(508) 675–7018.
Authentic Portuguese dishes in an authentic setting, sometimes even with live fado music, and dishes from $8.00.

**Turk's Seafood,**
82 Marion Road (Route 6),
Mattapoisett;
(508) 758–3117.
Giant portions of fried clams, fish-and-chips, or clam cakes with chowder at low-low prices. Food, not frills, at $5.00–$9.00.

### TO LEARN MORE ABOUT SOUTHEASTERN MASSACHUSETTS

Bristol County Development Council,
70 North Second Street,
P.O. Box BR–976,
New Bedford 02741;
(508) 997–1250.

Fairhaven Office of Tourism and Visitors Center,
27 Center Street,
Fairhaven 02719;
(508) 979–4085.

New Bedford Waterfront Visitors Center,
Pier 3,
New Bedford 02740;
(508) 979–1745 or
(800) 508–5353.

# Worcester County

Once you travel west of I–495, you've crossed a psychological barrier that is acutely felt by those who live here. Residents feel scorned, spurned, and ignored by Bostonians. Bostonians, in turn, think they've entered a primitive, provincial place of no interest or importance.

Worcester, New England's second-largest city, has historically been seen as a poor cousin to Boston. But Worcester is a pleasant surprise, with a handful of excellent museums and a rich past. Worcester is where the dining car was invented, as well as the valentine and the birth control pill. The Worcester Centrum is now the rock music palace of New England.

Worcester County stretches all the way from New Hampshire to Connecticut and Rhode Island. Within its borders are not only the big-city environs of Worcester but also territory ranging from old industrial towns to apple orchards and wineries, together with a clutch of rural small towns featuring some of the loveliest town commons in New England.

## Old Sturbridge Village Area

The world has beaten a path to the entrance gates of *Old Sturbridge Village,* and rightly so. It is New England's premier period restoration, creating a mid-nineteenth-century village from historic homes, shops, mills, and public buildings—even a covered bridge—collected from throughout New England. This village is inhabited by costumed interpreters who go about the everyday lives of the people who would have lived here, stitching quilts and bonnets, hammering iron into hooks and hinges, making bread and cheese, cooking over an open hearth, planting and harvesting crops, and making buckets. Despite the number of visitors each year, the village—especially the back areas—never seems crowded. Even the green has a leisurely feel to it, and if you follow the paths beyond it to the *Freeman Farm* and the newly added *Bixby House,* home of the village blacksmith, you will find even fewer people in this quiet corner.

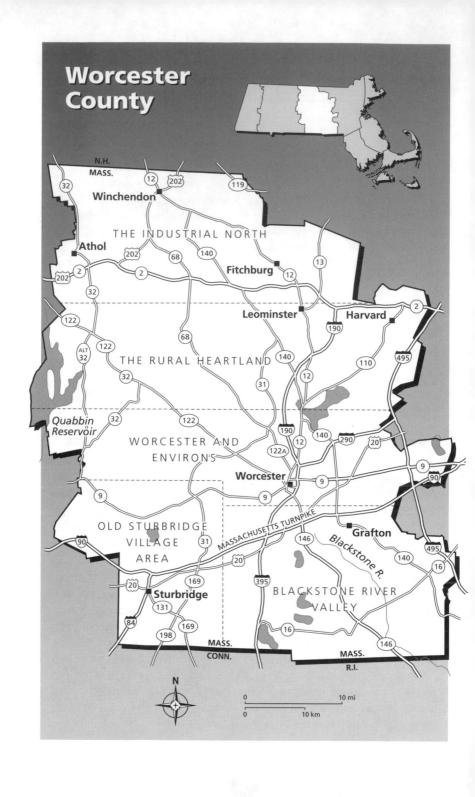

# Worcester County

N.H.
MASS.

32

12 202

119

**Winchendon**

THE INDUSTRIAL NORTH

**Athol**

202 68 140

13

**Fitchburg**

202 2

2

12

32

122

ALT 32

122

68

**Leominster**

**Harvard**

2

190

140

110

495

THE RURAL HEARTLAND

32

31

12

**Quabbin Reservoir**

32

122

190

140

290

20

WORCESTER AND ENVIRONS

122A

12

9

90

**Worcester**

9

9

9

OLD STURBRIDGE VILLAGE AREA

31

MASSACHUSETTS TURNPIKE

146

**Grafton**

*Blackstone R.*

90

20

395

BLACKSTONE RIVER VALLEY

140

495

16

169

**Sturbridge**

131

169

16

16

146

84

198

MASS.
CONN.

MASS.
R.I.

146

N

0        10 mi

0        10 km

# WORCESTER COUNTY

The "modern" enclave of mills here comes as a surprise to many people, who expect to see the farm and home industries of quilting, sewing, breadmaking, and cooperage, and even early skilled trades such as blacksmithing and tin-smithing, but don't realize how important the miller was in a community from the time of New England's earliest settlement. This industry had already begun to make life easier for the farmer and his wife by the early 1800s, harnessing water power to grind grain, card wool, and mechanize the laborious job of shaping timbers and sawing boards. Go down behind the carding mill and into its lower floor to see how the water powers the wheels. Cross the little bridge over the millrace to see how the gristmill operates on the weight of water, not its velocity.

You can have lunch in the *Tap Room* of the tavern from 11:30 A.M. until 3:00 P.M. daily, choosing from a $12.75 buffet of period foods that includes pot pies, ham, beans, cornbread, and Indian pudding. Old Sturbridge Village has a vast museum shop where, amid the predictable scented candles and other souvenir items, you can find kits for period crafts and a fine selection of books on early skills, New England, and New Englanders. Admission is $16 for adults, $15 for seniors, and $8.00 for ages six to fifteen; plan to spend the day in order to see everything. More than half the historic buildings are wheelchair-accessible. The village is open from 9:00 A.M. to 5:00 P.M. April through November, 10:00 A.M. to 4:00 P.M. Tuesday through Sunday November through December (closed Christmas Day), weekends only in January and early February, and 10:00 A.M. to 4:00 P.M. mid-February through March; *(508) 347–3362.*

*Hyland Orchard and Brewery* is a happy story of a family that reclaimed its farm—in more ways than one. The land their grandfather farmed more than 30 years ago had been sold, and its orchards fallen into disrepair, when two brothers joined with their brother-in-law and best friend to buy it back. "You couldn't even walk through the orchard, it was so overgrown," they recall, but you wouldn't know it today. They saved 400 of the old trees, and plant more each year. Along with the orchards, where they grow apples, peaches, pears, and berries, Hyland Farm has a microbrewery, which you can tour—and where you can taste the product. In fact, you can help bottle it if you're over 21. Exotic animals, including emus, miniature horses, and highland cattle, live here, too, and there's a nature trail to a bird sanctuary. The farm is open daily, and four times a year, there are family-oriented festivals with hayrides, a barbecue, and local bands. It's on Arnold Road, 2 miles off Route 20; (508) 347–7500.

On Saturday evenings in the summer, the town of Sturbridge presents free **Concerts on the Common,** on Route 131. The performers are professional musicians in all traditions—we recently heard the Latin trio Bambule, from Boston, but it might be a sixteen-piece "big band" or a German or New Orleans ragtime band. Concerts begin at 6:00 P.M., lasting for two hours, and you can bring a folding chair or sit on the grass. Pick up a schedule at the visitors center or call (508) 347–2506.

On Thursday, Friday, and Saturday evenings and Sunday afternoons in the summer, you can attend productions at the **Stageloft Repertory Company,** 530 Main Street (Route 20). Tickets are $12, $10 for seniors, and the schedule may include musicals, comedies, or a thriller; (508) 347–9005.

To stay in character with the ambiance of Old Sturbridge Village, you can stay or dine at **The Publick House,** facing the green on Route 131. This is a gracious old New England inn at its best, with well-decorated rooms in various sizes and an outstanding restaurant divided among several rooms. One has a walk-in fireplace where guests can watch their dinner cook in the winter. Traditional recipes are updated to contemporary styles and include newly available ingredients. Complete dinners are $20–$30 and the inn serves continuously from 7:30 A.M. to 10:00 P.M.; (508) 347–3313 or (800) PUBLICK.

For a change of pace from all the early American-ness, pick up a bottle of wine in the small shopping plaza near the visitors information kiosk and find the **Casual Cafe,** at 538 Main Street in Sturbridge. It's small (only ten tables) and its sign is easy to miss. You enter from the back of the building along an outdoor corridor to find a cozy room with small tables and fresh flowers. The menu reflects the ethnic diversity of the two owners, drawing from Italian and Japanese traditions, so you can begin with sushi and move on to a plateful of dramatic striped mushroom ravioli or tortellini with artichoke hearts in a spicy sauce of crushed fresh tomatoes. A plate of excellent sushi large enough to split (which you should do, since the entrees are very large) costs $5.95; entrees are $7.00–$9.00. No credit cards or liquor license, but you can bring your own wine. The restaurant opens at 5:00 P.M. Tuesday through Saturday, and reservations are a good idea; (508) 347–2281.

The Old Sturbridge Village Lodge, operated by the village, offers motel-style units or more atmospheric rooms in the historic **Oliver Wight House** with original stenciled walls and Federal furnishings. This lodging group is located at the entrance to the village, on Route 20, Sturbridge 01566; (508) 347–3327, fax (508) 347–3018.

Some believe in miracles. Their cast-off crutches and canes flank the white statue of Saint Anne at the **Saint Anne Shrine** in Sturbridge, where red and green votive candles glow in the dimness. The faithful believe a miracle took place here in 1887 when, with the help of Saint Anne, a woman parishioner was healed of dropsy. Ever since, pilgrims have flocked to the shrine in such numbers that an outdoor chapel was built for Sunday Mass.

Even if you don't believe in miracles, a visit here is well worth your while to see the museum of some sixty rare eighteenth- and nineteenth-century Russian icons. The icons feature elaborate artistry in lacquerware, gold and silver filigree, or mother-of-pearl. The most impressive of these exquisite and valuable pieces is a 5-foot-tall triptych in gold and silver of Christ, the Virgin, and Saint Nicholas.

Saint Anne Shrine is at 16 Church Street in the Fiskdale section of Sturbridge; call (508) 347–7338. The museum is open from 10:00 A.M. to 4:00 P.M. Monday through Friday, from 10:00 A.M. to 6:00 P.M. Saturday, and from 9:00 A.M. to 6:00 P.M. Sunday.

A shop of a different stripe is the **Oakwood Farm Christmas Barn** (508–885–3558) on Route 31 north in Spencer, a 175-year-old barn that sells ornaments, wreaths, garlands, music boxes, and nutcrackers. It's open from May 1 to January 1.

Just west of Spencer is a uniquely historical restaurant and inn, the **Salem Cross Inn.** The house was built in 1705 by a grandson of Peregrine White, the baby born on the *Mayflower* as it lay in Plymouth Harbor. The inn is richly paneled and extensively furnished with impressive collections of antiques: tin lanterns, portraits, redware, tall case clocks, and old prints, books, and maps. Come dinnertime, you can feast heartily on traditional dishes of beef, pork, chicken, seafood, fish, chowder, and Indian pudding, with meats cooked

---

## ANNUAL EVENTS IN WORCESTER COUNTY

**Late June and mid-September**

*Drover's Roast, Salem Cross Inn, West Brookfield, recreates the 1700s feast cooked over an outdoor fire, by reservation only; (508) 867–2345, fax (508) 867–0351.*

**Late June**

*Western Massachusetts Highland Games and Celtic Festival, Brimfield, with traditional contests, music, dance, and Scottish goods for sale; (413) 283–7250.*

**July 4**

*Independence Day Celebration, Old Sturbridge Village, Sturbridge, with a family picnic, parade, and reading of the Declaration of Independence; (508) 347–3362.*

**Late September**

*Agricultural Fair, Old Sturbridge Village, Sturbridge, where old-fashioned farm skills are demonstrated; (508) 347–3362.*

**Late September**

*Bolton Fair, Bolton, an old-fashioned agricultural fair held here annually since 1874. A farmers market features fresh local produce; (978) 779–0289*

## Capital Rock!

*Marble and limestone are common throughout this area, and were quarried in several places. Especially fine building stone came from quarries in nearby Lee, which supplied the marble for the wings of the Capitol building in Washington, D.C., in 1861 and 1862. Stone for the City Hall in Philadelphia also came from this quarry. A nearby mill cut thousands of stones for veterans buried in Arlington National Cemetery.*

over the open hearth on a 1700s roasting jack in the fieldstone fireplace. Apple pie bakes in the 1699 brick beehive oven. In summer, an old-time "Drover's Roast" is held, offering a side of beef cooked as it used to be—over an open pit—by drovers driving their cattle to market in Boston. On the six-hundred-acre farm, hayrides and sleigh rides are part of the festivities. The Salem Cross Inn is on Route 9 in West Brookfield. Dinner reservations are strongly advised anytime and are required for hearthside dinners on Friday nights. Call (508) 867–2345 or (508) 867–8337.

Also on Route 9 in West Brookfield is a Native American site, **Rock House Reservation.** Trails lead a short distance to a huge overhanging rock face, which was exposed by the last glacier that passed over Massachusetts more than 10,000 years ago. The cliff extends for some distance over a cave-like area at its base, and faces south, which protects the area under it from the coldest winds and also gives it sun in the winter. Its shelter was used as a winter hunting camp, and early digs here turned up implements and animal bones. You can climb to the top of the rock for a better view of how the glaciers moved the earth from around it like a giant bulldozer.

Other rock outcrops lie beside or above the trails, which you can follow on a forty-five-minute loop to the top of an overlook or on shorter loop segments. With luck, you might spot a scarlet tanager or eastern painted turtle in the reservation. Admission is free, and there is often a ranger at the entrance to explain the natural and human history of the site.

# *Blackstone River Valley*

**I**f you did not hear about *Lake Chargoggagoggmanchauggagog-gchaubunagungamaugg* in the fourth grade, now's the time. This is said to be the longest geographic name in the United States. It's an Indian word, translated as "You fish on your side, I fish on my side, nobody fishes in the middle." For short you can call it Webster Lake, since that's the town it's located near, on Route 197.

Clara Barton, founder of the American Red Cross, was born in a simple white farmhouse in North Oxford in 1821, now the *Clara Barton Birthplace Museum.* Amazingly, Barton never trained as a nurse. One story notes that she tended her bedridden little brother after he fell from a barn roof. She did not found the Red Cross until she was sixty. Before that, she was a teacher, and she was at the front lines in the Civil War. Besides nursing the soldiers and getting blankets and honey for them, she wrote their letters home, using a small wooden field desk that folded up so that it could be carried on a wagon.

The field desk is on view, as is a handmade quilt given to Barton with each of its twenty-seven blocks signed by Civil War officers. Much other family memorabilia and furnishings fill the house. The 1790 kitchen has an unusual indoor well with an oak bucket hanging from a rope. The museum is located at 68 Clara Barton Road, North Oxford; call (508) 987-5375. It's open from 11:00 A.M. to 5:00 P.M. Tuesday through Sunday, April 1 to late August, and by appointment. Admission is $1.00 for children and $2.50 for others.

A truly challenging hike can be had at *Purgatory Chasm State Reservation.* A huge ravine strewn with giant boulders, this dramatic chasm reaches down almost 80 feet. The steep, half-mile loop trail down from the parking lot takes you right through the middle of the gorge and gives your legs and lungs a real workout. Here and there, the boulders form a warren of little chambers and caves that children love to crawl into. The park also has picnic tables and a playground. Purgatory Chasm is on Purgatory Road off Route 146, about 10 miles south of Worcester; call (508) 234-3733. The chasm is closed in winter because of the danger posed by slippery rocks.

Somewhere in New England, you may have seen one of the famous clocks made by Simon Willard. Simon's three brothers, Benjamin, Ephraim, and Aaron, were all famous clockmakers too. The brothers Willard lived and worked in a cranberry red colonial house in Grafton, now the *Willard House and Clock Museum.* To get there, you drive through acres of stone walls and sheep pastures. The house began as one room in 1718 and still has a palpable quality of being lived in. You feel yourself a guest upon entering the stooped and narrow doorway. Clocks tick amiably from every room, periodically chiming in many voices. There are some seventy clocks made by an associated group of clockmakers, the largest such collection of this age in existence.

The Willard brothers invented and made clocks until 1839. Simon invented the "banjo" clock, named for its shape, although he never called it a banjo clock. The brothers became known for their tall case clocks—what most people call grandfather clocks—many with elegant brass finials and brass-filled stop fluting. The most splendid creation, made for the First Church of Roxbury, is a large round wall clock that is topped with a massive gold eagle. There's also a musical case clock, made by Simon, that plays one of seven tunes on the hour. Another Willard hallmark was decorative scenes on reverse-painted glass, such as Mount Vernon or Mary and her little lamb.

The brothers' workshop is much as it was, benches strewn with tools and works, the only eighteenth-century American clock shop still in its original location. The museum is at 11 Willard Street, a short distance from Grafton Center; call (508) 839–3500. It's open from 10:00 A.M. to 4:00 P.M. Tuesday through Saturday and from 1:00 to 5:00 P.M. Sunday. Admission is $3.00.

Uxbridge, south of Grafton at the intersection of Routes 16 and 12, sits on the Blackstone River, which was the corridor along which the American Industrial Revolution began. The entire Blackstone Valley is in the process of becoming a National Heritage Corridor, with a combination of historical and natural attractions highlighted, preserved, and interpreted. At the *River Bend Farm Visitor Center,* at 287 Oak Street, you can learn about the progress of this project, see how the canal locks worked, walk the towpath, or launch your canoe. Look for the excellent booklet "Canoe Guide for the Blackstone River," which maps the entire river with detailed text for paddlers and information on rapids, portages, and the environment. Contact the visitor center at (508) 278–6486.

Uxbridge is still known for its fiber industry, and you can buy knitting yarns at discounted prices at the *Uxbridge Yarn Mill Outlet,* in the mill at 27 Mendon Street (Route 16); (508) 278–5611.

At various times during the year, the riverboat **Blackstone Valley Explorer** takes passengers on a cruise through some of the earliest sites of the Industrial Revolution along the Blackstone River and Canal. Prices are usually around $7.00 for adults; (800) 619–2628.

# *Worcester and Environs*

Worcester's heritage is on view at the *Worcester Historical Museum,* at 30 Elm Street (508–753–8278). Though it's small, this museum packs a lot into its beautifully designed galleries. Holdings include many artifacts that belonged to Worcester residents in times past, such as furniture, memorabilia, clothing, artworks, and simple household items. Among the artifacts are an eighteenth-century delftware charger, a tricorn hatbox, the Lord's Prayer inscribed on a seashell, and a petrified buffalo horn brought back from the West.

Oil paintings show that Worcester was astonishingly rural until the mid-nineteenth-century manufacturing boom. Patent models represent some of the many clever machines invented in Worcester: a rolling mill, twine reels, a harness motion for a loom. Around 1900, Worcester also became the country's leading producer of lunch wagons. Four custom-made lunch wagon windows are lighted to show off their rich design painted in red and white. The museum opens at 10:00 A.M. Tuesday through Saturday and at 1:00 P.M. Sunday, and it closes at 4:00 P.M. Admission is $2.00.

Stephen Salisbury was a leading citizen of Worcester, and in 1772 he built an exquisite mansion in downtown Lincoln Square, later moved to 40 Highland Street. Besides being one of the few surviving eighteenth-century houses from Worcester's Main Street, the house is so gorgeous that people love to get married here.

The *Salisbury Mansion* has serenely symmetrical Georgian lines, with beautiful matching fanlight doorways front and rear, a pillared portico, and four tall chimneys. Patterned wallpapers and carpets, as well as paint colors, have been faithfully re-created using extensive family records. These records make the mansion one of the best-documented historic houses in New England.

Downstairs, Stephen ran a "hardware" store that sold imported teas and molasses, flax, sheep's wool, chocolate, ginger, beeswax, pewter, brass, and copper. In the original kitchen hangs the large wooden store sign bearing the Salisbury logo of a samovar. House tours are given from 1:00 to 4:00 P.M. Thursday through Sunday; admission is $2.00. For information, call the Worcester Historical Museum at (508) 753–8278. Year-round programs include vintage Christmas decorations, classical-music concerts, and afternoon teas. A joint admission ticket for the Worcester Historical Museum and the Salisbury Mansion is available for $3.00.

The romance of knighthood and chivalry lives on at the *Higgins Armory Museum,* one of the best collections of medieval armor in the country. The centerpiece is the Great Hall, which feels like a castle, with its stone Gothic arches, rose-patterned stained-glass window, and cathedral ceiling. An impressive array of shining suits of armor lines the Great Hall from end to end, as do halberds and lances, hauberks, and crossbows.

A sound-and-light show re-creates all the pageantry and heraldry of a tournament, featuring two life-size knights on horseback, their lances atilt. Trumpets blare, hooves gallop, and weapons clash resoundingly. It makes you think of Ivanhoe and Richard the Lion-Hearted.

An armored knight on horseback might wear as much as ninety-five pounds of armor. It's a wonder that anyone could even walk, let alone fight, in a getup like this. Some of the armor is surprisingly beautiful, such as a sixteenth-century Italian suit made of engraved and gilded blued steel, decorated with gold floral motifs.

The several thousand pieces in the collection also include some rare items, such as a Roman gladiator's helmet and Greek Corinthian helmets from about 550 B.C. Look too for the little white dog in armor, sporting a grand red head plume. One whole floor is devoted to hands-on fun for children, including trying on armor, making brass rubbings, and dressing up as Maid Marian or King Arthur. The Higgins Armory Museum is located at 100 Barber Avenue; call (508) 853–6015. It's open from 10:00 A.M. to 4:00 P.M. Tuesday through Saturday, from noon to 4:00 P.M. Sunday, and from 10:00 A.M. to 4:00 P.M. Mondays in July and August. Admission is $3.75 for senior citizens and children, and $4.75 for adults.

The **New England Science Center** blends the qualities of a zoo and a science museum, all spread out on spacious grounds ideal for a family outing. Around the grounds runs a bright red narrow-gauge train called the Explorer Express. Animal habitats house polar bears, primates, river otters, snowy owls, and bald eagles. There's a small picnic area and playground. Inside the museum, visitors see animal habitat exhibits such as intertidal zones, ponds and bogs, and African communities. There is a preschooler discovery room, a bird identification game, and several interactive computer and video exhibits on the environment. The museum is open from 10:00 A.M. to 5:00 P.M. Monday through Saturday and from noon to 5:00 P.M. on Sunday. Admission is $6.00 for adults and $4.00 for seniors, students, and children ages three to sixteen. Explorer Express tickets cost $1.00 extra. Call (508) 791–9211. The museum is located at 222 Harrington Way in Worcester.

What do you do with an old toilet? If you're Russell Manoog, a plumbing distributor who followed his father into the business, you save it, along with dozens of other vintage fixtures. Russell exhibits them all at his **American Sanitary Plumbing Museum,** the country's only such museum, opened in 1988.

Russell's father collected antique fixtures for sixty years. The oldest item is a section of a centuries-old wooden water main installed in Boston around 1652. An early, primitive indoor toilet looks more like an outhouse seat. By contrast, an 1891 earthenware toilet is elegantly painted with green and white floral motifs embossed with gold tracings. And an enamel hopper boasts beautiful scenes, painted in blue, of people, trees, buildings, and forests—a duplicate of a hopper at Mount Vernon. Among the museum's chamber pots is one made of white Limoges china that came from the French ocean liner *Ile de France.*

Besides toilets, there are early copper-lined and claw-foot bathtubs, lavatories, kitchen sinks, and sitz baths, along with a large collection of plumbers' tools and blowtorches. An "electric sink" invented in 1928 was the first try at a dishwasher. As part of its "Win the War" line in 1943, Kohler offered an iron kitchen sink, iron being a noncritical material. The museum is at 39 Piedmont Street. Hours are 10:00 A.M. to 2:00 P.M. Tuesday and Thursday, except July and August. Call (508) 754–9453.

In the countryside west of Worcester, Route 9 joins up with Route 56. Follow it north to Paxton and south on Route 31 to a very special spot, **Moore State Park.** This four-hundred-acre park was a private estate in the 1930s, landscaped with thousands of rhododendrons and azaleas. A dramatic, tree-lined drive leads down past open meadows to a swift-running brook, the site of an eighteenth-century mill village. Around a sawmill and gristmill, early settlers built a tavern, one-room schoolhouse, blacksmith shop, and mill owner's house. A self-guided tour passes among the remaining buildings and the crumbling stone foundations and cellar holes of those that are gone. The weathered blacksmith shop still sits along the brook, close to a waterfall, as does the sawmill, one of the oldest standing sawmills in New England still on its original site. Call (508) 792–3969 or (508) 368–0126 for information.

"Bring plenty of cash," warn the owners of **Spag's,** a discount bargain basement that sells a mishmash of everything in a warehouselike building, takes no credit cards or checks, and demands you bring your own bags or buy them. Still, shopping here is an adventure, turning up jumbo-size laundry soap, toys, fishing reels, tools, appliances, shoes, and furniture, in no particular order. Spag's is just beyond the eastern city limits, on Route 9 in Shrewsbury (no phone). Look for a giant sign bearing the smiling face of the owner.

# *The Rural Heartland*

A rural heartland of small towns, farmland, and apple country spreads out across all of Worcester County from the Route 495 beltway, near the town of Harvard, all the way west to the Quabbin Reservoir. Here you'll find town greens that look the same as they did a hundred years ago, remnants of Shaker settlements, and real working farms. Route 62 west travels right through the middle of this territory, and to see this area you can follow it with only a couple of detours.

Making your way through apple orchards on Route 110, you'll come to signs for **Fruitlands Museums,** a collection of four small museums that are little-known gems. Set high on rolling green hills with a stunning view of Mount Wachusett, the museums are surrounded by woods with nature trails. Down the hill stands the red colonial farmhouse where Bronson Alcott and like-minded others tried out their transcendentalist dream, thinking hard while the women tended the house and crops. Plain and primitively furnished, the **Alcott House** is pervaded by the spiritual feelings of its past occupants. The 1790s **Shaker House** was used as an office by the Shaker community in Harvard. It is filled with exhibits of Shaker handicrafts and industries, such as growing seeds and herbs. There's also a chair that belonged to Mother Ann, the sect's founder, who lived briefly in Harvard. The **American Indian Museum** holds countless decorated shields, clothing, baskets, and pottery. Finally, an ivied brick building houses the **Picture Gallery,** where you can see primitive portraits of children done by itinerant artists, as well as landscape paintings by artists of the Hudson River school.

Even if you don't tour the museums, the grounds are a wonderful place for picnicking. In summer, there are old-fashioned bandstand concerts on the lawn. The museum shop has some unusual, quality handicrafts. There's also a lovely tearoom enhanced by a white lattice doorway and an outdoor patio. The tearoom serves light lunches, snacks, and afternoon tea (3:00 to 4:00 P.M.) with pastries and desserts. The museums, at 102 Prospect Hill Road off Route 110, are open from 11:00 A.M. to 3:00 P.M. Monday through Saturday from mid-May through mid-October. Admission is $6.00 for adults, $4.00 for seniors, and $3.00 for children. Call (508) 456–3924.

You can see some of the houses built by Harvard's Shaker community on Shaker Road, in the **Shaker Historic District.** These plain but attractive clapboard dwellings are painted in pastel colors and complemented by stone stairs, barns, and tall pines. Some other Shaker land has been set aside as the **Holy Hill Conservation Area,** on South Shaker Road, just off Shaker Road. The sanctuary gets its name from a Shaker holy hill, where religious services were held outdoors. The worship area, sometimes called "the dancing ground," is half a mile up a trail. The grounds also include a stone bridge, a Shaker barn foundation, and a Shaker cemetery. For information, call the Harvard town clerk at (508) 456–4103. A trail guide is available for $5.00 at Town Hall on the town common.

For more than fifty years, puppet shows of the most loved of children's stories have been presented at the *Toy Cupboard Theatre and Museum* in South Lancaster. "Puss in Boots," "The Three Bears," "Little Red Riding Hood," "Hansel and Gretel," "The Frog Prince"—the list of classics goes on and on. The man behind the strings is Homer Hosmer, whose one-man show began in the summer of 1941. Grandchildren of his first audiences now come. The show goes on in a tiny theater hardly bigger than a toy box.

Hosmer also has a collection of memorabilia surrounding "The Remarkable Story of Chicken Little" ("The sky is falling! The sky is falling!") in a museum next door, where author John Greene Chandler once lived. Chandler was Hosmer's great-granduncle. The theater is at 57 East George Hill Road, just off Main Street. Puppet shows cost $3.00, including the museum tour; a museum tour alone costs 90 cents. The puppet show includes free punch, cookies, and lollipops. Shows are usually held every Sunday, Wednesday, and Thursday at 2:00 P.M. during July and August. Call ahead (978–365–9519) for program times.

On Route 62 west just before Route 70, you'll come to the *Wachusett Reservoir and Dam.* The dam here is so large it will remind you of the Grand Coulee Dam—Massachusetts-style, of course. And the reservoir itself is scenic and wild, ringed with tall pines and a rocky shoreline like that in Maine. The dam was built starting in 1900 and at its base is 185 feet thick. The structure stands 415 feet tall. A green park with a fountain lies at the base of the dam, down steep stone steps. There's a wide path along the spillway that makes for a pretty stroll as you look out on white houses hugging the shore.

By following Route 70 south, you'll come to Boylston. Here, high on a windswept hill with a breathtaking view of Mount Wachusett and the Wachusett Reservoir, the most ambitious botanical garden in New England is taking shape. The *Tower Hill Botanic Garden* is a fifty-year project of the Worcester County Horticultural Society.

Begun in the late 1980s, the botanical garden showcases the best plants of all kinds the gardener can find that will grow in Massachusetts. There are the Cottage Garden, planted with vegetables; the Wildlife Garden, with a pond and bird feeders; and the Lawn Garden, filled with flowering plants and shrubs. Walking and nature trails wind through the 132 acres.

An orchard contains more than a hundred antique flavorful varieties of apples that once grew all over New England. Above the Lawn Garden, a blue stone terrace set with urns steps up to an eighteenth-century white farmhouse that serves as society headquarters.

A large and luxurious visitor center holds a library, rooms for programs and classes, and a cafe that serves light fare. The cafe's flagstone terrace, a splendid place to dine, sits straight out over the view of the Wachusett Reservoir.

The Tower Hill Botanic Garden is at 11 French Drive; call (508) 869–6111. It's open Tuesday through Sunday from April through December and Tuesday through Friday from January through March. Hours are from 10:00 A.M. to 5:00 P.M., and admission is $4.00 for adults and $2.00 for children.

A wonderful family visit can be had at *Davis's Farmland Petting Zoo* in Sterling. Set way out on a country road surrounded by miles of pastureland, apple orchards, and the family's 150-year-old dairy farm, the petting zoo exhibits 250 farm animals. Children can see and touch most of them, including rabbits, ducks, pygmy goats, sheep, llamas, deer, pot-bellied pigs, and donkeys. There's a picnic area and playground in the middle for the children, and the $3.95 ticket includes a free hayride, where kids can see a scarecrow waving at them. The Davis family also breeds endangered farm animals that date back centuries, such as the Scotch Highland cow and the Belted Galloway cow, and a number of these are on display as well.

The Davises expect to open a new park across the street called Davis's Farmland, America's First Children's Discovery Farm, which will re-create farm life for children. At the park, kids will try such farm activities as planting and harvesting corn, running a farm stand, and milking a cow. The petting zoo is open from 10:00 A.M. to 5:00 P.M. Thursday through Sunday, from May 14 to October 31; call 978–422–6666. To get to the farm, follow Route 62 west to Sterling. Just past the Deershorn Farm Stand on the left, turn left onto Redstone Hill Road. The petting zoo is less than a mile up on the right.

If you keep going just past the petting zoo, you'll see a lefthand turn just past the apple orchards. On this corner stood the little red schoolhouse where Mary Sawyer of "Mary Had a Little Lamb" went to school. The schoolhouse is no longer there, but a small plaque tells her story. If you continue down this road about half a mile, on the first corner on the right you'll see the small white *house where Mary Sawyer lived.*

Continuing west on Route 62, you'll come to Princeton, a nineteenth-century summer resort with many hotels. At one time, there was even a three-story hotel on top of Wachusett Mountain. Today, there's a park, *Wachusett Mountain State Reservation* (508–464–2987), with 20 miles of hiking trails and alpine and cross-country skiing. The visitor center is a cozy refuge for hikers, with a huge, four-sided fieldstone fireplace. Views from the top are spectacular: Boston to the east and the Berkshire hills to the west. Wachusett is also a great place for seeing hawks, ospreys, falcons, and eagles, because it's along the migration route of these raptors.

More outdoor pleasures await at *Wachusett Meadow Wildlife Sanctuary,* a Massachusetts Audubon property. Though there isn't much farmland left in Massachusetts, you can see a traditional farm landscape here. The farmland is habitat for bobolinks, whose numbers have declined along with farm acreage. A nature trail passes through a red-maple swamp over a boardwalk with observation platforms for viewing the special plants and animals that live here. Another highlight is the *Crocker Maple,* one of the country's largest and more than three hundred years old. Though its ancient, gnarled limbs look as if they should spread next to a haunted house, the maple is an impressive sight, especially when its leaves are aflame with color in autumn. Wachusett Meadow is also a good place for snowshoeing. To get to the sanctuary, follow Route 62 west for three-quarters of a mile and turn right at the Massachusetts Audubon sign. Admission for adults is $3.00; for children, $2.00. For information, call (508) 464-2712.

Princeton has some excellent restaurants. A quiet gourmet dinner in the countryside is a hallmark of the *Harrington Farm Country Inn.* This mountainside farm was built on the western slope of Wachusett Mountain in 1763 and still has hand-painted stenciling on its walls. It's surrounded by thousands of acres of protected land ideal for hiking, berry picking, and cross-country skiing. In keeping with its setting, the restaurant's menu gives a country flair to such nouvelle American dishes as grilled pheasant with rosemary, roasted tenderloin with candied shallots, roast pork loin with sautéed apples, and occasional quail and venison entrees. To take advantage of the freshest seasonal ingredients, the menu changes weekly. The restaurant is closed Mondays and Tuesdays. The six guest rooms (doubles, $75 to $110) are furnished with original farm antiques. The inn is at 178 Westminster Road; call (978) 464-5600.

Tiny Rutland, in the heart of farm country, has a most historic property in the *General Rufus Putnam House,* a bed-and-breakfast inn built in 1750. The house belonged to one of George Washington's generals, Rufus Putnam, who served in the French and Indian War, and designed defenses for the American Revolution. The Georgian colonial home is largely untouched and still has its original wide pine floors, raised paneling in every room, and eight working fireplaces. The parlor, library, and dining room are beautifully painted and decorated with period antiques, as are the two guest rooms. The 7.5 acres of grounds include a nature trail through woods and a pond. The four-course breakfast is a feast of fruits and juices, homemade breads, coffee and juice, and eggs or pancakes. For reservations (double $100 to $125), call Folkstone Bed and Breakfast Reservation Service at (800) 762–2751 or (508) 480–0380.

Outside of a movie, you've probably never seen a herd of buffalo. But way out on a winding country road in Rutland is a buffalo farm, called **Alta Vista Farm,** where owners Howard and Nancy Mann have been raising buffalo since 1968. They have a herd of 62 bison and a small store where they sell bison steaks, roasts, kabobs, corned bison, and ground bison. Bison meat is often prescribed for heart patients because it is low in fat and cholesterol, the Manns explain. The store also sells gifts with bison or Indian themes, such as belt buckles, stickers, books, earrings made of buffalo head nickels, and American Indian *man del la* good-luck shields and dream catchers. Buffalo hides go for $175. You can see the buffalo out in the pasture and visit the store from 10:00 A.M. to 6:00 P.M. Wednesday through Sunday; call (978) 886–4365. To get to the farm, take Route 56 south .8 mile from Route 122A in Rutland Center. Just past a Citgo station, turn left onto Prescott Street, which turns into Hillside Road, and follow it 1.3 miles to the farm.

Although the town of Barre, reached via Route 62, has a pretty town common and lots of shops, a more interesting stop is the family-owned **Hartman's Herb Farm,** which sells one of the most extensive selections of herbs you'll ever see. Its catalog lists 20 kinds of thyme, 17 kinds of mint, and 13 kinds of basil. Like Yosemite, the farm sprang back after a massive fire in 1989 that claimed the shop and house. But everything grows greener now, say the Hartmans. The cluster of farm buildings commands a rustic setting down a narrow blacktop road. From the new shop's beamed ceiling hang tied bundles of yellow, pink, and purple flowers and of dried herbs, all giving forth an exquisite redolence. The shop also sells plants and garden accessories, books on herbs, soup and salad herbs, herb dips, herb teas, and such handmade crafts as dried-flower arrangements and wreaths, flower-decorated straw hats, raffia dolls, and, at Christmastime, herb wreaths and potpourri. On your visit, don't overlook the farm's resident pig, goats, sheep, rabbits, chickens, ducks, cats, and dog. The farm is particularly resplendent and fragrant at Christmastime, when mulled cider is served. To get there, go west on Routes 122 and 32, turn left onto Old Dana Road, and follow it until you come to the heart-shaped green sign. The shop is open from 10:00 A.M. to 5:00 P.M. daily. The Hartmans also have a small B&B—very small, accommodating just two people, at $85 a night. Call (978) 355–2015 for information.

The town of Petersham, too, has a *picturesque common,* complete with bandstand and Greek Revival mansions. The common is surrounded by interesting shops. A short hop from the common on North Main Street, the *Petersham Craft Center* (508–724–3415) offers a wide variety of crafts and art. The galleries in this more-than-seventy-year-old center housed in an antique white farmhouse have a homey, community feeling. Their offerings range from watercolors, blue-and-white flowered pottery, and heart-shaped, hand-forged iron hooks to linens, wooden toys, clothing, cotton rugs, and jewelry. The center is open from 11:30 A.M. to 4:00 P.M. daily except Monday. Directly opposite the common, the *Country Store* (508–724–3245) stands behind tall white pillars and offers such traditional products as maple syrup and cheddar cheese. A cozy, postage-stamp-size dining room in back serves sandwiches, soups, and chili and features enormous glass jars of homemade cookies.

Unknown to many is the fact that Harvard University has owned land in Petersham since 1907 for the purpose of forestry research. In 1941, a museum opened in the Harvard Forest, the *Fisher Museum of Forestry,* designed to interpret the history of New England forests. The museum is dark inside, to better show the lighted windows housing twenty-three unique dioramas. A preliminary color slide show gives background about the dioramas and showcases some beautifully artistic shots of tree canopies and forest plants.

As you go around the room, each diorama shows a particular phase of history in New England's forests, starting with a dense primeval forest of 1700 and moving on through farming, reforestation, and clear cutting. Other dioramas portray forestry management techniques, erosion, wildlife habitat, and forest fire devastation.

In addition to the dioramas' teaching intent, they are rare jewels whose like will never again be created. Hours of hand labor went into each display, and they are filled with purely artistic touches, such as people and vehicles, animals and birds. The trees and branches look so natural that you'd swear they were real. But even the tiniest pine needles are made of copper. One diorama looks just like a painting of a scenic spot among the trees on Harvard Pond, aflame with the reds and oranges of sunset.

The *Harvard Forest* also has nature trails and cross-country ski trails—wonderfully uncrowded spots. The forest and museum are on Route 32; call (508) 724–3302. Museum hours are from 9:00 A.M. to 5:00 P.M. weekdays and from noon to 4:00 P.M. Saturday and Sunday, May to October.

For a lovely oasis in the northern part of the county, stay at *The Inn at Clamber Hill,* a bed-and-breakfast in an estatelike stone-and-shingle "cottage" set in woodlands carpeted in beds of fern. Rooms or suites have queen-sized beds, and breakfast breads are freshly baked. Rates are $85 for doubles with a shared bath, $145 for suites with sitting rooms and private baths. Tea and dinner are served by prior arrangement. The inn is at 111 North Main Street, Petersham 01366; (978) 724–8800 or (888) 374–0007, fax (978) 724–8829, e-mail: clamber@Tiac.net.

# The Industrial North

B y 1914, the town of Winchendon was making so many toys that mail would arrive addressed simply to "Toy Town," its widely known nickname. Winchendon's Morton E. Converse Company, named after its founder, was the largest toy manufacturer in the country and sent wooden rocking horses all over the world. Memorabilia surrounding this heyday are exhibited at the *Winchendon Historical Society,* in the basement of the library at 50 Pleasant Street. The glass cases in the musty basement are crammed with Converse toys: dollhouses, toy trunks, drums, tea sets. Other toymakers followed on the heels of Converse's success.

Eventually, visitors to Toy Town numbered so many that Converse built a resort called the Toy Town Tavern, about which there's a scrapbook. The historical society's collection is wide ranging and also includes artifacts from the Revolutionary War, the Civil War, and World War II; eighteenth-century pewter; antique tools; clothing; portraits; and household goods. The library collection is open from 6:00 to 8:00 P.M. Tuesday in July and August, or you can call the library at (978) 297–0300 for an appointment.

A proud symbol of Toy Town, a *12-foot rocking horse,* stands under a canopy on Route 12, two blocks north of the library; a copy of the 1914 original, this giant replica was made as a parade float to celebrate the company's 150th anniversary.

As you drive down Elm Street in Gardner, you'll come upon a *giant wooden ladder-back chair,* so tall that it may remind you of Lily Tomlin's comedy prop for her routine about a little girl in a giant rocker. Townspeople joke that when the wood deteriorated, the chair was rebuilt bigger to maintain its Guinness world record as the world's largest chair. The two-story-high chair symbolizes Gardner's heritage as a large manufacturing center known as "Chair City."

The story of this chairmaking tradition is outlined at *Gardner Heritage State Park.* One man, James Comee, began crafting chairs by hand at his Pearl Street home in 1805. The apprentices he trained went on to open their own companies. A century later, there were almost forty chair companies in Gardner, making more than 4 million chairs a year. Gardner still makes chairs today.

A video details the craft of chairmaking, and on display are locally made chairs of bentwood, rush, rattan, wicker, and pressed-back oak, as well as Windsor, side, bedroom, ladder-back, and hand-painted and stenciled chairs. There's also an exhibit detailing Gardner's silversmithing history. The park is at 26 Lake Street; call (978) 630–1497 or (978) 632–2099 (a recording). The park is open Tuesday through Saturday from 9:00 A.M. to 4:00 P.M., as well as Sunday and Monday from noon to 4:00 P.M.

Another legacy of the chairmaking heritage is the many *furniture factory outlets* in Gardner, Winchendon, and Templeton, great places to find bargain furniture. For a map and brochure listing them, contact the Worcester County Convention and Visitors Bureau. (See page 144.)

At 102 Main Street in Gardner is a vintage diner in mint condition, the *Blue Moon Diner* (978–632–4333). Built by the Worcester Lunch Car Company in 1948, the diner has a handsome blue-and-cream exterior, oak-trimmed booths with blue leather seats, and the original art deco, steel diner's clock. The Italian owner, a former police officer who loves people, makes the rounds of the counter stools, booths, and tables to chat and joke with customers. Besides breakfasts of home fries, eggs, and fresh-fruit pancakes, the diner has blackboard specials such as meat loaf and pork pie, and homemade soups and pies.

Toy Town Horse, Winchendon

Nineteenth-century novels are full of references to women keeping their long, upswept hair in place with ornamental hair combs. Such combs have largely disappeared nowadays, but the

***Leominster Historical Society*** has the largest hair-comb collection in the country. Once home to a hair-comb factory, Leominster was known as "Comb City of the World."

Hundreds of hair combs fill two whole walls. It's hard to believe they came in so many styles. Some are 6 inches high or more, carved of tortoise shell with scrolled floral designs. Others are made of silver and filigreed in minute detail. And still others are made in the shapes of butterflies or dragonflies and studded with rhinestones or pearls. There's an ivory comb too, cut with the design of a fire-breathing dragon, that probably hails from China or India.

Other exhibits detail the plastics industry in Leominster, combmaking machinery, and the story of Johnny Appleseed, who was born here. While many know Johnny Appleseed only as a folk hero, he was a skilled nurseryman who distributed thousands of apple trees to settlers and started many nurseries throughout the Midwest. The historical society's museum is at 17 School Street (978–537–5424) and is open from 9:00 A.M. to 2:00 P.M. Monday through Friday and from 8:00 A.M. to noon Saturday, or by appointment.

Enough plastic bashing already. Ever since the first plastic—celluloid— was manufactured 125 years ago, plastic has found uses from toys to medical products to space flights. The country's only museum to chronicle the history of plastic is the ***National Plastics Center and Museum*** in Leominster, where the first celluloid plant was built. A "Plastics Hall of Fame" honors pioneers in the industry. Children can play with thousands of Legos and DuPlos and learn how plastics become popular toys they can recognize. A micromolder grinds up plastic milk bottles into souvenirs visitors can take home. The museum is at 210 Lancaster Street (Route 117). Hours are 11:00 A.M. to 4:00 P.M. Wednesday through Saturday. Tickets cost $2.00 for adults and teens and $1.00 for children ages four to twelve. Call (978) 537–9529 for information.

**MORE PLACES TO STAY
IN WORCESTER COUNTY**

*Elias Carter House,*
on the Common,
Brimfield 01010;
(413) 245–3267,
fax (413) 245–7619.
A homey bed-and-
breakfast, with summer
rates at $80 except during
Brimfield Flea Market
weekends, when they
jump to $115.

*Converse House,*
7 Brookfield Road,
Brimfield 01010;
(413) 245–7812.
An 1825 Federal–style
home, with summer rates
at $90, $120 on flea market
weekends.

*Commonwealth Cottage,*
11 Summit Avenue,
Sturbridge 01566;
(508) 347–7708.
A Queen Anne–style
cottage on a hilltop, serving
guests homebaked breads
at breakfast and a civilized
afternoon tea. Rooms begin
at $85 (low season).

*Charles Capron House,*
2 Capron Street,
Uxbridge 01569;
(508) 278–2214.
On the National Register
of Historic Places, this
seventeen-room Victorian
Gothic–style home is fur-
nished in antiques and
serves a full breakfast.

**MORE PLACES TO EAT
IN WORCESTER COUNTY**

*Le Bearn Restaurant
Français,*
12 Cedar Street,
Sturbridge;
(508) 347–5800.
A classic French restaurant
with warm hospitality to
go with the excellent food;
look for coquilles
St–Jacques, frogs legs, veal
cordon bleu, boeuf bour-
guignon, and other Gallic
entrees, most under $20.

*The French Bakery,*
Main Street (Route 20),
Sturbridge, is our choice for
fresh croissants in the
morning, or for its very
inexpensive cookies (25 to
45 cents) or fudgy brown-
ies (30 cents). Large square
pastries artfully laden with
stripes of raspberry, blueberry, or apricot are under
$1.00. On weekdays the
bakery opens at 6:30 A.M.,
on weekends at 8:00 A.M.

*The Sunburst,*
484 Main Street,
Sturbridge;
(508) 347–3097.
An upbeat place for
breakfast (ham and eggs,
omelettes, hot muffins,
french toast, granola) or
lunch (soups, quiche,
sandwiches) at
reasonable prices.

*Shorah's Ristorante,*
27 Foster Street,
Worcester;
(508) 797–0007.
Don't be misled by the
plain setting—the food is
anything but plain, with
imaginative dishes based
in Italian tradition.
Entrees are $13 to $17.

**Thai Orchid Restaurant,**
144 Commercial Street,
Worcester;
(508) 792–9701.
Long before Thai was a household word in restaurants, we were enjoying the spicy bite of crisp vegetables and tender meats here. The decor matches the food: stylish, authentic, and with lots of attention to detail; entrees from $9.00.

## WORTH SEEING IN WORCESTER COUNTY

**Brimfield Flea Markets,** held in May, July, and September, are like no other flea market or antique show. Plan well in advance for lodging and expect inflated room prices or a long drive; (413) 245–9329.

## TO LEARN MORE

Blackstone River Valley National Heritage Corridor Commission; (401) 762–0250.

Blackstone River Valley Visitors Bureau; (800) 841–1919.

Worcester Convention and Visitors Bureau, 33 Waldo Street, Worcester 01608; (508) 753–2920.

# Pioneer Valley

No one outside the Pioneer Valley seems to know where it is. The Pioneer Valley is actually the Connecticut River Valley; it follows the river's course the whole length of the state.

In its distance from Boston, this area may as well be another country. Residents know that Bostonians can't think of a good reason to come here. People here say "grinders" and "soda" instead of the Bostonian "submarines" and "tonic" and, unlike the Kennedys, pronounce their "*r*"s.

Still, it's hard to find another region in this state more markedly diverse. There's farmland here so isolated you wonder if anyone lives there. There are the large industrial cities of Springfield and Holyoke, ethnic rainbows. A centuries-old tradition of craftsmanship has drawn some fifteen hundred artists and craftspeople to live in the Pioneer Valley. Five of the state's best-known colleges are clustered here, and their thousands of students have kept the 1960s alive like another Cambridge or Berkeley. For this unique blend of outlooks, the region is also nicknamed "the Happy Valley."

## The Mohawk Trail

The Mohawk Trail (Route 2), originally an Indian footpath, today stretches 63 miles from Millers Falls to the New York border. A scenic delight to drive on, it passes through miles of farmland, apple orchards, and maple sugar houses. Because of its brilliant fall foliage display, it's a popular tourist path for leaf-peeping and is often crowded in the fall. The first part of the Mohawk Trail passes through Franklin County in the northern part of the Pioneer Valley.

Despite the bumper-to-bumper traffic on the Mohawk Trail in the fall, lots of little nooks and crannies are tucked away to explore. Perhaps the least-known section of this scenic valley lies to the east of the river, in the not-so-gently rolling hills along the New Hampshire border, north of the Quabbin Reservoir. Northfield lies along the Connecticut River, and a unique power plant/nature center uses its waters.

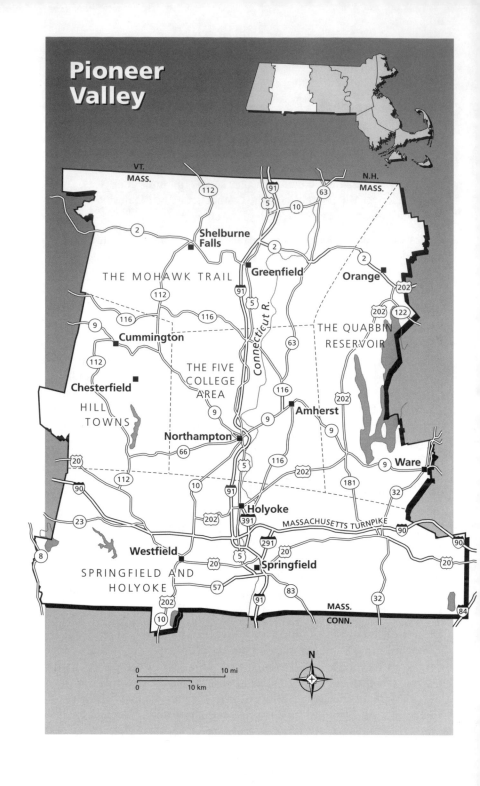

# Pioneer Valley

VT.
MASS.

N.H.
MASS.

112

91

63

5 10

2

112

Shelburne
Falls

2

THE MOHAWK TRAIL

Greenfield

2

Orange

202

91

5

202 122

112

116

116

63

THE QUABBIN
RESERVOIR

9

116

Cummington

THE FIVE
COLLEGE
AREA

112

9

116

202

Chesterfield

9

Amherst

9

HILL
TOWNS

Northampton

9

Ware

66

9

5

116

20

202

181

32

112

10

91

90

23

202

391

MASSACHUSETTS TURNPIKE

90

90

8

291

20

90

Westfield

20

5

Springfield

20

20

SPRINGFIELD AND
HOLYOKE

57

83

32

202

91

MASS.
CONN.

84

10

Holyoke

Connecticut R.

N

0                    10 mi

0                    10 km

# PIONEER VALLEY

AUTHORS' FAVORITES IN PIONEER VALLEY

"The Quad" Springfield
Museums

Historic Deerfield

The Bridge of Flowers,
Shelburne Falls

From Route 63, turn off at the *Northfield Mountain Recreation and Environmental Center,* established by Northeast Utilities. A visitor center that holds interesting exhibits on ice harvesting and logging also explains the operation of the company's hydroelectric plant. You can see how the water is pumped from the river to the top of the mountain during off-peak times, then used to generate electricity for peak-hours use, either in the exhibits in the visitors center or on a tour to the top of the mountain. You can't drive there yourself, but a bus takes those on the free tour. Call ahead for a reservation; (800) 859–2960. Throughout the year, the center sponsors nature programs on everything from wild animals and plants to wilderness survival and astronomy. For a list of these, and their fees, call the number above. You'll find some of the area's best cross-country skiing on Northfield Mountain trails; also here are a picnic area, campgrounds, and nature trails. One of these leads to a century-old quarry, and the Rose Ledge Trail leads to a scenic overlook above the river, about a forty-five-minute climb.

But the highlight of a visit to this area is a scenic 12-mile ride along the Connecticut River on the *Quinnetukut II,* an open-air riverboat with wooden benches. The ride is splendid on a sunny day, with the sunlight flashing on the waves and the breeze in your face. The wide expanse of river is flanked by unbroken green forests of pine and hardwoods, turning to rock cliffs imprinted with low-growing plants and mosses and, later, to marsh grasses. You pass under the French King Bridge, a graceful iron structure spanning 750 feet, built in 1932. You might spot a bald eagle among the many migratory birds and will certainly see geese and ducks. For information, contact Northeast Utilities, RR 2, P.O. Box 177, Northfield 01360; (413) 659–3714. The boat ride costs $7.00 for adults and $3.00 for children.

Downtown Northfield, sprawled out along Route 63, is home to the campus of nearby Northfield–Mount Hermon School, a prestigious school founded by evangelist Dwight Moody, who ran summer religious conferences in Northfield. A follower of Moody's built an extravagantly ornate house out in the woods to stay in only two weeks each summer during the meetings.

The house is now the *Northfield Country House* bed-and-breakfast inn. A dirt road shaded by towering pines imparts an otherworldly quality of peace and tranquillity to this nineteenth-century manor. The large house is handsome and comfortable inside and out. The outside is

## Hostel Territory

*The first American Youth Hostel was opened in Northfield in 1934 by Monroe and Isabel Smith, who founded the U.S. organization. A membership card was $1.00 for those under age 25, $2.00 for those older, and $3.00 for a family. There is still an AYH hostel in town, opened in 1981 in a large Victorian home at Pine and Highland streets. Lodging is $13 a night, and the hostel is open only in the summer; (413) 498–3505.*

fronted by rough stone columns and hundred-year-old hydrangeas with startlingly huge white blossoms. Inside are exquisitely carved cherry-wood moldings and china closets, as well as a 12-foot fieldstone hearth. Rooms are decorated with floral wallpapers, iron and brass bedsteads, and antiques. Some have fireplaces. Innkeeper Andrea Dale will be happy to point you to the best local antiques shop. Write the inn at School Street, Northfield 01360, or call (413) 498–2692 (double $60–$90).

One of Dale's favorite antiques shops is **Northfield Antiques** (413–498–5825), at 37 Main Street. It's tough to move around in this big old barn because it's so stuffed with antique tools, collectibles, and furniture.

South along the river is **Barton's Cove,** also part of the Northfield Mountain project, with a campground shaded in tall pines and several carry-in sites for those who prefer to camp in quiet seclusion. For visitors who arrive by boat, Munns Ferry offers riverside campsites. Reservations for these sites, which cost $10 a night and have a two-night maximum stay, should be made in advance through Barton Cove Campground at (413) 863–9300. Campsites at Barton Cove are $15, and the area, which has picnic sites and nature trails, is open for day use from 8:00 A.M. to 8:00 P.M. A canoe rental and shuttle service is also available at the campground, so you can travel by water between the two facilities and arrange for a ride back upstream.

Routes 2 and 2–A lead east to the work-a-day town of Athol. Leave Athol heading northeast, following Crescent Street to Chestnut Hill Road, on the way to Royalston, and you will eventually cross a stone bridge and see the trail leading to **Doane's Falls.** If the water here only knew it was headed for the endless eddies of impoundment in Tully Dam below, it might not be in such a hurry to rush over the series of abrupt ledges that make up this dramatic 200-foot waterfall. As you head down the trail alongside the falls, you will pass the foundation stones of mills that used power from the rushing waters to grind grain, saw lumber, process cloth, and make wooden buckets from 1753 into the 1800s. Be careful here any time but especially in wet weather or in the spring. The falls have been left in their natural state, without fences and restraining rails, by the Trustees of Reservations, which owns the property.

## Annual Events in Pioneer Valley

**Mid-March**

Central Massachusetts has two major **St. Patrick's Day Parades,** usually held on different days. Worcester's begins on Park Avenue at Mill Street and includes twenty-five floats and twenty marching bands; (508) 753-7197. The second largest St. Patrick's Day parade in the United States is in Holyoke, beginning at the K-Mart Plaza on Route 5; (413) 534-3376.

**Mid-July**

**Green River Festival,** Greenfield Community College, presents folk, country, and ethnic music; (413) 586-8686.

**July–August**

**Summit House Concerts,** Skinner State Park, Route 47, Hadley, presents Thursday evening concerts of Dixieland, folk, "big band," and barbershop music; (413) 538-9914.

**Mid–September**

**The Big E,** West Springfield, is the all–New England agricultural fair/ exposition; (413) 787-0271.

**Early October**

**Zoar Outdoors Annual Used Equipment Sale,** Route 2, Charlemont, with the company's own used kayaks, rafts, and canoes, plus those consigned by other owners; (800) 532-7483.

**Late November**

**Annual 17th Century Celebration,** Historic Deerfield, includes tours, demonstrations, and crafts, as well as period music; (413) 774-5581.

The unnumbered road leads on uphill to the lovely village of Royalston, a cluster of stately old homes and meeting houses around a wide green. From Route 68, between the village and its intersection with Route 32, Falls Road heads north, diminishing as it goes. Those without four-wheel drive should stop at the end of the town-maintained road (a sign marks this point) because a serious washout is ahead, and on a hill where backing out or parking is quite difficult. Follow the road on foot to the trailhead for **Royalston Falls,** about fifteen to twenty minutes from your car. The trail through the woods is another half-mile; you will hear the falls on its seventy-foot drop before you see it. This falls has a fence along its precipitous brink. You can also reach the falls from Route 32, north of its intersection with Route 68, from the Newton Cemetery. The sign for this trail is all-but-hidden on the east side of the winding road, and although the walk to the falls is shorter from here, the climb back out will make you wish for the longer, but kinder and gentler, route from the other side.

If you rode on the *Quinnetukut II,* you probably noticed a dam along the river. Just below the dam is the **Turners Falls Fishway** (413–659–3714), where fish ladders built by Northeast Utilities help anadromous fish make it back upriver to spawn. (Anadromous fish are fish born in fresh water that swim downstream to feed and grow in the ocean before returning upstream to reproduce; examples are shad and salmon.) The fish have been in great decline on the Connecticut River, and the fish ladders are helping to increase the population.

From mid-May through mid-June, you can watch the fish through viewing windows as they fight the current on their way upriver to spawn; the hours are 9:00 A.M. to 5:00 P.M., Wednesday through Sunday. Along the riverbank is a small, grassy picnic area with a serene view of the river. You might pick up a lunch at the *Shady Glen Diner,* at 7 Avenue A in downtown Turners Falls (413–863–9636).

For some moderately priced food that's plain but good, stop in at *Turnbull's Restaurant* at the Route 2 and Interstate 91 rotary in Greenfield (413–773–8203). The fare includes sandwiches, fish, steaks, and salads, in a country setting, with prices ranging from $14 to $19.

Before heading west on Route 2 from Greenfield, make a detour south along Route 5. Parallel to Interstate 91, which relieves it of most through-traffic, Route 5 travels through flat riverbottom farmlands where you will see stands selling the season's freshest produce. These grow thicker south of Deerfield, but your destination here should be *Historic Deerfield*. Though this is a well-known tourist attraction, it's still a special place to visit. The faithfulness and purity of its surroundings give a powerful sense of the past. The original Deerfield was a farming community founded in 1669. Twelve of its eighteenth- and nineteenth-century houses have been preserved and opened as house museums. The clapboard houses with mullioned windows and imposing Connecticut Valley doors stand serenely in oases of green lawns, neatly contained by wooden fences. When you look out in the distance, you see nothing but cornfields, just as you would have centuries ago. Cars look out of place driving along the main street—called simply "The Street"—where no trace of modernity intrudes. Families still live cheek by jowl with the house museums on The Street and still use the old post office and church.

Each house offers its own treasures—remarkable collections of American decorative arts. The *Stebbins House,* the first brick house built in the county, features a carved freestanding staircase, painted ceiling garlands, Chinese export porcelain, tasseled swag draperies, and hand-painted French murals showing the voyages of Captain Cook in the Sandwich Islands. Another house holds dozens of glass cases full of exquisitely repoussé and engraved silver, from the seventeenth century on up. Besides coffeepots and candlesticks, there's a pagoda-shaped, filigreed epergne so beautiful it could be a piece of sculpture.

In the fall of 1998, Historic Deerfield opened a new, state-of-the-art-building to house the overflow collections and mount creative exhibitions in other-than-historic house settings. This is a radical departure from the town's past policies and gives as many as 5,000 pieces not normally on display a chance to be shown. The first special exhibition, which is on display through 2001, examines the pursuit of refinement and sophistication in rural New England in the century beginning in the 1750s. The exhibit's unusual stage-like design is intended to show not only the objects but also the way in which early New Englanders perceived their value and importance.

Historic Deerfield also includes a museum shop that sells some nice reproductions, books, and handicrafts. Historic Deerfield is open daily from 9:30 A.M. to 4:30 P.M. A ticket to all twelve houses costs $10; (413) 774–5581.

In the village, and part of the National Historic District, is the restored *Deerfield Inn,* built in 1884. Furnished in antiques and reproductions of furnishings appropriate to various periods of Deerfield's history, the inn gives visitors to the town a chance to complete the sensation of moving back in time. The restaurant is far from old-fashioned, however,

Historic Deerfield

with creative seasonal entrees and a very good wine and beer list, featuring the products of a number of New England microbreweries. To reserve a room at the inn, call (413) 774-5587 or DestINNations at (800) 333–4667.

Another short detour off the Mohawk Trail, up Routes 5 and 10, will bring you to an excellent restaurant in Bernardston, the **Four Leaf Clover Restaurant** (413–648–9514). A country place full of good cheer, this little restaurant, founded in 1949, has wooden booths and excellently priced homemade food. Lunches feature generous hot and cold sandwiches, as well as salads. At dinner, you can get chicken potpie, seafood, or veal cutlets, among the other classic dishes. Top it all off with homemade puddings and pies or a sundae. Be prepared to wait in line on a Saturday night, but main courses will only cost you $8.00 to $15.00.

Instead of returning to Greenfield, you can continue up Route 5, where you will pass **Carriage Barn Antiques.** Just as you think you have seen all the furniture in the barn, you notice another building. Be sure to explore them all, not only for the chance to see some very nice antiques but also for the reasonable price tags on them, unusual for this antiques-conscious region.

Before the road crosses the border into Vermont, you'll come to an unnumbered road to your left, marked **Brook Road**. If you're really serious about seeing off-the-beaten-path Massachusetts, take it. You may get lost, but you can't get too far without meeting Route 112, crossing the Vermont border, or finding yourself back in Greenfield. To add to your sense of adventure, the road isn't even on the state's "Official Transportation Map" (which is about as poor an excuse for a road map as we've seen outside the Third World).

## Free Love in the Hills

*I*f *you think life is dull in these little villages, read on. Late in the 1700s, William Dorrell moved to the hilly town of Leyden and began to preach a doctrine based on free love and the sanctity of life—animal as well as human. He attracted a group of followers who approved of his philosophy and practiced his new religion. The people of Leyden were a tolerant lot and ignored his unusual doctrine until his followers began to demonstrate their religion publicly, in ways their neighbors found profoundly shocking. A town elder named Ezekiel Foster put an end to Dorrell's preaching once and for all, but Dorrell continued to live in the community, presumably a chastened man, until his death at age 94.*

Brook Road begins by climbing through the woods, with a rocky ledge on its north side and a brook to its south and a few pullouts that would make nice spots for a picnic on a hot summer day. When you reach a crossroad, after the road becomes gravel at the Vermont line, turn left and you'll be back in Massachusetts—and on a paved road. Look for Zimmerman Hill Road, which takes you to the unusual town of *Leyden Center,* perched on a very small hilltop.

Bear right at the church and head downhill until you reach a T, where you should go right. Go left at the fork and follow the signs to Colrain. At the foot of a steep hill, go right, then left at a three-corners. All the while, you will be traveling past hill farms with pastures of grazing cattle, red barns, and hillside orchards. In the late summer, you may find peaches for sale beside the road. When you reach the first wide road you've seen during this journey, go right and you will literally drop into the town of Colrain.

A left turn above Colrain will take you to *Pine Hill Orchards,* a farm stand, and *West Country Winery,* which specializes in fruit wines from locally grown apples, blueberries, and peaches, and in hard cider; (413) 624–3481. You can sample its tasty drinks at the winery. In the restaurant, which opens at 7:00 A.M. on weekdays and 8:00 A.M. on weekends, remaining open until 4:30 P.M., you can have sandwiches, apple pie, or shortcake of the season's fresh fruit. Outdoors your children will enjoy meeting the array of animals and birds, which includes goats, rabbits, ducks, and geese.

Downhill past the church with the blue roof (everyone uses that as a landmark in town), you'll find *North River Antiques,* with furniture and smaller items in the front and a used-book store hiding around back; (413) 625–2210. Open Friday, Saturday, and Sunday afternoons or by appointment, this is a good place to look for old books about the area, which has quite a surprising history. (You'll hear more about it in Shelburne Falls.) On Lyonsville Road is a tiny covered bridge, one of only three original nineteenth-century covered bridges left in Massachusetts. Restoration of the bridge was done using hundred-year-old methods—teams of pulling oxen hauled it from its footings. Another, the *Arthur Smith Covered Bridge,* sits unrestored beside the river, visible from Route 112, which you should take into Shelburne Falls to connect with the Mohawk Trail.

If, instead of going on this adventure through the hill borderlands, you leave Greenfield on Route 2, the Mohawk Trail, you will begin to climb almost immediately. About halfway up this long hill is *Old Greenfield Village,* a new museum of old things, collected and created with remarkable foresight by Wayne Morse. In 1962 Morse began buying not just an item here and there but entire shops as craftspeople and artisans retired or old properties were sold. He began constructing buildings to house them, often out of old timber and fixtures—a door from here, a set of windows from there—until he now has a total of fourteen buildings housing a complete village of shops, with a church and schoolhouse.

The most remarkable thing about this museum, apart from its being the work of one person, is the range of things you will find here, from common everyday items to the most comprehensive collection anywhere of taps and dies, an industry that made Greenfield the thread-cutting capital of the world. The general store looks much more real, with its stacks of wooden crates and its glass cabinet full of tobacco—another local product—than those clean-countered replicas in most museum villages. In the original pharmacy, you really expect a bewhiskered pharmacist in his rumpled white jacket to step out from behind the rows of glass bottles. It's the kind of place you could poke around in all day, which you are welcome to do; each building has a recorded narrative and often signs and diagrams to show how things worked. Admission is $5.00 for adults, $4.00 for seniors, and $3.00 for ages six to sixteen, and

## Recycling on a Major Scale

*T*he Bridge of Flowers has an interesting history, which involves Colrain. In 1896, Shelburne Falls had a trolley line, and was a station on the Boston & Maine Railroad. The town of Colrain, for reasons not quite clear, had become a major center for washing the oils out of cotton, grown in the South and transported to Shelburne Falls by train. Because Colrain is so much higher in altitude than Shelburne Falls, it was impossible to carry the cotton there by train, so a trolley line was built from the B&M railyard to the mills in Colrain, and a bridge was built beside the iron road bridge to carry the trolley line over the river. It also carried a water main—as it still does.

Until 1926, the cotton moved back and forth on trolley cars, which also carried apples, cider, coal, oil, and passengers, although it was primarily a freight line. In 1927, the line was abandoned after trucks became more efficient, and all the cars were burned—except one, which was bought by a local farmer as a pre-fab chicken coop. The bridge, too narrow for automobile traffic, soon became an eyesore, but was purchased by the Fire District because of the water supply it provided. In 1929, Mr. and Mrs. Walter Burnham began the effort to turn the bridge into a public garden, which the Women's Club agreed to maintain. Although it still does, the bridge has become a source of pride to the whole community, and when the structure needed major restoration in the 1970s, community groups and businesses all contributed.

the museum is open from May 15 through October 15 from 10:00 A.M. to 4:00 P.M. Wednesday through Monday; (413) 774–7138.

Just to the south of the Mohawk Trail is the town of *Shelburne Falls,* with several interesting places to visit. The village is blessed with really nice shops, galleries, and restaurants, along with two strikingly unusual attractions. The first is the *Bridge of Flowers,* a graceful, five-arch span over the Deerfield River. Three seasons of the year, beautiful blooming plants line both sides of this old bridge, making it a wonderful spot for a stroll. More than five hundred species bloom here, including crocuses and other spring bulbs, chrysanthemums, delphinium, foxglove, and wisteria. It's also nice to look at from the riverbanks, and the bridge is lighted at night.

Across the street from the Bridge of Flowers is a great place to stock up on picnic fixings: *McCusker's Market and Deli* (413–625–9411). Freshly made pasta and tabouli salads are specialties, as are gourmet coffees and teas and homemade ice cream.

The other truly unusual sight in Shelburne Falls is the *Glacial Potholes.* These are round holes carved into stone millions of years ago by the glacial action of water swirling rocks along the ground. Besides being an interesting natural phenomenon, Shelburne Falls's glacial potholes make great swimming holes. The potholes vary from a few inches to almost 40 feet in diameter, scattered along the riverbed with little waterfalls here and there. The rock surface is a moonscape of smooth curves, perfect for sunning. To get to the potholes, walk down the steps behind Mole Hollow Candles on Deerfield Avenue.

The *Salmon Falls Artisans Showroom* (413–625–9833), 1 block from the Bridge of Flowers, on Ashfield Street, is housed in an old three-story granary that nicely showcases the high-quality work of more than 150 regional artists and craftspeople. Wares include paintings, jewelry, pottery, weaving, sculpture, and furniture. The showroom is open daily May through December and closed Mondays in winter.

The *Shelburne Falls Trolley Museum,* past the Salmon Falls Artisans Showroom on the hill overlooking the river, is devoted to restoring the one remaining car from the Colrain trolley line, rescued after 65 years' service as a chicken coop. Some of the basic structure of the car was in surprisingly good shape, other parts nearly irreparable. For a utilitarian car, it has a lot of fine detail, including brass fittings and mahogany paneling which volunteers have painstakingly repaired and restored. It is a work in progress, but visitors can go inside and see the interior, which is largely in place. In the building are photographs of the car as found and of the restoration process, as well as other materials relating to railroads and trolleys in the area. Hours vary, but the museum is usually open weekend afternoons or by appointment; (413) 625–9443 or 625–6707. The long-range plan is to operate the trolley as a shuttle for visitors between a parking lot at the railroad yard and the Bridge of Flowers.

As you travel the Mohawk Trail, you'll see lots of signs for maple sugar farms. One of the best to visit is **Gould's Maple Farm** (413–625–6170), 7 miles west of Interstate 91. Gould's has been making maple syrup for more than thirty years and lets visitors watch each spring. A shed behind the 1827 barn holds the old-fashioned, wood-fired evaporators that boil down the maple sap in March. You can have "sugar on snow," a traditional New England treat, and buy homemade syrup and maple sugar candy. The biggest treat, though, is breakfast in the **Gould Sugar House.** The country-style dining room could not be more rustic, with oxbows hanging from the rafters, wooden picnic tables covered with red-and-white-checkered tablecoths, an old woodstove, and the smell of maple syrup hanging warmly in the air. Feast on homemade pancakes, corn fritters, and waffles, all served with the sweet golden liquid. Large windows offer spectacular vistas of the surrounding forests. Gould's is open daily from March 1 through October, except for May. Maple-sugaring months are March and April.

In Charlemont, **Zoar Outdoors,** handily located facing the Mohawk Trail (Route 2) an one side and the Deerfield River on the other, rents kayaks, gives kayak lessons, and offers guided kayak and river rafting trips. All-day clinics are about $110 with graded sessions designed for beginners as well as those who need to polish their paddling skills. Zoar Gap, on the Deerfield River, is ideal for beginning and intermediate rafters, with class II and III rapids. Trips include all equipment and a riverbank picnic lunch, for $69. Check the Web site at www.zoarout@aol.com or call (800) 532–7483.

# Hill Towns

Driving through the "hill towns" of Franklin County is pure pleasure. These tiny villages are some of the most rural and traditional in all of New England. In particular, take Route 112 south from Route 9 through **the Worthingtons:** Worthington Corners, Worthington Center, and South Worthington. As it heads south from Route 9, Route 112 is barely one lane wide and is lined with thick-trunked trees that grow right out to the edge of the road. Sheep graze, and farmers harrow their fields. You'll pass a pick-your-own blueberry farm, Cumworth

Farm. At Worthington Corners there's an old-fashioned general store, the Worthington Corners Grocery.

A turnoff from Route 112 leads you to the **William Cullen Bryant Homestead** (413–634–2244) in Cummington, boyhood and country home of the famous poet and *New York Evening Post* editor. This home was a splendid retreat for Bryant, and he derived much inspiration for his poetry here. Handsome, tall maples line the long drive up to the rambling, twenty-three-room white house with open-air porches and gambrel roof. The house commands superb views of the countryside and is at such a high remove that it seems to float in its own green sea. In Bryant's day, the homestead was very much a working farm, with productive orchards and fields. The house is filled with Bryant's belongings and with souvenirs of his travels around the world. Among them are his Empire canopied, four-poster maple bed, a fit bed for a poet. His straw hat for berry picking still rests on a corner of his oak desk in the study, which has a view of the Hampshire Hills in the distance. The Bryant Homestead is open from Friday to Sunday in summer and only on weekends between Labor Day and Columbus Day; hours are 1:00 to 5:00 P.M. Admission is $5.00 for adults and $2.00 for children.

The most rugged spot in the hill towns is **Chesterfield Gorge.** A deep canyon carved into sheer granite cliffs, the gorge courses with tumbling white water. Looking down into its swirling depths is a dizzying experience. You can also see the crumbling stone remnants of a bridge over the gorge, built in 1739, a part of the Boston-to-Albany Post Road. Thick forests of pine and hemlock shelter picnic tables here and there. The gorge is a Trustees of Reservation property; call (413) 684–0148 or (413) 298–3239 for information.

## *The Five-College Area*

Naturally enough, there are five college campuses here: Mount Holyoke, Smith, Hampshire, Amherst, and the University of Massachusetts. The campuses all have interesting museums, and the lively student life means there are plenty of restaurants, shops, and arts events. You can start in the small towns north of Amherst and Northampton and work your way south through the Connecticut River Valley, passing by farmland and old tobacco barns.

Don't you always want to sit down and read in a bookstore? At the **Montague Book Mill,** you can. This unique spot is a book lover's paradise. It's housed in an 1834 grain mill overlooking the Sawmill River, a building that also did duty as a manufacturer of industrial machinery. The mill's old wooden floors, massive ceiling beams, and floor-to-ceiling windows have been kept, and now they hold three floors of used and discount books on every conceivable subject. Comfortable old chairs have been placed in reading nooks overlooking the river and a waterfall. A cafe serves coffee, baked goods, soups, and sandwiches, as does an outdoor deck in season. The Book Mill hosts jazz, folk, and classical-music concerts in its basement. Off Route 63 on Greenfield Road in Montague Center, the Book Mill is open from 10:00 A.M. to 6:00 P.M. daily. Call (413) 367–9206.

While exploring the Pioneer Valley, you couldn't find a more splendid or peaceful home base than the **Hannah Dudley House** in North Leverett, a bed-and-breakfast inn secluded on its own 110 acres of woods. Simply arriving here is an experience, as you drive up through 75-foot-tall pines to the 1797 farmhouse with slate roof and working fireplaces. The landscaped grounds feature a tea garden with an in-ground pool, waterfall, and frog pond. Wildlife and birds show themselves everywhere about the lawns and woods, where there are nature trails for hiking.

Once an Arabian-horse farm, the property still has pastures and barn with two horses, Pepper and Roman, who love to be fed apples and carrots. The spacious backyard offers restful spots on two hammocks and a glider, as well as a patio with barbecue grill. The front brick terrace with four white wicker chairs is another nice spot to enjoy the outdoors. The innkeepers set out a three-course breakfast, which might be home-baked apricot croissants or raspberry stars, plates of fresh fruit, and freshly squeezed juice. The inn is located at 114 Dudleyville Road in North Leverett. Call (413) 367–2323 for directions and reservations (doubles $155 to $175).

For a truly wild ride, drive on the aptly named **Rattlesnake Gutter Road.** To get there, follow the sign for Rattlesnake Gutter Road at the intersection of Dudleyville, North Leverett, and Church roads a short distance from the inn in North Leverett. Rattlesnake Gutter Road is a dirt road that climbs more than 1.5 miles through a steep, densely wooded ravine. The road falls away sharply on either side, almost 100 feet down. Tangles of massive boulders and the huge, moss-covered trunks of fallen trees line the sides of the ravine. The temperature drops noticeably as you drive in the dark shadow of looming pines.

You might think a small farming town an unlikely place for a major monument to world peace. But in the woods of North Leverett stands a three-story **Peace Pagoda** built by Buddhist monks and nuns. Its white dome shape has a gold statue with a shrine underneath on each of three sides, and there are stairways to climb for a closer view. The grounds hold a small landscaped pond with goldfish. The Buddhists are building a large temple to serve as an altar and residence for the pagoda's caretakers. From the height of this hill, you can see for miles, as far as the Berkshire Hills. To get to the Peace Pagoda, from Moore's Corners in the center of North Leverett, go about two miles on North Leverett Road. Opposite the North Leverett Baptist Church, turn left onto Cave Hill Road. Go .9 mile, until you see a tiny white sign

Peace Pagoda, North Leverett

for the Peace Pagoda, and then turn left onto an unmarked dirt road that leads to a small parking area.

"Pig Out in Style" announces the billboard outside **Bub's Bar-B-Q** on Route 116 in Sunderland. This low-lying shack serves some of the best southern-style barbecue you'll find anywhere in New England: barbecued chicken, ribs, pulled pork, and burgers, with a secret sauce and an "unlimited" menu of side dishes, including hickory-smoked potatoes, collard greens, spicy dirty rice, ranch beans, orange-glazed sweet potatoes, black-eyed-pea salad, dill potato salad, and bread and butter. Most dinners are only $7.95 or $8.95. Picnic tables serve as seating, and rolls of paper towels on each one serve as napkins. Bub's is open daily.

Just south of Bub's on Route 116, you'll see a sign on the right for **Red-Wing Meadow Trout Farm,** a fine spot for family fishing. The farm stocks several ponds with trout and bass, making it easy for children to catch them. On a Sunday afternoon, you'll see families with small children excitedly reeling them in. The bass have to go back in the water, but any trout caught can be purchased for $4.25 a pound. You can ask for lessons, too. Red-Wing Meadow is open from 9:00 A.M. to 4:00 P.M. weekdays and from 8:00 A.M. to sunset weekends, from April to November. Fishing fees are $2.00 per person or $5.00 for a family; 75 cents rents you a fishing rod. The farm is at 500 Sunderland Road; call (413) 549–4118.

"Because I could not stop for Death, / He kindly stopped for me— / The Carriage held but just Ourselves / And Immortality." These lines were written by "the Belle of Amherst"—poet Emily Dickinson, who spent her whole life here. At the **Emily Dickinson Homestead,** you can see where she lived and worked. The brick mansion with white trim is so heavily shaded by thick-growing trees that it looks as secretive as Emily herself. The poet lived a strange, reclusive life, spending most of her time at home. In her later years she dressed all in white and never left the house. Still, she wrote powerfully of life and death, love and nature. Unknown and virtually unpublished in her lifetime, she became one of America's most famous poets after her death.

Although most of the house is an Amherst College faculty home, you can see several rooms. In the poet's spare, simple bedroom are the sleigh bed she slept in and one of the white dresses she wore. The house, located at 280 Main Street, is open for tours at 1:00, 2:00, 3:00, and 4:00 P.M. Wednesday through Saturday, March through mid-December. Reservations are advised. Call (413) 542–8161. Admission is $4.00, $3.00 for students, and $2.00 for children.

Northampton's Main Street bustles with activity day and night, and this is where you'll find yourself spending most of your time.

You'll know immediately that you're in a different museum when you step in the front door of the **Words & Pictures Museum,** at 140 Main Street in Northampton, and come face to face with a larger-than-life-size figure of the Predator from the Arnold Schwarzenegger film of the same name. This museum is dedicated to sequential art, which, as its four floors of galleries will explain, starts with cave paintings and medieval paintings and progresses to today's comic books and graphic novels. Founded by Kevin Eastman, co-creator of the Teenage Mutant Ninja Turtles, the museum has a permanent collection of ten thousand pieces from fifty artists, which are featured in rotating exhibitions. You'll see works by the artists of *Spiderman, Batman, Aliens,* and *Swamp Thing,* among many others. An "interactive zone" is a streetscape with the Ninja Turtles climbing its walls where kids can design their own comics using computer and video games. Admission costs $3.00 for adults, $2.00 for students and seniors, and $1.00 for anyone eighteen and under. The museum is open from noon to 5:00 P.M. Tuesday through Thursday and on Sunday, from noon to 8:00 P.M.; and from noon to 8:00 P.M. Saturday. Call (413) 586–8545.

Right next door to the museum, at 150 Main Street, **Thorne's Market** is where everybody goes, sooner or later. A century-old office building that's been made over into four floors of boutiques, the Thorne's complex still looks interestingly old. Here, you'll find half the population of

Northampton, as well as gourmet kitchen items, arts and crafts, clothes, toys, and home goods.

Main Street is so loaded with restaurants that it's hard to choose among them. For good food at reasonable prices, you might try the Italian fare at *Spoleto,* located at 12 Crafts Avenue (413–586–6313). Classics such as fettuccine carbonara and saltimboca share the menu with a risotto of chicken and porcini or grilled swordfish on arrugala with caramelized onions, most around $13. Vegetarian and natural foods at *Paul and Elizabeth's* in Thorne's Market (413–584–4832) are always reliable. It's a popular place whose decor features earth colors and wood tables.

Calvin Coolidge was an Amherst grad and lived many years in Northampton, up until his death in 1933. Before becoming president, he practiced law and served as mayor and governor. A collection of his personal mementos, family photos, and souvenirs of office is exhibited in the *Calvin Coolidge Memorial Room* in the Forbes Library. Amid these family memorabilia, "Silent Cal" seems a little more human. Although the official White House oil portraits of Coolidge and his wife hang on the wall, there are also many black-and-white photos of the Coolidges, who had two sons, one of whom died very young. Also in the collection is a full Indian feather headdress that a descendant of Sitting Bull gave to Coolidge in Black Hills, South Dakota, where Coolidge kept a summer White House. Although many constituents thought he looked pretty funny in the headdress, Coolidge was not too proud to be photographed wearing it. The library is located at 20 West Street; the memorial room is open from 1:00 to 5:00 P.M. Monday and Tuesday and from 2:00 to 4:00 P.M. Wednesday.

While all the campuses have their attractions, one of the nicest places to visit is the *Lyman Plant House* at Smith College in Northampton. It gives you a real lift no matter what the season to walk into these labyrinthine greenhouses and smell the potting soil and growing things. Besides scads of common plants like begonias and African violets, the thirteen greenhouses hold tropical plants from Africa, cacti from the Peruvian desert, and tree ferns from Tasmania–thirty-five hundred species in all. Outdoor gardens and an arboretum surround the 1890s greenhouses. They're open daily from 9:00 A.M. to 4:00 P.M.; call (413) 584–2700.

The *Arcadia Nature Center and Wildlife Sanctuary* is a pleasant place to spend a morning or an afternoon. Located on an ancient oxbow of the Connecticut River, it has trails leading through floodplain forest, meadowland, and a marsh, with an observation tower overlooking it.

All kinds of programs are offered, including canoe excursions on the Connecticut River, hawk watches, and wildflower walks. The sanctuary is located at 127 Combs Road in Easthampton. Admission is $3.00 for adults and $2.00 for children. Call (413) 584–3009.

A favored student eatery, because it's so cheap, is the **Miss Florence Diner** on North Main Street (Route 9) in Florence. This is an authentic vintage diner, with bright yellow sides lettered in red art deco style, green awnings, and glass-block corners. Yankee pot roast, meat loaf, or baked stuffed peppers usually won't set you back much more than $5.00.

The town of Williamsburg, whose white nineteenth-century buildings range attractively along Route 9, has three points of interest. The first you'll come to is the **Williamsburg General Store.** This nineteenth-century store lives up to a general store's expectation of being a purveyor of almost everything, in a historic wooden building with a columned porch. In its two cramped rooms, there's barely room for the merchandise, let alone the customers. The store sells everything from dozens of kitchen gadgets to candy and baked goods, children's books, Christmas items, soaps and shampoos, candles, and jewelry. It's a fun place to browse and shop.

Right across the street from the general store is one of those rare finds, a country restaurant where the food costs next to nothing. The **Woodside Restaurant** has a small and cozy dining room with plain wooden tables and a counter. It serves breakfast (all day), lunch, and dinner, offering such down-home fare as hamburgers and hot dogs, BLTs, pot roast, and homemade chicken pie, with dinners averaging $6.95 to $8.50.

Continuing west on Route 9 brings you to the **Williamsburg Blacksmiths,** where wrought iron has been crafted since the late 1800s, in the same building. A small showroom sells its wares: hooks and hinges, fireplace tools, lamp stands, even bedsteads, as well as some pewter, tin, and brass pieces. The shop gives blacksmithing demonstrations several times a season on weekends. Call (413) 268–7341.

# The Quabbin Reservoir

f you head east out of Amherst on Route 9, the road will bring you to the **Quabbin Reservoir,** a 55,000-acre watershed that supplies greater Boston's drinking water. This vast tract also offers splendid recreation: fishing, hiking from most of its fifty-two gates, biking, and picnicking. There's a spectacular array of wildlife in its thick woods, from white-tailed deer and beaver to wild turkeys and hawks. The Quabbin is also the best place in Massachusetts to see bald eagles, which were reestablished here as a nesting species in the state, as were wild loons.

A sign on Route 9 marks *Quabbin Park,* a small peninsula of the reservoir that has a lookout tower, a dam, and a visitor center (413–323–7221). In the visitor center, a colored board shows the serpentine journey the water takes from the Quabbin to Boston. To create the reservoir, four towns in the Swift River Valley were flooded in 1939; on display are aerial photos taken of those towns in 1930. A video presents oral histories of former town residents. (Mementos from the four towns are preserved up the road a piece at the Swift River Valley Historical Society, which is discussed later in this chapter.) The *Quabbin Park Cemetery* is where all the graves of the Swift River Valley were moved, some dating back to colonial times. The visitor center also has trail maps, as well as books and brochures on the Quabbin. Located at 485 Ware Road in Belchertown, the visitor center is open from 8:30 A.M. to 4:30 P.M. weekdays and from 9:00 A.M. to 5:00 P.M. weekends.

Route 9 intersects with Route 202, which winds around the western half of the reservoir and offers several interesting stops along the way. A great lunchtime stop off Route 202 is *Hamilton Orchards* (508–544–6867), a family operation since the 1920s. There are all kinds of treats and activities here. You can pick your own apples, raspberries, and blueberries or watch the making of cider or maple syrup in season. A unique "doughnut robot" turns out cider doughnuts by the hour. In the barn and shop, the irresistible smells of warm apple pie and turnovers waft through the air. There are free apples for "kids of all ages" and a cafeteria serving apple dumplings, baked beans, hot dogs, and sundaes. The cafe is a cheery, hearty place, with a woodstove, apple print tablecloths, and a wall of windows looking out on a clean sweep of mountain and forest.

A restaurant that could not be more a part and piece of this area is the *New Salem Store and Restaurant* (508–544–6618). The rustic dining room has a massive fireplace and old wooden booths and tables. The walls are a Quabbin art gallery: historic black-and-white photos of Swift River Valley families of 1910, beautiful color photos of wild birds and animals at the Quabbin, and aerial views of the scenic reservoir. At lunch, the restaurant serves good homemade soups and breads, hot and cold sandwiches, and salads. Dinner is a more gourmet affair.

If a visit to the Quabbin Reservoir whetted your curiosity about the four towns flooded to create it, you can find out about them at the

*Swift River Valley Historical Society* (508–544–6882), on Elm Street off Route 202. Three small buildings cluster together in a clearing: a white, early-nineteenth-century house, a church, and a red barn, all holding memorabilia from the four towns—Greenwich, Dana, Prescott, and Enfield. The church originally stood in North Prescott.

When I first visited, there were still people living who hailed from the Swift River Valley. An elderly man was able to show me his house on a diorama of the valley. The four towns were officially tolled out of existence in 1938. All twenty-five hundred residents had to leave, and their homes were razed or relocated, businesses torn down, and cemeteries dug up. Nothing remained but old lanes and cellar holes. Such a sacrifice would be unheard of today. Among items saved by the historical society are a handwoven palm-leaf hat made in Dana, hatmaking having been one of its principal industries; wedding gowns and lace handkerchiefs; and cameos and jewelry. The historical-society buildings are open Wednesday and Sunday in July and August and only on Sunday from September to mid-October. Hours are 2:00 to 4:00 P.M., and admission is $2.00.

In the nineteenth century, the town of Orange was a hive of industry. Like a miniature Lowell, it was laced with canals and brick factories and mills. Many mementos of this industrial past are kept at the *Orange Historical Society,* at 41 North Main Street. The museum is in a large Victorian home that rambles on forever. It was built in 1867 for Stephen French, cofounder of the first sewing machine company, the New Home Sewing Machine Company of Orange. A handful of New Home sewing machines, elaborately painted and housed in solid oak cabinets, are on exhibit.

By 1832, Orange had a wooden-pail factory, a carding mill, a sawmill, a gristmill, a blacksmith, tanneries, a wheelwright and carriage shop, and a scythe factory. Orange is also where Minute Tapioca was invented, in 1894. The museum has a coffee grinder that was used in the first production of the tapioca and has pictures of the tapioca plant and vintage ads for the product. At the turn of the century, Orange made Grout Steam Cars, steam-powered vehicles that started with a match and won prizes for hill climbing, speed, and endurance all over the world; on display at the museum is a 1904 Grout Steam Car.

Besides these hallmarks of industry, the museum holds large and varied collections of decorative arts and household memorabilia too numerous to list completely. They include china, pewter, and porcelain; dolls and dollhouses; antique iron cookware; hats, shoes, and jewelry; and military memorabilia. A barn houses antique fire vehicles, old plows and farm tools, and a 1915 World War I caisson. The museum is open from 2:00 to 4:00 P.M. Sunday and Wednesday, mid-May through September; admission is $2.00. For information, call (508) 544–3141.

# Springfield and Holyoke

Interstate 91 goes bombing right through the heart of these two busy cities. It's hard to find your way about here, but do take the trouble, because you'll be well rewarded. For travel information, contact the Greater Springfield Convention and Visitors Bureau, 34 Boland Way at Baystate West, Springfield 01103; (413) 787–1548.

The **Hadley Farm Museum** is a delightful assemblage of the implements and daily objects of early rural living. From a well-preserved Concord Coach and fully equipped peddler's wagon to cranberry rakes and a tool used to remove apples from the throats of cows, every detail of farm and small town life is here. The barn in which all this is displayed is as interesting as its contents, a three-story estate barn built in 1782. Many of the implements highlight the early agriculture of the valley—a broom-making machine recalls the town's prominence as a grower of broomcorn. You can browse about the museum at your own speed Tuesday through Saturday 10:00 A.M. to 4:30 P.M. or Sunday 1:30 to 4:30 P.M., mid-May through mid-October. Admission is free, but your donation is welcome. It's at 147 Russell Street (Route 9), Hadley; (413) 584–8279.

The world's only "dinosaur quarry," **Nash Dinosaur Land,** is in South Hadley, just outside Holyoke. Although scientists recoil in horror at the idea, entrepreneur Carlton Nash has made a fifty-year business of selling real, 200-million-year-old dinosaur tracks found here by a local farmer in 1802. Nash has sold the tracks to such celebrities as the late General George S. Patton, at prices varying according to size and rarity, up to thousands of dollars. What do you do with dinosaur tracks? Use them as paperweights, edge your pool or garden with them, keep them as conversation pieces. Nash Dinosaur Land is on Route 116; call (413) 467–9566. The quarry and the museum are closed between Christmas and March.

The next stop is **Holyoke Heritage State Park** (413–534–1723), which colorfully chronicles the industrial history of Holyoke. In the nineteenth century, the city built a three-level canal system 4.5 miles long to channel Connecticut River water, first to its cotton mills and later to its paper mills. Holyoke once had so many paper mills—some two dozen—that it was known as "Paper City" and made a great deal of the world's fine writing papers. You'll find lots of memorabilia of city residents, papermaking

## Yikes! Dinosaurs!

*The Connecticut Valley has yielded some of the most interesting of New England's prehistoric animal finds, the first of which was in 1865, when a workman noticed strange three-toed imprints in sandstone slabs quarried in Montague, which he was laying for a walkway.*

*A site in Gill and a third near Turners Falls added more, and further finds were made later in Northampton. In addition to Nash's, dino-searchers will want to visit the Springfield Science Museum, which has a life-sized replica of Tyrannosaurus Rex and a dinosaur footprint the kids can climb into; (413) 263–6800.*

machinery, and a slide show about the industrial and social history of Holyoke. A train with vintage 1920s passenger cars occasionally runs through the park and through town. (Call for the schedule.) The landscaped grounds, which overlook a canal and several century-old redbrick mill buildings, are also a fine spot for a picnic. The park is located at 221 Appleton Street. Hours are noon to 4:30 P.M. daily.

Adjacent to the park is the *Volleyball Hall of Fame* (413–536–0926), a tribute to the fact that volleyball was invented in Holyoke in 1895. Boldly painted, contemporary exhibits explain that volleyball was invented by a local YMCA physical-education director who used a tennis net and the inside of a basketball and called his new game "mintonette." The museum, at 444 Dwight Street, is open from 10:00 A.M. to 4:00 P.M. Tuesday through Friday and from noon to 4:00 P.M. weekends.

A bright jewel not to be overlooked in Holyoke is the *Wistariahurst Museum,* an elegant Victorian mansion that was the home of a wealthy silk manufacturer. Lavishly decorated with stained glass, parquet floors, coffered ceilings, and a marble lobby, the home also holds many period furnishings and paintings. A Renaissance-style music hall is a frequent venue for concerts, as this fine mansion serves as a cultural center for the city.

Also on the grounds are landscaped gardens and a carriage house containing North American Indian and natural-history exhibits. Wistariahurst is at 238 Cabot Street in Holyoke; call (413) 534–2216. Admission is $2.00 for adults and $1.50 for children. Hours are from 1:00 to 5:00 P.M. Wednesdays and weekends, except in the winter, when the museum closes at 4:00 P.M.

Downtown Springfield boasts a cultural centerpiece in four important museums, all handily arranged in a cluster off State Street and Chestnut Avenue called the *Springfield Museum Quadrangle.* There are not one but two major art museums. The *George Walter Vincent Smith Art Museum* houses the collection of the Victorian gentleman it's named after, who collected what he liked: Japanese arms, Chinese cloisonné, and Oriental jades, textiles, and ceramics. The *Museum of Fine Arts* holds twenty centuries of art, including impressionist, expressionist, and early European paintings, and works by Helen Frankenthaler and Georgia O'Keeffe. A more fun place for children is the *Science Museum,* which invites children to touch many exhibits and also has a planetarium. At the *Connecticut Valley Historical Museum,* you can see many fine decorative artworks made by Connecticut River Valley residents, including pewter, silver, furniture, and the work of itinerant portrait painters. Early valley life is illustrated by a colonial kitchen, a Federal dining room, and two nineteenth-century tavern rooms brought here. The museums are open from noon to 4:00 P.M. Thursday through Sunday. Admission is $4.00 for adults and $1.00 for children and teens ages six to eighteen. For information, call the Springfield Library and Museums Association at (413) 739–3871.

In the late nineteenth century, Springfield had so many fine Victorian homes set on tree-lined streets that it earned the nickname "City of Homes." Hundreds of these houses still stand, and two areas are now historic districts. One of them, the *McKnight District,* has almost nine hundred Victorian houses built between 1870 and 1900. Huge, rambling affairs, they have wide porches and, often, carriage houses and stables. The McKnight District centers on Worthington Street; call (413) 736–8583 for information.

The *Student Prince and Fort Restaurant,* at 8 Fort Street (413–734–7475), has been a much-loved local institution since 1935. Its Old World German feeling is created by stained-glass windows, wood-paneled booths, and a priceless collection of some fifteen hundred antique beer steins lining the shelves of its dining-room walls. Some steins are one of a kind; one once belonged to a Russian czar. The stained-glass windows show classic scenes of Springfield and Germany.

The German and American menu lists such specialties as oxtail soup, hasenpfeffer, jaeger schnitzel, and sauerbraten. You'll find all kinds of German beers on draft, as well as many wines and European liqueurs. To add to the fun, the restaurant throws festivals several times a year. In February, a Game Fest features pheasant, buffalo, venison, and bear. A May Wine Fest and an Oktoberfest are also popular. And at Christmastime, the Fort puts up decorations and brings in carolers.

Even if you're not a military buff, you'll find the *Springfield Armory National Historic Site* an interesting place. George Washington chose

Springfield as the site for a national arsenal in 1794. The small arms and weapons made there played a major role in American wars thereafter. On and around the armory green stand a number of original buildings, including the Main Arsenal, the Commanding Officer's Quarters, and the Master Armorer's House.

The weapons housed in the Main Arsenal form the world's largest collection of small arms. Here you can see the Springfield rifle used in World War I and the famous M-1 rifle used by millions of servicemen in World War II. The armory is located at One Armory Square and is open daily from 10:00 A.M. to 5:00 P.M. Call (413) 734-8551.

Springfield is also the birthplace of the motorcycle—invented in 1901 when bicycle-racing champion George Hendee teamed up with C. Oscar Hedstrom to open the Indian Motocycle Manufacturing Company (they dropped the *r* as an advertising ploy). The famous Indian Motocycle the company produced was known worldwide for quality and beauty. In World War I, more than half the army motorcycles in use were Indians. In its heyday, the company also made airplane engines, bicycles, and outboard motors. You can see a large collection of Indian Motocycles, toy motorcycles, and memorabilia at the *Indian Motocycle Museum,* at 33 Hendee Street (413-737-2624). An annual Indian Day rally attracts proud Indian owners from all over the country. The museum is open from 10:00 A.M. to 5:00 P.M. daily; admission is $3.00 for adults and $1.00 for children.

Although not so well known as Old Sturbridge Village, *Storrowton Village Museum* was established much earlier. It is a collection of nine eighteenth- and nineteenth-century buildings brought here in the 1920s from all over New England and arranged like the heart of an old New England village. Besides a meetinghouse and church, there are a blacksmith shop, tavern, and school. Because of its small size, this attraction offers a much more intimate experience than Old Sturbridge Village. Storrowton Village is on the grounds of the Eastern States Exposition, off Memorial Avenue in West Springfield; call (413) 787-0136. Admission is $5.00 for adults and $3.00 for children. Tours are given from 11:00 A.M. to 3:30 P.M. Monday through Saturday, from mid-June through Labor Day.

Author Thornton Burgess, who wrote tales of Peter Rabbit and *Old Mother West Wind,* once lived in Hampden. His former home can be toured and is now part of *Laughing Brook Education Center and Wildlife Sanctuary.* Several miles of hiking trails take you through woodlands and fields, past streams and a pond. An intriguing addition made in 1990 is the ***Northeast Habitats Exhibit,*** an arrangement of boardwalks and observation towers that let you see animals in their habitats, just as sophisticated zoos have taken to doing. Among the animals here are white-tailed deer, bobcats, coyotes, turkey vultures, and barred owls. The sanctuary, located at 789 Main Street in Hampden, is open year-round from 10:00 A.M. to 5:00 P.M. Tuesday through Sunday. Admission is $3.00 for adults and $1.50 for children. Call (413) 566–8034.

**MORE PLACES TO STAY
IN PIONEER VALLEY**

***Allen House Inn,***
599 Main Street,
Amherst 01002;
(413) 253–5000.
A Victorian bed-and-breakfast, decorated in Eastlake and William Morris styles, within walking distance of the center of Amherst; rates are $45 to $135.

***The Lord Jeffrey Inn,***
on the Common,
Amherst;
(413) 253–2576 or
(800) 742–0358.
A classic upscale New England inn, with rates starting below $100.

***The Johnson Homestead Bed-and-Breakfast,***
79 Buckland Road,
Shelburne Falls 01370;
(413) 625–6603.
A late 1800s home, a mile and a half off Route 112, with rooms at $65, including a full country breakfast.

***1797 House,***
Upper Street,
Buckland
(Shelburne Falls) 01338;
(413) 625–2975.
A historic home with full country breakfasts; rooms $60 to $80.

**MORE PLACES TO EAT
IN PIONEER VALLEY**

***The Copper Angel Cafe,***
2 State Street,
at the Bridge of Flowers,
Shelburne Falls;
(413) 625–2727.
Healthy dishes, many of them vegetarian, 11:30 A.M. to 9 P.M., with breakfast on Sunday.

***Paul and Elizabeth's,***
Thorne's Market,
150 Main Street,
Northampton;
(413) 548–4832.
Popular for lunch.

***¡Cha Cha Cha!,***
134 Main Street,
Northampton;
(413) 586–7311.
South-of-the-Border regulars, plus vegetarian selections ($5.00–$8.00), open from 11:30 A.M. to 10:00 P.M. Tuesday through Sunday.

***The Lord Jeffrey Inn,***
on the Common,
Amherst;
(413) 253–2576.
Continental classics here may include veal Madeira, braised pork tenderloin in Pernod, or chicken Dijon, most under $20.

**WORTH SEEING IN
PIONEER VALLEY**

***Basketball Hall of Fame,***
Springfield,
(413) 781–6500,
a high-tech museum that's fun even if you're not a fan.

*Yankee Candle Car Museum,*
South Deerfield;
(413) 665–2020.

*Memorial Hall Museum,*
Deerfield;
(413) 774–3768,
which includes the famed
door with tomahawk
marks in it.

## TO LEARN MORE

For travel information on
the Mohawk Trail and
Franklin County areas, con-
tact the Franklin County
Chamber of Commerce,
P.O. Box 790, 395 Main
Street, Greenfield 01302;
(413) 773–5463.

# The Berkshires

I f the crowded, manicured lawns and black tie of Tanglewood are not your style, don't despair. That kind of mannered existence centers in the Stockbridge and Lenox area, where most tourists head. The rest of the Berkshires, north and south, is hidden territory, friendly and casual.

The countryside of the southern Berkshires is about as bucolic as it gets. Country roads disappear into the trees; small villages with white-steepled churches appear at rare intervals among the fields and meadows of rural farmland. Not a few artists and craftspeople have chosen this lovely hinterland for their home.

Almost no one thinks of heading north from Tanglewood. But if you do, you'll find some splendid natural wonders and old mill towns with a patina of industrial history. And your travels there will be wonderfully uncrowded.

Still, the central Berkshires is no place to sneeze at. It's here that world-famous cultural sophistication and scenic beauty come together in a unique amalgam, an amalgam you won't find anywhere else in the state. Acres of greenery and stately mountains embrace dance and theater festivals and the summer home of the Boston Symphony Orchestra. The inspiring beauty of the mountains attracted Nathaniel Hawthorne, Herman Melville, Edith Wharton, William Cullen Bryant, and Henry James. They in turn attracted the wealthy, who found it chic to build enormous summer "cottages" in the Gilded Age.

## Southern Berkshires

W inding country roads make it impossible not to double back on your tracks around here, but you won't mind in this scenic New England of yesteryear, composed of farms, ponds, meadows of Queen Anne's lace, and pastures full of cows. Going south on Route 102 from Lee, take a right onto the narrow Tyringham-Monterey Road. Eventually you'll come to a little thatched cottage, densely shadowed by

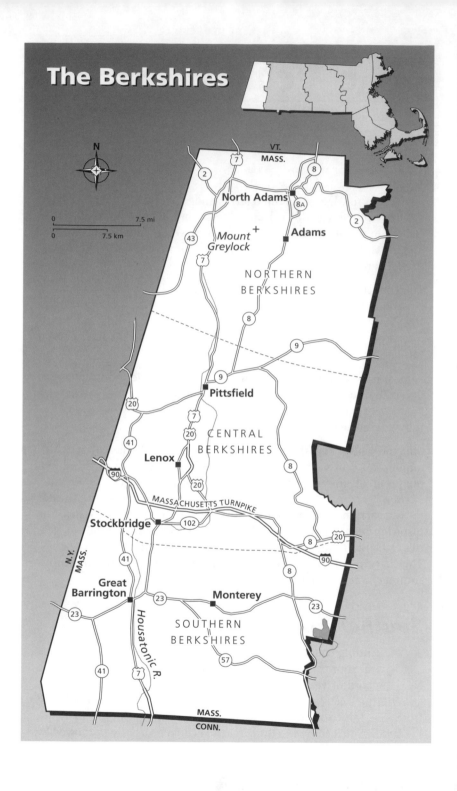

a grove of trees, that looks for all the world exactly like the fairy-tale house of Hansel and Gretel. Grottoes of stone reach up the walls to the rolling curves of its roof. **Santarella** belonged to the late sculptor Sir Henry Kitson, an unusual person who used it as his studio.

Kitson sculpted the *Minute Man* at Lexington and also the *Pilgrim Maid* at Plymouth. Here at his studio, a stone walk with abstract sculpture leads to wild gardens and a little pond where Sir Henry kept goldfish—he fed them oatmeal and called them by name. While the outside is intriguing enough, the gallery exhibits paintings, sculpture, and ceramics of artists from local and regional to national stature. The galleries have a mystical, medieval feeling, with Gothic-arched stone doorways, stained-glass windows, a stone floor, and a beamed cathedral ceiling. Behind the cottage a path leads past two improbable round tower structures with witch-hat roofs. Beyond these is a garden with large sculptures, mostly abstract, set among the plants, often with facing benches so you can sit to contemplate them. At the end is a pond with benches where you can watch frogs play in the water. You can visit the galleries from 10:00 A.M. to 5:00 P.M. daily, Memorial Day to Labor Day and then weekends only until Columbus Day. Admission is $1.00. Call (413) 243–3260.

Tyringham is a pretty town with a number of very old homes and farmhouses dating from the mid-1700s. But be very careful to travel well under the posted speed limit as you go through the village, since there is usually an officer waiting at this notorious speed trap.

A little farther south on the Tyringham-Monterey Road, you come to a dirt road on the left called Art School Road. It leads to the historic **Bidwell House,** high on a hill in the forest. In a region not overflowing with historic houses, this one is a real jewel.

The Reverend Adonijah Bidwell built the house around 1750, soon after he came to Monterey to set

Santarella

up a church. The luxury of this white Georgian saltbox house is illuminating to those of us expecting ascetic surroundings. Son of a wealthy merchant, Reverend Bidwell furnished his house with nothing but the best: elegantly carved paneling, beautiful colors of cranberry and blue, and two beehive ovens. Among the fine goods are imported gold and embroidered fabrics, patterned carpets, canopied four-posters, redware, pewter, English delft china, and six punch bowls. Listed on the National Register of Historic Places, the house was opened to the public in 1990. Hours are 11:00 A.M. to 4:00 P.M. Tuesday through Sunday and holidays, May 26 through October 14. Admission is $4.00 for adults, $3.00 for seniors and students, and $2.00 for children. Call (413) 528–6888 for information.

Also on Art School Road you'll find *Joyous Spring Pottery,* a unique, one-man gallery. Many pairs of visitors' shoes sit on the deck outside the glass doors, removed in honor of the Japanese-style salon. Owner Michael Marcus works in a most unusual vein, an ancient Japanese technique called *yakishime,* which he studied in Japan; only a handful of craftspeople in this country know it. Rather than using glazes, this method lets molten ash from a wood-fired kiln create random patterns in tans, browns, pale yellows, and siennas. Marcus built his own Japanese-style, multichambered climbing kiln to get these results. His showroom is filled with many curved and rounded pieces based on such traditional forms as sake bottles, sushi plates, and tea ceremony pieces. Although this pottery is expensive, it's also exquisite. The gallery is open from 10:00 A.M. to 5:00 P.M. daily in summer and by appointment from November to Memorial Day; call (413) 528–4115.

A few miles down, a right-hand fork off the Tyringham-Monterey Road turns into the Monterey Road, which, naturally enough, brings you into tiny Monterey. The center of town, on Route 23, is the *Monterey General Store,* right next door to the post office. The store's white-columned porch shelters two wooden benches and a sign listing the goods of 1780, when the store was established: spices, molasses, beeswax, hops, tinware, burlap, awls, castor oil, seeds, and rock candy, among others. Inside is more modern merchandise, as well as a small coffee shop that is a popular gathering place for socializing and gossip.

One of the best goat cheeses is produced right in Monterey: Monterey Chèvre, made at *Rawson Brook Farm* (413–528–2138). Wayne Dunlop and Susan Sellew like living off the land in a simple way and raising their young daughter on a farm. They keep a herd of French and American Alpine goats, with their names printed on green collar tags—Vanilla, Azaline, Anisette, and Mocha, for example. You are welcome to visit the

# THE BERKSHIRES

farm and see the pretty goats out in the fields. You can watch them being milked in the "milk parlor" from April 1 through November 1, around 5:00 P.M. Five kinds of chèvre are sold from a tall, steel refrigerator in the milking parlor: plain chèvre, chèvre with chives and garlic, chèvre with no salt, chèvre with thyme and olive oil, and peppered logs of chèvre.

To reach Rawson Brook Farm, follow the signs just past the general store, taking the first right off Route 23 heading east. Because Wayne and Susan live there, you can visit the farm almost anytime, but they ask that you not be unreasonable about this.

Head back out to Route 23 west and go a little more than 2 miles to see a unique little restaurant, the **Roadside Store and Café,** with two gas pumps out front. The tiny dining room, with its old wooden tables and butcher-block counter, is always crowded. A favorite haunt of locals, bicyclists, and fishermen, the Roadside Store is owned and operated by the Gould Farm Community, a working farm for people with psychiatric problems. The "guests," as they are called, live and work on the farm and wait on tables in the restaurant to gain work experience. On the breakfast menu are buckwheat pancakes that hang over the edges of a 10-inch plate, french toast (made with the farm's homemade bread and served with its own maple syrup), omelettes, and lots of baked goods. For lunch, there are burgers and sandwiches. The store is open from 7:30 A.M. to 3:00 P.M. daily; call (413) 528–2633.

In the lovely little village of New Marlborough is the **Old Inn on the Green and Gedney Farm,** Village Green, New Marlborough; (413) 229–3131. Both on the same property, one is a former stagecoach inn and general store, the other a Percheron barn. The barn's high ceilings make the perfect setting for dramatic decor while the inn is furnished traditionally in antiques and oriental rugs. Some of the inn's rooms have fireplaces.

## ANNUAL EVENTS IN THE BERKSHIRES

**Mid-July**

*Berkshire Choral Festival,* Berkshire School, Route 41, Sheffield, presents a variety of music including Broadway show tunes and works by Handel and Beethoven; (413) 229–1136.

**Mid-August**

*Summer Festival and Flower Show,* Berkshire Botanical Garden, Stockbridge; (413) 298–3926.

**Late September**

*Autumn Fair,* Hancock Shaker Village, Hancock, celebrating the season with Shaker skills and traditions; (413) 443–0188.

**Early to mid-November**

*Christmas Around the World,* Chesterwood; (413) 298 3579.

**December 26**

*Holiday House Tour,* Lenox, with eight historic inns and homes open to the public on a self-guided tour; (413) 637–3646.

**December 31**

*First Night* festivities in Pittsfield ring in the New Year with a parade, music, and fireworks; (413) 443–6501.

More unexpected in this quintessential little New England town is *Parada Vida,* an authentic Puerto Rican cantina with eight items on the menu, including rice and beans, and good margaritas. Open in the summer Tuesday through Sunday from 5:30 P.M., weekends only during the rest of the year, it's on Route 57, just out of the village center; (413) 229–2743.

Tiny **Mill River** takes its name from the many paper mills here in the mid-1800s. It's no longer an industrial center; now it's just a charming village with an antique general store and town hall.

If you're in need of a quiet respite, you'll find it not far from the village. About 1 mile south of the bridge into Mill River, on the Clayton–Mill River Road, there's a sign saying UMPACHENE FALLS. A dirt road leads to a rushing river by a small park. The falls lie a short walk away under a mantle of pines. Large boulders offer nice vantage points to gaze at the falls and listen to the play of water falling from terrace to terrace over its half-mile course. In the pool below, small children swim in hot weather.

The southwest corner of the southern Berkshires embraces two lovely spots, **Bartholomew's Cobble** and the historic **Colonel John Ashley House,** adjoining properties of the Trustees of Reservations (413–229–8600) in Ashley Falls.

The word *cobble* means rocky-topped hill—and it's a remarkable natural phenomenon. Bartholomew's Cobble is only the second National Natural Landmark to be so designated in Massachusetts (the first was Gay Head Cliffs on Martha's Vineyard). The two marble outcroppings here formed 500 million years ago from recrystallized limestone. The limy soil nurtured many unusual ferns and other rock-dwelling plants, including maidenhair spleenwort, columbine, and harebells. Besides some 53 kinds of ferns, there are almost 500 species of wildflowers and 100 species of trees.

This sylvan setting is a wonderful place to walk, with about 6 miles of trails. The very short Eaton Trail up the cobble can be climbed in a few minutes, rewarding the climber with a peaceful view of the Housatonic River Valley and grazing cows on green meadows. Take time to visit the rustic little museum holding animal and plant specimens, along with Indian relics.

Bartholomew's Cobble is open from 9:00 A.M. to 5:00 P.M. daily from mid-April to mid-October. Admission is $3.00 for adults and $1.00 for children.

In colonial days, Bartholomew's Cobble was owned by Colonel John Ashley, a wealthy merchant and lawyer and the leading citizen of

Sheffield. His two-story wood-frame house, built in 1735, is the oldest in Berkshire County.

As you step into the cool, dim interior of the Ashley House, the years fall away to that much more primitive time. Still, Colonel Ashley imported craftsmen from far and wide to create intricately carved paneling and moldings, boxed ceiling beams, and, in his study, an exquisite, sunburst-topped cupboard. There's a fine collection of redware and Benningtonware in the buttery.

In his study, Colonel Ashley and a committee drafted the Sheffield Declaration of 1773, which prefigured the Declaration of Independence. It also inspired an Ashley family slave called Mum Bett to seek her freedom. With Colonel Ashley's help, she became the first freed slave in Massachusetts. The Ashley House adjoins Bartholomew's Cobble, off Route 7A in Ashley Falls, and is well marked by signs. It's open from 1:00 to 5:00 P.M. Wednesday through Sunday and holidays, from the last Wednesday in June through Labor Day, and then weekends only until Columbus Day. Tickets cost $5.00 for adults and $2.50 for children.

Make your way west on Salisbury Road to Route 41 south to find a great base for further explorations. Housed in a renovated nineteenth-century barn, *Race Brook Lodge*—864 South Undermountain Road, Sheffield—calls itself a "chintz-free zone." The original hand-hewn beams define all its rooms, which are finished with stenciled walls and country-style comforters, rugs, and furniture. The whole effect is comfortable and casual, and rooms are quiet and private, tucked into various corners of the barn. The inn sits at the foot of Race Mountain next to a small brook, which you can hear from your window at night. One appeal of staying here is that you can hike up along the brook and pick up the Appalachian Trail where it traverses the ridge of Race Mountain. The ridge offers unparalleled views of both the Housatonic River Valley and the Hudson River. About 45 minutes from the back door of the lodge is Race Brook Falls, a secluded spot, and the top of the ridge is about a 2.5-mile climb. The owners of Race Brook Lodge, a congenial couple who spend time with their guests, can give you information on the trails, and will loan you snowshoes for your winter hikes. Cyclists should look here for an excellent Berkshires biking map. Call (888) 725–6343 or (413) 229–2916.

Just north of Route 41, strung out along narrow and winding Route 23, *South Egremont* is like a little village lost in time. The whole downtown, including a pretty white church and town hall, is a National Historic District.

The nineteenth century lives on at the *Gaslight Store* (413–528–0870), where you can still buy an egg cream and purchase penny candy for a penny. An egg cream has neither egg nor cream in it but tastes delicious all the same. Like an ice-cream soda without ice cream, it's made with syrup, seltzer, and milk. The owner makes no profit on his penny candy but prices it that way anyway to keep tradition alive.

The store has been there for 150 years and still has the original marble ice-cream counter. On shelves stand antique boxes of Rinso and Ivory Snow, Royal baking powder, and Lydia Pinkham tablets, along with old-fashioned glassware. Ice-cream-parlor chairs with heart-shaped backs add to the vintage feeling, as do the red-and-white-checkered table-cloths. An antique cash register in beautiful repoussé bronze sits ready to ring up purchases.

Several doors away, *Mom's Country Café* (413–528–2414) offers down-home cheer exuded by friendly waitresses, homemade food, lace curtains, and tables made out of old sewing machines. Breakfast is served all day.

In distinct contrast to its rustic surroundings, *John Andrew's* is a gourmet restaurant to equal any in the big city. On Route 23 about 2 miles south of the Route 41 intersection, John Andrew's is a real surprise. Housed in a white colonial house, it looks cutting-edge contemporary on the inside. An artist designed its interior with deep pink sponge-painted walls, which make the dining room feel warm, and chic black wall sconces. The young and talented chef changes his eclectic menu every couple of months. You might start with an appetizer of whole roasted garlic with peasant bread, goat cheese, sun-dried tomatoes, and black olives, then move on to a green salad with baked buffalo mozzarella. An entree might feature tortelli with artichokes, spinach, and mascarpone; or perhaps a risotto with wild rice, Portobello mushroom, potato, and grilled radicchio. Desserts are luxurious: white-chocolate raspberry tart or strawberry napoleon with crème anglaise, for example. For reservations (which are strongly advised on weekends), call (413) 528–3469.

Tucked into the very southwest corner of the state, bordering on New York, is the wildest countryside you'll encounter in the southern Berkshires. A narrow, rutted road with dizzying switchbacks dips and swoops up and down Mount Washington, winding through a towering dark forest. Long before you get to the spectacular 80-foot waterfall that barrels down the mountainside—*Bash Bish Falls*—you'll swear you're lost in the wilderness.

Indian legend has it that a beautiful Indian maiden, White Swan, hurled herself into the falls to her death. Two paths lead down to the falls. One is so unbelievably steep that it looks as though only world-champion rock climbers should attempt it; the other, a wide gravel path, descends to a point just above the falls. From Route 23, take Route 41 south and then make an immediate right onto Mount Washington Road. Follow signs first for Mount Washington State Forest and then for Bash Bish Falls. Call (413) 528–0330 for information.

Busy Great Barrington brims with restaurants, some of the nicest of them on *Railroad Street,* just off Route 7 downtown, a little enclave that also mixes in several intriguing boutiques. Among the eateries here are *La Tomate* (413–528–3003), an upbeat little bistro that feels very French and serves excellent French food, and *Martin's* at number 49 (413–528–5455), offering all-day breakfast, blackboard specials and homemade muffins, soups, and desserts. Around the corner from Railroad Street, at 10 Castle Street, is the *Castle Street Café* (413–528–5244), a citified cafe whose sophisticated chef makes such ambitious dishes as grilled Cornish game hen marinated in garlic and herbs, and roast duck with black currants and cassis, as well as other American and Continental fare.

Our favorite of these is the *Helsinki Cafe,* hidden in the back of a building that faces onto Main Street. Cozy, noisy, and very Finnish, the cafe makes a fine art of tea, with an excellent selection and proper brewing. The food is not necessarily Scandinavian (rather like food in Helsinki restaurants) and may include chicken with Calamata olives and capers with risotto or pan-seared salmon with a generous topping of leeks, mushrooms, and chèvre, as well as a Finnish dish of Karelian lamb with cardamom, served with almond couscous. Entrees are priced from $15 to $20, and daily specials include soup or salad. At lunch the menu offers sandwiches, wursts, and gravelaks; (413) 528–3394.

## *Central Berkshires*

On your way to Stockbridge, you'll see *Monument Mountain Reservation* on Route 7, about 2.5 miles south of town. This mountain was the scene of what has been called the world's most famous literary picnic. Herman Melville, Nathaniel Hawthorne, and Oliver Wendell Holmes climbed it on an August day in 1850. Dressed in their frock coats, they admired the view, lunched among the rocks, and toasted William Cullen Bryant. This craggy mountain rises some 1,700 feet to wonderful scenic views. At the entrance are picnic tables shaded by pines.

In Stockbridge, hordes of tourists clump about the porch of the **Red Lion Inn** and congregate around the shops on Main Street. It's worth a step inside the Red Lion Inn to see its colonial-looking lobby and a grand collection of Staffordshire china lining the edge of the ceiling. Originally built as a stagecoach stop in 1773, the inn is one of the few continuously operating in New England since before 1800 and hosted five presidents in its day. It was rebuilt after a fire in 1896.

Staying at the Red Lion Inn is expensive, as is dining there. But tucked downstairs, the **Lion's Den** pub is a cozy and inexpensive spot to grab a bite. In dramatic red and white surroundings, with a pressed-tin ceiling, wainscoting, and Tiffany lamps, the restaurant offers a pub menu of homemade soups and sandwiches and such daily specials as meat loaf and shepherd's pie. Call (413) 298–5545.

Right on Main Street are two attractions that most people don't pay any attention to. One is a tall stone tower, sort of Gothic-looking. It's the **Children's Chimes,** a carillon given to the town in 1878 by David Dudley Field, Jr., in honor of his grandchildren. Field left money for the chimes to be played, by hand, from apple blossom time until frost.

The other site, located across the street in the town cemetery, is one of the country's most unusual family plots—the **"Sedgwick Pie."** It's indeed shaped like a pie, with dozens of headstones and monuments in varying shapes and sizes placed in concentric rings, all facing toward the center. Legend has it that this design was intended to make sure the Sedgwicks saw only Sedgwicks when they woke up on Judgment Day, but that notion has been categorically denied by more than one Sedgwick. Generations of Sedgwicks have been buried in the pie, eschewing fancy coffins and wearing their pajamas. To see the pie, walk through the cemetery toward the right back corner.

Once you step away from Main Street, you can find many secluded areas in Stockbridge. One, the **Ice Glen,** is a great place for a walk on a hot day. The Ice Glen was carved out by a glacier that left massive boulders where the sun never reaches. It has been said that you can find ice crystals there even in summer, although more likely the rocks are just moist. When you stand in front of these moss-covered stones, it's as cool as opening a refrigerator door. This mystical place used to be the site of Halloween bonfires and torchlight parades.

To reach the Ice Glen, turn onto Park Road off Route 7 just south of downtown Stockbridge. Park at the end of the turnaround. Over the wooden footbridge, the right branch of the trail leads up to the Ice Glen, about a fifteen- to twenty-minute walk.

Just north of Main Street are yet two more inviting places. One of the most beautiful spots in town is the *Marian Center* monastery on Eden Hill, founded by an order that originated in Poland. A long drive leads up to grassy lawns surrounding the abbey and an exquisite stone chapel. The grounds are an inspiring place for a walk or picnic, and no one should miss seeing the chapel. Inside it are marvelous stained-glass windows of saints, frescoes, marble altars, gospel scenes, and a magnificent Rose Window. The craftsmanship of all these creations rivals that of the great cathedrals of Europe, and indeed the work was led by an Italian master stonecutter. Call (413) 298–3691.

The second inviting spot stands across from the Marian Center—*Naumkeag,* a turretted mansion designed in 1885 by Stanford White for lawyer and diplomat Joseph Choate, who served as ambassador to England. The twenty-six-room house is full of offbeat personality, as White intended it to be. Turrets and bay windows are asymmetrical and appear at odd places.

Inside and out, this Norman-style, shingled-and-gabled mansion radiates the extravagance of the Gilded Age. The spacious rooms have high ceilings and mahogany trim. A Waterford-crystal chandelier and silk-damask-patterned walls highlight the drawing room. Rare Chinese porcelains collected by Choate's daughter, Mabel, are on view, as are drawings and paintings by Choate's wife, who was an artist. An elegant, red-carpeted staircase with rope-turned balusters leads up to the seven bedrooms. President William McKinley stayed in the master guest bedroom when he visited the Choates.

On the veranda, you can admire the expansive views of the azure Berkshire Hills dropping off below you. The gardens are among the loveliest in America, graced with a topiary promenade, Venetian-style posts, a Chinese pagoda, and a linden walk archway. The most significant feature of the landscape design here is the multi-tiered staircase leading up a steep hillside between sheltering birches, with a fountain playing down its center. This and the way the garden has been designed to frame the view of the Berkshires make this among New England's finest landscaped gardens. On the upper level, near the entrance to the house, is a Japanese garden with a moon gate, added later. Naumkeag is located on Prospect Hill Road. The house and gardens are open daily except Monday from mid-May through Columbus Day. Hours are 10:00 A.M. to 5:00 P.M. with the last tour beginning at 4:15 P.M. Adults and teens pay $7.00 for admission to the house and gardens or $5.00 for the gardens only, and children ages six to twelve are admitted to both for $2.50. Call (413) 298–3239.

The much-loved illustrator and artist Norman Rockwell lived and painted for the last twenty-five years of his life in Stockbridge, where he was fond of using local people as models. A palatial new headquarters for the **Norman Rockwell Museum** opened in 1993 to display the world's largest collection of his paintings. Housed in a white, New England–style building, the museum shows off early illustrations and drawings, as well as instantly recognizable *Saturday Evening Post* covers. The red studio that Rockwell fashioned out of a carriage barn has been moved to the thirty-six-acre grounds as well, so you can see his art library and easel. The attractive grounds offer scenic views of the Berkshire Hills and include a picnic spot. The museum is open daily 10:00 A.M. to 5:00 P.M. from May through October. From November through April, hours are 11:00 A.M. to 4:00 P.M. weekdays and 10:00 A.M. to 5:00 P.M. weekends. Admission in high season is $8.00 for adults and teens and $2.00 for children over age five; in winter, it drops to $7.50 for adults. For information, call (413) 298–4100. To get to the museum, head west on Route 102 out of town and go about half a mile south on Route 183.

About a half mile south of the Rockwell Museum on Route 183, you'll see signs for **Chesterwood,** the former summer estate of sculptor Daniel Chester French. French, who worked here for more than thirty years, was most famous for his statue of Abraham Lincoln for the Lincoln Memorial in Washington D.C., and the *Minute Man* in Concord. In his studio are the plaster "sketches" for Lincoln and for several others. This estate, on beautifully landscaped grounds, is still truly a country home, almost half a mile down a dirt road. A pair of 23-foot-tall doors and a modeling table that rolled outdoors on railroad tracks let the artist view his work in natural light and from the perspective it would later be viewed from. Chesterwood is open daily from 10:00 A.M. to 5:00 P.M. May through October. Admission is $7.50 for adults, $4.00 for teens up to nineteen, and $2.00 for children ages six to twelve, or $17.00 for an entire family. Call (413) 298–3579.

Before you leave Stockbridge, stop in at the **Berkshire Botanic Garden,** 2 miles west on Route 102. At the visitor center, you can get a self-guiding map to the gardens and greenhouses. Among the prettiest displays are a massive stand of daylilies in glowing pinks, yellows, and oranges; a primrose walk; a rose garden; and a small pond thickly growing with pond lilies and cattails. Also here are a diminutive herb garden, wildflowers, and many trees and shrubs. The gardens are a nice place to spend an afternoon or have a picnic. The center and gardens are open May through October from 10:00 A.M. to 5:00 P.M. Admission is $5.00

for adults. (Greenhouses stay open year-round, and admission is free in winter.) Call (413) 298–3926.

If you keep going west on Route 102, you'll end up on the main street of **West Stockbridge,** a small village that is always less crowded than Stockbridge and is much more quaint. West Stockbridge still has its library and town clerk's office in a white house dating to 1774. A cluster of crafts shops, art galleries, antiques stores, clothing boutiques, and restaurants lines both sides of the street, going back several blocks.

East of Stockbridge along Route 102 lies Lee, a town often bypassed by those on their way to Lenox or Stockbridge. An unusual bed-and-breakfast is to be found here out in the country. **Devonfield** is a Federal-era mansion that served in 1942 as the summer home of Queen Wilhelmina of the Netherlands and the Princess Beatrix, now queen. The inn's rolling green grounds encompass acres of lawn, a swimming pool, tennis courts, a flagstone terrace, stands of white birch, and views of the Berkshires. The house is spacious, elegant, and welcoming, retaining such touches as wide, oak-pegged floors, black iron hardware, and 2-inch-thick doors. A number of the very large rooms have gorgeously patterned wallpapers, working fireplaces, canopied four-posters, and window seats with views of the grounds. The living room and dining room are large enough for many guests to spread out without crowding each other. Breakfast is a three-course affair of fruits and juices, homemade muffins, and a cooked entree, perhaps blueberry pancakes. Although this is a beautifully appointed manor house, there is nothing stiff or formal in its atmosphere. After ten minutes you feel as though it is your own home. Winter packages make it a fine place to escape to. Rooms begin at $105, the penthouse and guesthouse at $155. Reserve by calling (413) 243–3298 or (800) 664–0880 or through DestINNations at (800) 333–4667.

Main Street in Lee holds a number of eateries. If you like Mexican food—a rare find in these parts—head for the **Cactus Café** (413-243–4300), a convivial spot all done up in pink and green, with serapes and sombreros on the wall. Its wide windows look out on Main Street. Diners can order a full range of traditional choices: enchiladas, chiles rellenos, fajitas, guacamole, and an excellent flan for dessert.

Lovely **Lenox** was once a nucleus of millionaires' mansions, helping to win the Berkshires its nickname of "the Inland Newport." Novelist Edith Wharton had her home at The Mount, now open to the public and the setting for Shakespeare and Company productions of the bard's plays.

## Just a Little Place in the Hills

*To qualify as a "Berkshire Cottage," a summer home must have at least thirty rooms and be surrounded by more than twenty acres of estate lands. But that was the bare minimum. Shaddow Brook, the largest before it burned in 1956, had a nice even one hundred rooms and sat on upwards of 700 acres. More than ninety summer estates qualified for the title, including Naumkeag, Chesterwood, The Mount, and Arrowhead, all open today as museums. When noted actress Fanny Kemble suggested a benefit for the village poor, she was told, "But we have no poor."*

Today Lenox is a verdant place, still used to the well-heeled. Fine shops and restaurants stand ready to serve them. Every summer, thousands throng the lawns of nearby Tanglewood to hear the Boston Symphony Orchestra.

Just outside Tanglewood, Hawthorne Street intersects with Lake Road, which winds along the **Stockbridge Bowl.** This large lake, ringed with forests and mountains, is so blue and beautiful that it will remind you of a Swiss lake.

The most entertaining thing about the **Pleasant Valley Wildlife Sanctuary** has to be the beaver dams and lodges you can see in two ponds. Besides nature's oldest engineers, the 7 miles of trails show off uplands and meadows, a hemlock gorge, a hummingbird garden, and a limestone cobble. There are also a natural-history museum and lots of special programs, including bird and wildflower walks. The sanctuary is located at 472 West Mountain Road. To get there, follow Routes 7 and 20 north till you see the blue-and-white Audubon sign on the left, opposite the All Season Motor Inn; then turn left onto West Dugway Road and follow signs to West Mountain Road. Pleasant Valley is open from dawn to dusk Tuesday through Sunday. Admission is $3.00 for adults and $2.00 for children. Museum hours are from 10:00 A.M. to 4:00 P.M. weekends, mid-May through mid-June and September through October, and daily in July and August. Call (413) 637–0320.

Hawthorne's new friend Melville lived not far north from him in a quiet country home outside Pittsfield called **Arrowhead.** From his piazza, Melville had a wide-open view of Mount Greylock, which he thought resembled a great white whale; the view inspired him to write most of *Moby-Dick* here in 1850 and 1851. In the Chimney Room, parts of the chimney are inscribed with words from Melville's short story "I and My Chimney." Upstairs, you can see his study, with some of his quill pens and his spectacles still on the table.

Behind this eighteenth-century yellow farmhouse stand stately trees, along with a red barn, a place where Melville was fond of chatting with Hawthorne. Arrowhead is at 780 Holmes Road off Route 7 just south of Pittsfield, clearly marked by signs. Tours begin on the hour from 10:00

A.M. to 4:00 P.M. daily from Memorial Day weekend to Labor Day, after which it opens during the same hours Friday through Monday until October 31. Admission is $5.00 for adults, $4.50 for seniors, and $3.00 for children ages six to sixteen, with a family rate of $15.00. Call (413) 442–1793.

The *Hancock Shaker Village,* 5 miles west of Pittsfield, is a major tourist attraction and often crowded. Still, this is the best place to learn about the unique chapter in New England history written by the Shakers. This unusual sect, founded in 1774, earned the derisive name of Shakers because of members' active style of singing and dancing at worship.

The Shaker community at Hancock reached its height in the 1840s with about 250 members. Women served alongside men as eldresses and deacons, and everyone worked together at dairying, furnituremaking, handweaving, and basketry. They became famous for the high quality of their products, particularly the furniture and oval-shaped wooden boxes.

Twenty of their original brick and wooden buildings stand scattered about the green landscape. A stroll among them on a sparkling sunny day is pleasant and in distinct contrast to the severity of their lives. In the *Brick Dwelling,* where the brethren and sisters lived, rising was at 4:30 A.M., but breakfast was not until 7:00. The sexes sat separately at plain wooden tables and ate in silence.

Drawing people like a talisman, the *Round Stone Barn* is a thing of beauty, topped with a white cupola, and yet is eminently practical: It allowed one man standing alone in it to milk fifty-four cows. Other buildings show the work of everyday life: the washhouse, the tannery, the icehouse, and the poultry house.

Most days, there's a program: Shaker hymn music, baking or boxmaking demonstrations, or spinning and weaving. Occasionally, Shaker-style candlelight dinners are served.

Hancock Shaker Village is open daily from April through November. Hours are from 9:30 A.M. to 5:00 P.M. Memorial Day weekend to October 31 and from 10:00 A.M. to 3:00 P.M. during April, May, and November. Admission is $10.00 for adults and $5.00 for children and teens ages six to seventeen. Call (413) 443–0188.

Right in the middle of downtown Pittsfield, at 39 South Street, is *The Berkshire Museum,* a community museum with significant exhibits in subjects from fine art to natural history. Particularly outstanding in the art category are collections of Hudson River School paintings, American primitives, silver, and ancient art—enough to put the fine art galleries right up there with the best art museums in New England. Local history is another strong area, with early tools, Native American artifacts, and early electrical equipment. (General Electric was once the city's major employer.) An aquarium joins more than 3,000 minerals and fossils in the natural-history section. Regular programs, lectures, and musical events fill the calendar; (413) 443–7171.

Outside the handsome brick downtown of Pittsfield are the large mills of Crane and Company, papermakers for almost two hundred years. Just past the mills, 5 miles east of Pittsfield off Route 9, there's a sign for the *Crane Paper Museum* in Dalton.

Crane is the only company that makes paper for the U.S. government to print money on, a contract it has held since 1879. Paul Revere was the company's first banknote engraver. The seventh generation of Cranes is at work in the mills. The company has made nothing but fine rag papers ever since the first mill was built in 1801. Because of its consistently high quality, Crane paper was traditionally used in the nineteenth century for official documents, deeds, titles, and financial instruments and came to be known as bond paper. Until 1845, the paper was entirely made by hand, a single sheet at a time.

The museum is in an ivy-covered stone building with stair-stepped gables, a former rag room. On view are historic currency samples, exhibits on papermaking, and many samples of letterheads and invitations. It's open from 2:00 to 5:00 P.M. Monday through Friday from June through October. Call (413) 684–2600.

Round Stone Barn, Hancock Shaker Village

There's no good way to get to **Becket.** And that's how townspeople like it. (You can get there by taking Route 8 south from Dalton.) The town of Becket is about as hinterland as it gets in the central Berkshires. Bypassed entirely by the Massachusetts Turnpike, Becket has kept itself in its own little time warp, remaining rural and undeveloped. Its population numbers only sixteen hundred. The few buildings that constitute downtown Becket huddle together for encouragement along a short stretch of Route 8. As an intriguing counterpoint, one of the most prestigious dance festivals in the world is held here—*Jacob's Pillow.*

If you're a connoisseur of general stores, you'll find the **Becket General Store** the most idiosyncratically genuine of the many to be found in the central and southern Berkshires. Local men and women line up at the small counter in the morning in a steady and constant stream. Some sit down to sip coffee and munch doughnuts; others buy newspapers. The shelves hem one in so narrowly that two people cannot pass each other without do-si-do-ing down the aisles. Cramming the shelves is a hodge-podge of merchandise that would do a nineteenth-century general store proud: fishing lures next to birthday candles; such toys as crayons, and Wiffle balls; shampoo and cough syrup; kitchen gadgets; and, in a nod to modernity, rental videos. Cardboard boxes full of potatoes, peaches, tomatoes, and bananas are stacked on the floor.

From Becket, you can take the Pittsfield Road right off Route 8, which eventually brings you back out to Routes 7 and 20.

# Northern Berkshires

*H*eading north on Route 7, you'll pass **Pontoosuc Lake** on the left. This is a nice place to sailboard or canoe, and there are rental outlets along the shore. For a scenic detour, take Peck's Road, a left turn that loops almost completely around the lake.

Mighty **Mount Greylock,** at 3,491 feet, is the state's highest peak. From its summit, you can see five states and up to 100 miles. The ten-thousand-acre reservation is popular for camping, for hiking and cross-country skiing along its 45 miles of trails, or for just plain seeking tranquillity from its rugged heights. A highlight of a visit here is the **War Veterans Memorial Tower,** built in 1932 at the summit and originally designed as a lighthouse. The Williams College Outing Club publishes a trail guide that describes all the local hiking trails; you can get a copy from the Outing Club, Baxter Hall, Williams College, Williamstown; (413) 597–2317.

You can drive up the south side of the mountain from Lanesboro, and down the north side in North Adams. From Route 7 north of Lanesboro, you'll see the entrance road. A short distance in, a visitor center holds displays on natural history. The season opens at Mount Greylock when "mountain spring" arrives, usually in mid-May, and closes in October. Call (413) 499–4262 for information. Those who love informality will welcome a stay at *Bascom Lodge* at the summit, a rustic stone-and-wood building constructed by the Civilian Conservation Corps in the 1930s. Bascom Lodge is run by the Appalachian Mountain Club, which offers private and dormitory-style rooms, plus family-style breakfast and dinner. For information, write AMC–Bascom Lodge, P.O. Box 686, Lanesboro 01237, or call (413) 743–1591.

Near the Massachusetts-Vermont border, Route 7 joins the Mohawk Trail (Route 2), formerly a Mohawk Indian invasion route and now a migration path for tourists seeking scenic fall foliage. When you reach the junction, you'll be in Williamstown, the site of the pretty *Williams College campus.* A drive along Main Street through the campus shows off its smooth green lawns and ivied brick buildings.

On the Williams campus, the *Williams College Museum of Art* has over 10,000 works, especially strong in ancient and modern arts, and featuring New England's finest collection of ancient Abyssinian sculpture. Extraordinary exhibits created and first shown here tour art museums throughout the country. This museum is an often-overlooked highlight in the Berkshires art scene; (413) 597–2429.

*The Orchards* is an upscale inn, its large guest rooms decorated in attractive furnishings with a tailored air. Many rooms overlook the courtyard which the inn completely encircles, a space filled with a well-manicured garden around a stone-lined pool. The plants are chosen for their year-round appearance so that the garden remains colorful and attractive even after the leaves have gone. Afternoon tea is served to hotel guests daily, and other genteel details—goosedown pillows, fresh flowers, and a library—set The Orchards apart. Rooms begin at $125. The Orchards is at 222 Adams Road (Route 2), Williamstown 01267; (413) 458–9611 or (800) 225–1517. Or you can reserve through DestINNations at (800) 333–4667.

Also on the edge of town, on Route 7, is a lodging of an entirely different character. *Riverbend Farm* was owned by a friend of Ethan Allen's, before the Revolution, and Allen stayed there often. Fortunately for us, the house has been restored to as close to its colonial interior as possible, so guests can enjoy the historic atmosphere (although in a lot more peaceful surroundings than the house would have offered when rowdy Ethan and his friends were in town.) Guests are invited to use the antiques and to sink into the wing chairs. Rooms characterized by fine paneling, homespun coverlets, braided rugs, and antique furnishings are $90 and include a breakfast of homemade granola and breads, with honey from the innkeepers' hives. The inn is open mid-April through October. Write to Riverbend Farm at 643 Simonds Road (Route 7 N), Williamstown 01267; (413) 458–3121 or (800) 418–2057.

A unique and welcoming place to stay outside of town is at the *Field Farm,* in the middle of a nature reserve, about 300 acres of valley wildland owned by the Trustees of Reservations, which also operates the B&B. Rooms are large and modern; some are private and others operate on a shared-lodging basis, designed for small groups or families. Two of the guest rooms have working fireplaces, and the building is wheelchair-accessible. The setting is idyllic, with gardens and birds and no other buildings in sight. The farm sponsors occasional weekend nature programs; 554 Sloan Road, Williamstown 01267; (413) 443–0011.

At the *Western Gateway Heritage State Park* (413–663–6312) in North Adams, the railroad history of North Adams comes alive in a thoroughly entertaining way. Housed in six old wooden railroad buildings, the park also includes a cluster of shops and restaurants, linked by a cobblestoned courtyard and black iron streetlamps.

The visitor center tells the story of the building of the $4^3/_4$-mile Hoosac Tunnel through 2,500-foot-high Mount Hoosac—one of the greatest engineering feats of the nineteenth century. The project claimed the lives of almost two hundred men and took twenty-four years to build. The ring of pickaxes, the shouts of men, and the dripping of water can be heard inside an old boxcar through an imaginative audiovisual presentation. Here in the eerie darkness, you experience the same working conditions the tunnelers did. The tunnel made North Adams "the western gateway" to commercial travel from the East, a long-sought goal. North Adams also became an important railroad town. Children can ride a miniature train around the freight yard in good weather.

The park is well marked by signs off Route 8. It's open daily from 10:00 A.M. to 5:00 P.M.

In a spot in North Adams, glacial melt rushing over limestone deposits carved out a deep chasm and left an arch above it—the only "natural bridge" of marble in North America. Now the centerpiece of a state park, the *Natural Bridge* is visible from a walkway high and narrow like a catwalk that lets you peer over and around the Natural Bridge from almost any angle. Chain-link fence ruins the photo opportunity; on the other hand, it keeps people from falling in and killing themselves. Despite the mighty forces that shaped it, the Natural Bridge itself is quite small—a span of some 20 feet—and so dark inside that it looks cavelike. Still, something about it mesmerizes. A few picnic tables spread about a grassy area in earshot of the water are a nice spot to lunch.

The park is open from 10:00 A.M. to 5:00 P.M. daily from Memorial Day to Columbus Day, and from 10:00 A.M. until 8:00 P.M. on weekends and holidays from May 15 to October 30. Call the Western Gateway park at (413) 663–6312 or (413) 663–6392 for information. There's an admission charge of $2.00 per car.

Undaunted by the cola giants, *Squeeze Beverages* of North Adams has been making its own brand of sodas since 1920, one of only a handful of independent bottlers left in New England. The thirty-six flavors include sarsaparilla, birch beer, watermelon, and cherry cola, all sold in glass bottles bearing Squeeze's own logo. Squeeze ships only eight of these flavors to retail stores, so if you want a real choice, stop by the store in back of the factory, at 190 Howland Avenue (Route 8). If you're lucky, you may get a glance at the bottling process. The store is open from 8:00 A.M. to 4:00 P.M. weekdays and from 8:00 A.M. to noon Saturdays; call (413) 743–1410.

Just east of North Adams, a few miles past the junction of Route 8, Route 2 takes a giant bend, almost 180 degrees. The loop-the-loop in the road practically derails buses and gives cars plenty of pause. It's called the *Hairpin Turn,* and it's an inspiring place to stop. It just happens to be situated at one of the most fabulous vantage points for viewing the Hoosac Valley. You're up so high here that it looks as though you could hang glide right down into the valley. Few houses mar the pretty bowl of greenery below, and the blue sky and clouds reach up in front of you forever. In the elbow of the turn, there's a small parking lot with observation telescopes set up for a closer look, behind which are a nondescript restaurant and souvenir stand.

As you come back down Route 8 into the center of Adams, just past the McKinley Statue on Park Street you'll see the *Miss Adams Diner* on the left. This is an original diner built in 1949 by the Worcester Lunch Car Company that has been nicely restored, with a green-and-white tiled floor, plenty of chrome, and the original Worcester Diner clock. The diner offers blue plate specials, vegetarian burgers, and eggs Benedict, among other items. Call (413) 753–5300.

As a last stop in the northern Berkshires, an unusual political footnote awaits you in the town of Cheshire. A local pastor decided that a nice gift for President Jefferson would be a cheese made by Cheshire farmers. A big one. Molding it in a cider press, the farmers made a 1,235-pound cheese—one day's product of the town's dairies. The cheese was drawn by oxen to Albany and was then shipped by water to Washington, D.C., where, on January 1, 1802, it was presented to the third president with great fanfare.

In commemoration of this moment of glory, the ***Cheshire Cheese Press Monument*** stands on a corner, a concrete replica of the cider press used to make the cheese. To get there, head south on Route 8 and turn left onto Church Street at the First Baptist Church. The monument is at Church and School Streets, just opposite the Cheshire Post Office. Slow down or you'll miss it; it's not very big, and it could be partly hidden by children climbing on it.

**MORE PLACES TO STAY IN THE BERKSHIRES**

***Red Bird Inn,***
Route 57
New Marlborough 01230;
(413) 229-2433.
A moderately priced bed and-breakfast in an old stagecoach inn amid beautiful gardens.

***Bow Wow Road Inn,***
570 Bow Wow Road
Sheffield 01257;
(413) 229-3339.
A well-appointed four-room inn with rooms at $110 to $150.

***Devonfield,***
85 Stockbridge Road
Lee, 01238;
(413) 243-3298 or
(800) 664-0880
or through DestINNations
at (800) 333-4667.
A spacious, elegant getaway you won't want to leave.

**MORE PLACES TO EAT IN THE BERKSHIRES**

***John Andrew's Restaurant,***
Route 23
South Egremont;
(413) 528-3469.
Mediterranean-style cooking complements local ingredients, served in a country setting; wines are moderately priced.

***Church Street Cafe,***
65 Church Street,
Lenox;
(413) 637-2745.
Healthy food needn't be dull, and it isn't at this "New American" stronghold where couscous and Japanese dishes share the menu.

***La Bruschetta Ristorante,***
1 Harris Street,
West Stockbridge;
(413) 232-7141.
Creative specials, such as chicken breast with grilled artichokes and roasted shallots, or raspberry goat cheese tart, are fresh and interesting at $16 to $20.

***Cheesecake Charlie's,***
83 Church Street,
Lenox;
(413) 637-9779,
serves breakfast and lunch, plus non-dairy cheesecakes in its selection of tea-time-any-time pastries.

***Hobson's Choice,***
159 Water Street,
Williamstown;
(413) 458–9101.
Casual, with a long menu
that includes several vegetarian entrees, and a good
beer list. Salad bar is
included with entrees.

***Theresa's Stockbridge
Cafe,***
40 Main Street (back),
Stockbridge;
(413) 298–3915.
Nice design-your-own deli
sandwiches, generous chef
salads, quiche, in a bright
cafe with a terrace. The
apple pie is really home-
made.

WORTH SEEING
IN THE BERKSHIRES

***Sterling and Francine
Clark Art Institute,***
Williamstown;
(413) 458–9545.
Admission is no longer
free, as many local
brochures still show it.

***The Mount,***
Home of Edith Wharton,
Route 7 at Plunkett Street,
Lenox;
(413) 637–1899.

***Mission House,***
Main Street,
Stockbridge;
(413) 298–3239.
A 1739 home with gardens.

***Tanglewood,***
Lenox;
(413) 637–1940.

TO LEARN MORE
ABOUT THE BERKSHIRES

Berkshire Hills
Visitors Bureau,
Berkshire Common,
Pittsfield, MA 01201;
(413) 443–9186 or
(800) 237–5747.
Skiers should ask for the
annual "Massachusetts Ski
Guide" by calling
(800) 227–MASS.
For ski conditions, call
(413) 499–7669.

# Index

Entries for Museums, Parks and Green Spaces, and Restaurants appear in the special indexes beginning on page 200.

## General Index

# INDEX

# INDEX

# *Museums*

# Parks and Green Spaces

# *Restaurants*

# INDEX

# About the Authors

After four years of college in Boston and Cambridge, respectively, Barbara and Stillman Rogers remained in the Boston area for several years and now live just over the line in the border town of Richmond, NH. They write about all New England for magazines and in their newspaper travel columns, and are authors of *New Hampshire: Off the Beaten Path, The Rhode Island Guide, Natural Wonders of Vermont,* and many other travel books.

# Devoted to Travelers
# Diverse in Nature